HEALING THE WOUNDS

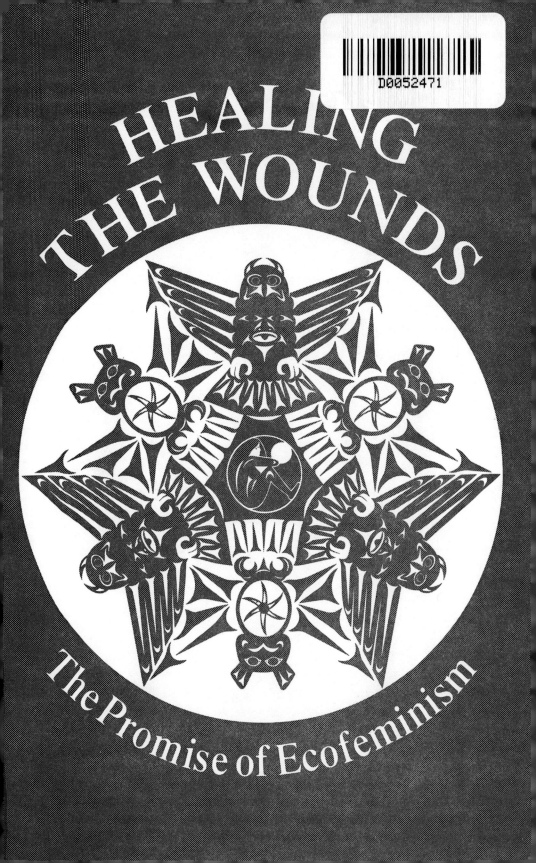

The Promise of Ecofeminism

HEALING THE WOUNDS: THE PROMISE OF ECOFEMINISM

Edited by Judith Plant

NEW SOCIETY PUBLISHERS

Philadelphia, PA   Santa Cruz, CA

Inquiries regarding requests to reprint all or part of *Healing the Wounds: The Promise of Ecofeminism* should be addressed to:
New Society Publishers
4527 Springfield Avenue
Philadelphia, PA 19143

ISBN 0-86571-152-6 Hardcover
ISBN 0-86571-153-4 Paperback

Printed in the United States of America on partially recycled paper by BookCrafters, Fredericksburg, VA.

Cover and book design by Tina Birky
Cover art, "Captive Maiden," by Susan Point
Other art:

Page 5	from "Captive Maiden," by Susan Point.
Page 49	"Two-Headed Serpent," by Susan Point.
Page 113	"She Goes Around, She Comes Around," by Roma Heillig Morris.
Page 187	"Food of the Thunderbird," by Susan Point.

To order directly from the publisher, add $1.75 to the price for the first copy, $.50 each additional. Send check or money order to:
New Society Publishers
PO Box 582
Santa Cruz, CA 95061

New Society Publishers is a project of the New Society Educational Foundation, a nonprofit, tax-exempt, public foundation. Opinions expressed in this book do not necessarily represent positions of the New Society Educational Foundation.

Table of Contents

PART THREE
She Is Alive in You: Ecofeminist Spirituality

PART FOUR
The Circle Is Gathering: Ecofeminist Community

Acknowledgments

There is an aging photograph hanging on my wall. It is of four generations of women—my mother's lineage—and I am the baby cradled in my mother's arms. From this image I have often drawn strength and gentleness. So it seems most fitting to give first thanks to my mother, to whom I owe my life.

There are many other people who have supported me, both spiritually and physically making this book possible. My love, my partner for a decade, my close friend, Kip, I can never thank enough. Our work together makes our love grow stronger. My heartfelt thanks also go to our household, which kept good food and good feelings flowing.

A major source of inspiration for this book has been the community in which I live; without its existence, without our collective struggle for a better world, the book would never have been born. I thank especially our women's circle, Paula Rubinson too, who encouraged me to believe in the project when my own confidence was lost. Close friends Eleanor, Hattie, Kip, Tschitschi, and Van gave generously of their time, and read and read, offering kind words of criticism and advice.

Many connections were made in the process of gathering together this anthology. I am grateful to Jim Cheney, Judy Goldhaft, Judith Kjellberg, Barbara La Morticella, Ruth Lechte, and Jennifer Sells for putting me in touch with potential contributors. Ellen and David from New Society Publishers have become my friends over this manuscript; I can never thank them enough for being there. And to Tina Birky, appreciation for her patient and diligent copyediting.

Grateful acknowledgment is made for permission to reprint previously published and copyrighted articles and material from the following sources:

"The Ecology of Feminism and the Feminism of Ecology," by Ynestra King, reprinted by permission of the author.

"Split Culture," by Susan Griffin, first published in *The Schumacher Lectures*, Vol. II, edited by Satish Kumar, Blond & Briggs, 1984. Reprinted by permission of the author.

"A New Movement—A New Hope: East Wind, West Wind and the Wind from the South," by Corinne Kumar D'Souza, first published in *Women in a Changing World*, No. 24.

"Women/Wilderness," by Ursula K. LeGuin, first published in *Dancing at the Edge of the World*, Grove Press, 1989.

"Women Act: Women and Environmental Protection in India," by Pamela Philipose, first published in *Women in a Changing World*, No. 24.

"Mama Coyote Talks to the Boys," by Sharon Doubiago, originally published in *The New Catalyst*, No. 10, and reprinted with permission from the publisher.

"Speaking for the Earth: The Haida Way," first published by *Ruebsaat's Magazine*, No. 20.

"Lakshmi Ashram: A Gandhian Perspective in the Himalayan Foothills," by Radha Bhatt, first published by *The Modern Churchman*, New Series, Vol. XXVI, no. 3.

"Toward an Ecofeminist Spirituality," by Charlene Spretnak, excerpts from *The Politics of Women's Spirituality*, edited by Charlene Spretnak. Copyright © 1982 by Charlene Spretnak. Reprinted with permission of Doubleday, a division of Bantam, Doubleday, Dell Publishing Group, Inc.

"Toward An Ecological-Feminist Theology of Nature," by Rosemary Radford Ruether, reproduced with permission, from *Sexism and God-Talk: Toward a Feminist Theology*, by Rosemary Ruether, Beacon Press, 1983.

"The Juice and the Mystery," by Margot Adler, first published, in part, by *The World: Journal of the Unitarian Universalist Association*, Vol. 1, No. 5.

"Sacred Land, Sacred Sex," by Dolores LaChapelle, first published by The Way of The Mountain Learning Center, PO Box 542, Silverton, Colorado, 81433, and available in quantity from this address. Reprinted with permission of the author.

"A Story of Beginnings," by Starhawk, excerpted from *Truth or Dare*, by Starhawk. Reprinted with permission of the author and Harper and Row, Publishers, Inc.

"Tampons," by Ellen Bass, first published in *Our Stunning Harvest: Poems by Ellen Bass*, Philadelphia, Pa: New Society Publishers, 1984. Reprinted with permission from the author and publisher.

"Consensus and Community" originally appeared in *The New Catalyst*, No. 12, and is reprinted with permission from the publishers.

Foreword

Linking Arms, Dear Sisters, Brings Hope!

This book is a book of hope, a book about healing wounds and about believing in your own strength, believing in the courage to do things together, to change and transform daily politics nonviolently. This book is about global ecological sisterhood! We need such books and such anthologies more than ever because we must illuminate *now* the vision of a world free of mass destructive weapons, free of sexism and racism, free of violence and repression.

The Intermediate Nuclear Force (INF) Treaty is a small and modest step toward nuclear disarmament. This treaty reduces nuclear weaponry (excluding, unfortunately, the nuclear warheads and the guidance systems) by only 3 percent, but at least it has begun to break the cycle of arms escalation in *one* area of nuclear weaponry.

The potential for a true path toward *at least* nuclear disarmament is now, for the first time, within sight—within our grasp. This is a time for being hopeful as the Cold War seems to thaw between East and West. . . . But it is also a time of being all the more watchful, because there are still plenty of patriarchal technocrats out there—in the military-industrial complex, within the ridiculous secret services, and within the bureaucracies like the Pentagon, wanting to *compensate* for the weapons being removed; about to "modernize" a new generation of more and more deadly precise mass destructive weapons! We need only to follow the debate on biological weapons development or watch what is being deployed in the world's oceans.

This is *not* a time for complacency. It is a time for continuing to *link arms* as global sisters—like the women in the Chipko Movement in India; like the women at Greenham Common, in England, who are *not* giving up their struggle against militarization; like the women of the Western Shoshone Indian Nation in Nevada who opposed nuclear testing by encircling the test grounds; like the women in the Pacific struggling for a nuclear-free future to prevent babies being damaged through French atomic bomb tests; like the women in the Krim Region of the Soviet Union demonstrating courageously against a new nuclear power plant.

To eliminate war and its tools, to eliminate racism and repression, we must eliminate its causes. Our call to action, our call for nonviolent transformation of society is based on the belief that the struggle for disarmament, peace, social justice, protection of the planet Earth, and the fulfillment of basic human needs and human rights are *one* and indivisible.

The great project of our time is to see wholly, to see "outsidedly," to hear and to transcend the cleavage between humanity and nature.

As Susan Griffin has put it in her contribution: "We are divided against ourselves. . . . We no longer feel ourselves to be a part of this earth. . . . In my resistance to pain and change, I have felt the will toward self-annihilation. And still the singing in my body daily returns me to a love of this earth. I know that by a slow practice, if I am to survive, I must learn to listen to this song. . . . "

We are learning to listen to this song. . . .

We are learning to heal our wounds. . . . That is what this courageous book is all about. Just repairing the existing system, whether capitalist or state socialist, cannot be an answer for us! Our aim is a nonviolent and ecological-feminist transformation of societal structures. Our aim is radical, nonviolent change *outside*—and *inside* of us! The macrocosm and the microcosm! This has to do with transforming power! Not power over, or power to dominate, or power to terrorize—but shared power; abolishing power as we know it, replacing it with the power of nonviolence or something common to all, to be used *by all* and *for all!* Power as the discovery of *our own strength*—as opposed to a passive receiving of power exercised by others, often in our name.

Creating a truly free society—based on ecological and feminist principles that can mediate humanity's relationship with nature—is our common aim. Sharing and giving solidarity across all ideological and geographical boundaries when our sisters and brothers are repressed and discriminated against is also our common aim. Living, producing, working, and living in comprehensible human dimensions is another common goal for us all.

I agree fully with Starhawk when she writes, "Compassion, our ability to feel with another, to value other lives as we value our own, to see ourselves as answerable and accountable to those who are different from us, has survival value. . . . " And I fully agree with her when she concludes: "Although the structures of war and domination are strongly entrenched, they must inevitably change, as all things change. We can become agents of that transformation, and bring a new world to birth." The women in this book are all agents of such a transformation and they make very clear that feminist spirituality, earth-based spirituality, is not just a theory, a philosophy—it's a practice, a way of life!

Ecofeminism must be practiced in our daily lives, and should thereby also contribute to an understanding of the connections between the domination of persons and the domination of nonhuman nature. Ecofeminism draws on the principles of *unity in diversity,* a most important aspect in times of social simplification.

This book is joining together *feminist visions* and *ecological politics:* it demonstrates that ecofeminists are taking action to effect transformations and radical changes that are, in the words of Ynestra King, " . . . immediate and personal as well as long-term and structural!" Thinking globally, acting locally, unifying our ecological and feminist thoughts and actions!

Linking arms, dear sisters, brings hope!

—Petra Kelly
August, 1988

Publisher's Note

I have often compared being the publisher's editor for a book to being a midwife. This feels particularly appropriate for me now, as my work on *Healing the Wounds: The Promise of Ecofeminism* has woven in and out of my pregnancy, and through the birth and infancy of my now fifteen-month-old daughter Aliyah. The promise of ecofeminism is a promise that I have made to my daughter by bringing her into this world, a commitment to struggle to build a community worth living in with all creatures of the earth.

This is a community that Ali sees easily, it is a part of her whole being. I imagine that as children we could all see that community, as I am reminded by the memories of my own childhood which came forth as I watch my daughter grow. For me, *Healing the Wounds* is about understanding the threats to that community and how we, together, can learn to overcome them.

One of my joys in working on this book has been the development of my friendship with Judith Plant. Judith strives hard to live out her values. This summer we visited Judith and her community on the Bridge River in central British Columbia. Theirs is a community trying to live in harmony with the land and with each other. We arrived just as Judith and the community finished hosting the Third North American Bioregional Congress, were gearing up for a fight against a planned toxic waste dump nearby, were keeping their gardens going, finishing this book, and having a good time. It's been great fun working with you, Judith, I look forward to much more work, play, friendship, and love.

Ellen Sawislak
New Society Publishers
3 February, 1989

Dedication

For my children, Julie, Shannon, and Willie

Toward a New World:
An Introduction

Judith Plant

Our cabin, which sits high on a knoll overlooking a narrow mountain valley, has a wide verandah around two sides. We often find ourselves sitting here, reflecting on our work, our lives, the state of the world. Sometimes we are simply sitting—listening to the sounds of birds, feeling the breath of warm winds, healing ourselves in the midst of the natural world. And suddenly there will come a roar and rumble so loud it is difficult to tell if a helicopter is overhead or an 18-wheeler is barreling through the valley. Almost always it's the latter, for we live on what the Ministry of Forests refers to as a "corridor." This corridor connects the forest with the sawmill—a path beaten hard from the weight of dead trees.

Each time a truckload of fir, pine, or spruce passes by—and it happens many times a day—we grieve for the loss of our sisters and brothers who are the forests. It is literally a part of us that is dying—we know this for a fact. We know that without the trees, the oxygen and water we humans need for our survival is threatened. More than our own interests are at stake, for our interests cannot be separated from the rest of life. Our pain for the death of the forests is simply, and most fundamentally, compassion for the senseless destruction of life.

This compassion that we feel is the essence of a new paradigm which ecofeminism describes in detail. Feeling the life of the "other"—literally experiencing its existence—is becoming the new starting point for human decision-making. This is a radical departure from the driving force behind the self-interested approach to the natural world that underlies the logging industry, the mining industry, the war machine—the entire realm of most modern human activities.

It is no accident that the minister of forests is a man, that the logging company is owned and run by men, that the logging truck driver is a man. For after all, this world is a man's world. Our language says it all, a virgin forest is as yet untouched by the hand of "man." And the world is rapidly being penetrated, consumed and destroyed by this man's world—spreading across the face of the earth, teasing and tempting the last remnants of loving peoples with its modern glass beads—televisions and tanks; filling the ears of poor people with doublespeak about security, only to establish dangerous technology on their homelands; voraciously trying to control all that is natural, regarding nature as a resource to be exploited for the gain of a very few. As the Amazon rainforest is bulldozed to provide cheap beef for American hamburgers, the habitat of peoples who once lived and loved with this earth is destroyed and the fragile womb of planet Earth is dealt yet another killing blow. This "man's world" is on the very edge of collapse. . . .

This is so because there is no respect for the "other" in patriarchal society. The other, the object of patriarchal rationality, is considered only insofar as it can benefit the subject. So self-centered is this view that it is blind to the fact that its own life depends on the integrity and well-being of the whole. This is the subject matter of ecofeminism, a key strand in the planetary shift away from the simple-minded selfishness of patriarchy.

While it is very clear that the majority of people still continue to operate within a patriarchal framework, it is extremely encouraging to note the many who are realizing that this way of being has had its day. Our son often hitch-hikes to town and, more often than not, he is picked up by a logging truck driver. He tells us that most of these men feel they'd rather be doing something else; that they, too, love the forests and believe that local people are getting a raw deal in the wholesale destruction of the trees for the benefit of mega-corporations. Then there is the case of the mining community in southern British Columbia who—with an 85 percent majority—spoke against uranium mining in their area in spite of the fact that this industry could have brought big bucks into their community. Or there's the logging-road engineer, who stopped into our office the other day and, among other things, said that if women ran the industry, we probably wouldn't have the problems we have today, because, he said, women have compassion. . . .

Connecting feminism with environmentalism is an eye-opener for many who might otherwise not have been able to listen to either issue. Taking the feminist critique of human relationships and putting it side by side with an analysis of human and nonhuman relationships, showing that both women and the earth have been regarded as the object of self-interested patriarchs, is making a lot of sense to a lot of people. Men—our brothers, fathers, lovers, and friends—need not be the enemy. Though they have been groomed since early childhood to become the enactors of patriarchy, they began life in the arms of women and, as little boys, they undoubtedly loved the freedom of the outdoors, were thrilled at the sight of a nest of baby birds, for instance, or ecstatic with fresh-fallen snow. It breaks many a young boy's heart to find out that the slingshot he so innocently plays with actually kills the little bird. Male human beings have the capacity to have compassion for life, but they will have to struggle long and hard to overcome their own upbringing. More and more men are embracing ecofeminism because they see the depth of the analysis and realize that in shedding the privileges of patriarchy they do more than create equal rights for all; that this great effort may actually save the earth and the life it supports.

It is true that women have been socialized in such a way that allows them to experience compassion. This experience is, however, often skewed by the subordinate, deferential position given to women that somehow loads the responsibility of caring for others with guilt and anxiety. For this compassion that women have been allowed does not carry with it any power to make decisions. Because of this skewed situation, caring often becomes entangled with personal frustrations over feelings of powerlessness, leading to an inability to take responsibility.

Thus it is that neither the present understanding of what is female or male is an adequate characterization of what it is to be human. For both genders are fraught with pathological behaviors which serve to perpetuate the system of domination and oppression. So women, too, must struggle to claim those aspects of our socialization that are of benefit to the species, believe in them even though they have been so undervalued and scorned even by ourselves, and impress upon men their own responsibility to change. For we women will not be held responsible for cleaning up the patriarchal mess by ourselves because we are told we are more able. No, not this time. The message of ecofeminism is that we *all* must cultivate the human characteristics of gentleness and caring, giving up patriarchy with all its deadly privileges.

This means valuing diversity above all else. It means we have to take our own authority, be responsible for ourselves, our communities. And more and more this is becoming a reality. Being part of a publishing collective that produces a quarterly alternative magazine which focuses on regional issues of planetary concern, it is becoming increasingly apparent to me that people all over the world are organizing at the local level against logging, toxic wastes, mining, nuclear power plants—any corporate invasion that threatens the well-being of its citizenry. And the methods that they are using to make decisions and to take action are, more often than not, a reflection of the consensus of the group. Differences—if not useful in the defense of the local community—fall off as unimportant. Thus, on the front lines are people of different cultures, colors, ages, sexes, and political persuasions. Here is power-from-within expressing itself—the power to find unity in diversity.

This anthology in no way fully represents the wide spectrum of thought that is ecofeminism. It does, however, begin to define a truly international movement that has the power to radically transform our human perceptions of our species and its place in the natural world. It begins to open the door to human cultural possibilities as yet uncharted but which hold the promise of a world built not on fear but on love; which thrives not on self-interest but on the joyful experience of differences; which values not money and materialism above all else, but the real security of mutual interdependence. It is surely very confusing to be in this period of human history, this age of transformation, but we must, with determination and our increasing power-from-within, continue the struggle to heal the wounds in ourselves and the sweet earth from which we draw our life and breath. This book is a step along that path.

PART ONE
REMEBERING WHO
WE ARE: THE MEANING
OF ECOFEMINISM

> Long ago we gave up ourselves. . . . We have traded our real
> existence, our real feelings for a delusion. Instead of fighting for our
> lives, we bend all our efforts to defend delusion. We deny all evidence
> at hand that this civilization, which has shaped our minds, is also
> destroying the earth.
>
> —Susan Griffin, "Split Culture"

Making the connection between feminism and ecology enables us to
step outside of the dualistic, separated world into which we were all
born. From this vantage point, this new perspective, we begin to see
how our relations with each other are reflected in our relations with
the natural world. The rape of the earth, in all its forms, becomes a
metaphor for the rape of woman, in all its many guises. In layer after
layer, a truly sick society is revealed, a society of alienated relationships
all linked to a rationalization that separates "man" from nature.

At the same time, by understanding that we are all part of the same
organic flow of life, we are reminded, with a stirring that excites our
deepest selves, of who we really are. We are part of this earth, and
thus the world becomes a place of infinite mystery, of delight to the
senses and the intellect.

Susan Griffin describes how the old paradigm has divided us against
ourselves and how, though we are on the edge of death, we are our
own worst enemies. Yet she also reminds us of our capacities for love,

pleasure, and joy, that are so much a part of being human. Ecofeminism as a praxis of hope is the basis upon which Ynestra King begins to develop a theory of ecological feminism. Extending this theory to the Third World, Corinne Kumar D'Souza's contribution shows how the dualistic perspective from the West, so destructive to women, has submerged and erased other cultures. Sharon Doubiago takes on the voice of Mama Coyote and speaks especially to male ecologists, urging them to connect feminism with their work. Lastly, Ursula K. LeGuin speaks for what has been unspoken, left out of civilization, for that experience that has not been shared with men.

1
Split Culture
Susan Griffin

We who are born into this civilization have inherited a habit of mind. We are divided against ourselves. We no longer feel ourselves to be a part of this earth. We regard our fellow creatures as enemies. And, very young, we even learn to disown a part of our own being. We come to believe that we do not know what we know. We grow used to ignoring the evidence of our own experience, what we hear or see, what we feel in our own bodies. We come into maturity keeping secrets. But we forget this secret knowledge and feel instead only a vague shame, a sense that perhaps we are not who we say we are. Yet we have learned well to pretend that what is true is not true. In some places the sky is perpetually gray, and the air is filled with a putrid smell. Forests we loved as children disappear. The waters we once swam are forbidden to us now because they are poisoned. We remember there was a sweet taste to fruit, that there used to be more birds. But we do not read these perceptions as signs of our own peril.

Long ago we gave up ourselves. Now, if we are dying by increments, we have ceased to be aware of this death. How can we know our own death if we do not know our own existence? We have traded our real existence, our real feelings for a delusion. Instead of fighting for our lives, we bend all our efforts to defend delusion. We deny all evidence at hand that this civilization, which has shaped our minds, is also destroying the earth.

The dividedness of our minds is etched into our language. To us, the word *thought* means an activity separate from feeling, just as the word *mind* suggests a place apart from the body and from the rhythms of the earth. We do not use the word *animal* to describe human qualities. Our word *spirit* rises in our imaginations above the earth as if we believed that holiness exists in an inverse proportion to gravity. The circumstance of our birth is common to us; we are all of woman born. But we have a word *race* which suggests to us that human beings belong to different categories of virtue by birth. Through the words *masculine* and *feminine*, which we use to designate two alien and alienated

7

poles of human behavior, we make our sexuality a source of separation. We divide ourselves and all that we know along an invisible borderline between what we call Nature and what we believe is superior to Nature.

Now we find ourselves moving almost without recourse toward a war that will destroy all of our lives. And were this not true, we have learned that the way we live has damaged the atmosphere, our bodies, even our genetic heritage so severely that perhaps we cannot save ourselves. We are at the edge of death, and yet, like one who contemplates suicide, we are our own enemies. We think with the very mind that has brought disaster on us. And this mind, taught and trained by this civilization, does not know itself. This is a mind in exile from its own wisdom.

According to this worldview—a view whose assumptions are so widely accepted by this civilization that we do not even think of it as an ideology—there is a hierarchy to existence. God and the angels, things pure in spirit and devoid of any material content, come first. Everything earthly is corrupt. But among the corrupt, human beings are of the highest spiritual order, more significant, valuable, and trustworthy than animals, or certainly trees or, of course, tomatoes, and obviously more intelligent than mountains, or oceans, or particles of sand. Among human beings, a similar order exists. Those of the human species who belong to what is thought of as the white race, and those who are part of the masculine gender, are at the top of this hierarchy. Various glosses on this fundamental belief place the rest of us in different descending orders.

We have learned of the scientific revolution that it was a victory over the irrational, over magical thought that led to the Inquisition and the witch burnings. And we do not commonly associate the philosophy of St. Augustine about men and women with the scientific worldview because we are accustomed to thinking that science and religion are at opposite positions in a polemic that expressed itself in the trial of Galileo. Despite the fact that Galileo recanted to the church, we no longer believe the world was literally created in seven days, nor do we place the earth at the center of the solar system.

But what we have not considered is that a civilization may suffer a great transformation in its institutions and its philosophy—power can shift from church to state, and the authority for knowledge from priest to scientist—and yet still retain, in a new guise and a new language, the essence of the old point of view. Such is the case with the scientific revolution, so that many assumptions, methods, and even questions we take to be scientific, actually partake of the same paradigm that in an earlier age we described as Christian.

Let us look at Newton's *Optics* for an example. Before Newton's work on optics, many different ideas about vision were believed, including the notion that a ray of light emanated from the human eye and illuminated the world. Through observation and experiment, Newton concluded that color is not a property of the eye nor the property of any object but is instead produced by the retina, sensitive to light refracted at different angles. This and like discoveries in the seventeenth and eighteenth centuries fell into a philosophical doctrine that was taken to be an experimentally proven vision of the true nature of the world. The scientific point of view argued that we cannot trust our senses, that we are deceived by the appearance of the material world, that color is a form of illusion, that color is simply a figment of our minds and does not exist.*

Thus if religion told us that the earth was a corrupt place, that our true home was heaven, that sensual feeling was not to be trusted and could lead us to hell and damnation, science did not in essence contradict that doctrine. For science, too, told us not to trust our senses, that matter is deceptive, and that we are alien to our surroundings. If, then, religion told us that our own senses could not be trusted and that therefore we must bow to scripture and the authority of the priest, now science tells us that we must bow to the truth of objective experimental data and the authority of scientific experts. In both systems, not only are we alienated from a world that is described as deceiving us; we are also alienated from our own capacity to see and hear, to taste and touch, to know and describe our own experience.

Such is the strength of this old way of thinking—that the earth and what is natural in ourselves is not to be trusted—that it hardly occurs to us that there is another way to interpret Newton's discovery; we have confused his discovery with our old paradigmatic vision.

For indeed one can make a very different interpretation of Newton's observations of the nature of optics. Instead of believing we are deceived by matter or our senses, instead of deciding that color does not exist, we can assert, since we do experience color, that in our experience of color we have entered into a union with what we perceive. That together with matter we create color. That our sense of color is indeed evidence of a profound, sensual, and emotional connection we have with all that

---

*"I cannot sufficiently admire the eminence of those men's wits, that have received and held it to be true, and with the sprightliness of their judgements offered such violence to their own senses, so that they have been able to prefer that which their reason dictated to them, to that which sensible experiments represented most manifestly to the contrary.... I cannot find any bounds for my admiration, how that reason in Aristarchus and Copernicus, to commit such a rape on their senses; as in despite thereof to make herself mistress of credulity." (From Galileo's *Dialogues Concerning the Two Great Systems of the World*, Vol. I, as cited in E. A. Burtt, *The Metaphysical Foundations of Modern Science*, New York, 1954.)

is part of this earth. That the joy color gives us is perhaps part of the balance of the universe.

There is another example of how the old paradigm affects what we take to be impartial science, from Francis Bacon's argument that science ought to proceed by experimentation. It must be close to self-evident, one can object here, that scientific experimentation is a movement toward respect of the material world. Before the idea of experiment, the nature of the material world was not even considered worthy of observation. Speculation and deductive reason were the sources of truth. I must digress for a moment to point out that if one is part of Nature oneself, speculation, especially when it involves self-reflection, *is* a kind of experiment. And perhaps this is not really a digression. For indeed, what is missing in Bacon's idea of scientific experiment is any self-reflection. He assumes that a superior objectivity, a state of emotional and physical detachment, can belong to the scientist who performs an experiment.

In different ages, both religion and science have been the focus of our hopes and the arbiters of what we call truth. Because they have expressed the consciousness of a whole civilization, both institutions also carry with them and epitomize, in their ideas and traditions, the troubled conflict, the dividedness, of our consciousness. Both institutions within Western civilization have been shaped by and have deepened our alienation from this earth.

If the church once offered the denigration of incarnate life as a solution to the human condition, now science offers us the control of matter as our rescue. But what can be wrong with cultivating either the human spirit or the soil we live on? Human creativity is a part of Nature, but rather we think of ourselves as working against Nature. The paradigm that tells us we are apart from and above this earth is not simply an intellectual response to Nature. It is instead a deeply fearful attitude. And the fear that lies under this thought, like all fear, turns into rage.

The pursuit of scientific knowledge in our civilization is beset by an emotional dilemma. In order to control Nature, we must know Nature. But just as we are seeking to know, there is a knowledge we fear. We are afraid to remember what we, in our bodies and in our feelings, still know, but what, in our fragmented, civilized consciousness we have been persuaded to forget. That, like the forests we destroy, or the rivers we try to tame, *we* are Nature.

The discovery of the solar system, of gravitational law, of evolution, of the microscopic world of the cell, of the genetic information that is part of matter, of the nature of light, and of the continuum between matter and energy, should transform consciousness so that we in this civilization might begin to regard the human condition with humility rather than arrogance. The thinkers who made what we call the scientific revolution had begun to discover a vast matrix of natural order, a very large wisdom whose boundaries we cannot even imagine. Just as the Earth is not the center of the solar system, so the biosphere is not centered on the human species nor circumscribed by human culture. We are dependent on the universe around us not only to breathe and eat, but even to keep our feet on the ground. For we do this not at will but because we exist in a field of energy. All that we do is shaped by and partakes of that field. And our perceptions and what we experience as real depend upon the nature and movements of matter and light. Not only are we mortal, but the very human form suffers a slow change over generations. Between my arm and the air, between the movements of a flame and what we call the solid mass of wood, there is no boundary.

But we have come to rely upon another image of ourselves: as discrete static beings. And we have learned to think that we must take control of our environment in order to survive. We believe that it is a cultural order, the order we have willed, and not natural order, the order of which we are a part, that makes us safe. Thus, if the discoveries of modern science have given us the means to manipulate Nature, they have also terrified us. And this is why, in the fourteenth century, when science began to challenge our old idea of who we are, the witch burnings began. The slave trade began in the sixteenth century at the height of this revolution in thought. And in the twentieth century, when science again questioned the old notion that we are above Nature, the Nazi Holocaust and now the nuclear holocaust have commenced.

But in separating Nature from culture within himself, the man who believes this delusion has split his own needs and desires from his intelligence and from all meaning. Thus his own desires return to him as meaningless, as cruel and senseless violations. Out of the lost fragments of his own psyche, he has created a monstrous image to contain his own self-loathing. Thus the pornographer creates out of his own sexual desires a meeting between two bodies that is without emotion, without any deep or soulful connection. And when he invents a woman, a pornographic heroine, he gives her a body without a spirit, without any sensibility, without a significant consciousness. She is like the dead matter, the brute matter, of scientific theory.

And the modern mind invents the same image of Nature itself. Matter is dead. A forest has no spiritual life. When Reagan was governor of California, he said in response to ecologists who were trying to preserve the great coastal forests, "If you have seen one tree you have seen them all." Believing a mountain to have no inner reason, no sacredness unto itself, the modern technologist takes coal out of the soil simply by cutting away half of the face of the mountain. Suddenly the whole of the mountain begins to erode. Chemicals from this erosion enter the streams in an unnatural balance. Trees, plants, fish, animals die. The countryside, once breathtakingly beautiful, begins to look like a place of devastation. He transforms the mountain into what he believed the mountain to be.

In the same way, society transforms those who have become symbols of Nature into objects of degradation. If a woman is a symbol of Nature wherever she is pictured as submissive or wherever she is disempowered in the social order, we can believe that culture has a supernatural power over Nature. If the Jew, who we imagine plots against us, is stripped of all civil rights, we can believe that we have control over natural power. Even those of us who suffer materially and psychologically from this delusory system of control have been educated to feel a false sense of safety from it.

Yet indeed none of us are safe. Now our lives are, every one of us, endangered by this delusion. For the delusion itself cannot rest. It is like the hungry tiger of our fearful dreams: devouring.

When the technologist destroys the mountain, he must feel, momentarily, a false sense of triumph. Like the explorers of an earlier age, he has conquered this piece of earth. He has wrested from her what he wanted. He has beaten her. And yet now, as he looks on the devastation he has caused, he cannot help but see there an image of his own inner life. His soul has been robbed by this theft. The death he sees before him must at one and the same time remind him of the part of himself he has murdered and his own inevitable mortality which, in the very act of controlling Nature, he has tried to deny.

The very images and avenues that express our power over Nature take us back to our own memory and knowledge of Nature's power both inside and outside of ourselves. Therefore our delusion demands that we gain a greater control over Nature. We must escalate our efforts. We must improve our technology.

One can see the dimensions of this madness more clearly in the development of the nuclear power industry. At each turning point, when a piece of human technology was seen to fail, the architects of this industry never questioned the fundamental premise that we are meant to make use of the energy inside the atom by splitting matter apart. Instead, another technological solution was offered. And each technological solution has in turn posed a greater danger.

Repeatedly one reads in the newspapers that an error in the design of a nuclear power plant has been covered over by the men who build and operate the plants. In many cases the economic motivation for such a denial is clear. To design the plant properly would take many more millions of dollars. But even given this economic motive, one wonders why these men, who often live in the area of the plant and

work there every day, are not afraid for their own lives or the lives of
their families. But the answer is that they rely for a feeling of safety
not on rational information about natural law, but on the delusion
that culture, through technology or any other means, can control
Nature.

The mind that invents a delusion of power over Nature in order to
feel safe is afraid of fear itself. And the more this mind learns to rely
on delusion, the less tolerance this mind has for any betrayal of that
delusion. For we must remember that this mind has denied that it
itself is a thing of Nature. It has begun to identify not only its own
survival, but its own existence with culture. The mind believes that
it exists because what it thinks is true. Therefore, to contradict delusion
is to threaten the mind's very existence. And the ideas, words, numbers,
concepts have become more real to this mind than material reality.

Thus when this mind is threatened by a material danger, it does
not respond rationally. For this mind has lost touch with material
reality. It is a mind possessed by madness, by a hallucinated idea of
its own power. We can see such a mind at work in Stalin, during the
period of Soviet industrialization. In this period, the Soviet Union as
a nation faced the grave material danger of hunger and starvation. And
yet, as a solution, Stalin chose to destroy real and operating farms
before the new, sanctioned way of farming was functioning. Issac
Deutscher writes vividly of this cast of mind, "The whole experiment
seemed to be a piece of prodigious insanity, in which all the rules of
logic and principles of economics were turned upside down. It was as
if a whole nation had suddenly abandoned and destroyed its houses
and huts which, though obsolete and decaying, existed in reality, and
moved lock, stock, and barrel, into some illusory buildings."

But what is essential to understand about this mind is that it is in
a panic. It will go to any lengths to defend its delusory idea of reality.
Those who opposed Stalin's plans for collectivization were sent to prison
camps or murdered.

And the extent to which a belief in ideas over reality is a part of
this century was predicted by George Orwell in his novel, *1984,*
through the humorous but now distressingly accurate parody of a
governmental slogan he invented, "Peace is War." Thus today it is
actually presented as a rational argument that a buildup in arms, or a
"preventative" invasion of another country, is the best way to keep
peace.

We all understand economic motivation as fundamental to human
nature. And yet we are making a mistake if we believe that this is the
only motivation. For economics touch upon reality. It would, after
all, be of no economic profit to anyone living to destroy the earth.
Such a destruction could only be seen as profitable by a madman.

But it is madness and the motivations of madness that I am describing here.

It is only when we understand how economic motivation can be shaped and changed by this madness that we can begin to see the real danger that our culture's state of delusion poses for us. Let us take the slave trade for an example. There is an obvious economic profit to be gained by adventurers from the sale of other human beings. And yet we must question whether simply self-interest leads naturally to such a violation of other beings. Is it not a soul already distorted that can consider enslaving another human being?

Self-interest, the desire to survive, is simply part of flesh, an emotion that arises in us by virtue of our material existence, by virtue even of our love for life and for this earth. But early in childhood we are taught that our survival depends on a freedom from natural power. We are taught that we live not through the understanding of Nature but through the manipulation of Nature.

If one studies the definitions of liberty in the *Oxford English Dictionary* one sees that liberty, first defined as an "exemption or release from captivity, bondage or slavery," later becomes "the faculty or power to do as one likes," and then becomes "an unrestrained use of or access to"—as in "to take liberties with a wench"—and finally, liberty means "at one's power or disposal."

Like the Inquisition and the witch burnings, the slave trade began at the time of the scientific revolution, in the sixteenth century. This revolution threatened to change the old worldview that men ordered Nature and replaced it with an understanding of a natural law to which we are all subject. The delusion that we are free from natural law was endangered. But that freedom could be regained symbolically by enslaving a people whom this culture conceived of as symbols of Nature. At this time and through the nineteenth century it was both a scientific and a general belief that Africans were closer to Nature than white men and women. In the nineteenth century, after evolutionary theory, scientists argued that Africans had descended more directly from primates.

That the slave trade was not motivated by simple economic self-interest becomes more clear when one studies the conditions that had to be endured by the men, women, and children taken into captivity on the slave ships. So many died during these trips across the water, not only from disease and exposure to the elements, but also from the brutality of the slave traders. Had these men valued their cargo from a simple economic motive they might have taken more care to preserve these lives. But, instead, an unwonted measure of cruelty entered their acts.

Ruth and Jacob Weldon, an African couple who experienced a slave passage, recorded an incident of a child of nine months who was flogged continuously for refusing to eat. Because this beating failed to move the child to eat, the captain ordered that "the child be placed feet first into a pot of boiling water. After trying other torturous methods with no success, the captain dropped the child and caused its death. Not deriving enough satisfaction from this sadistic act, he then commanded the mother to throw the body of the child overboard. The mother refused but she was beaten until she submitted."

That Bell Hooks called this behavior sadistic is entirely fitting. Clearly, to murder a child in order to get that child to eat is not rational behavior. Rather, the motive lay elsewhere, with the desire to inflict cruelty for its own sake. But why is it that a slave trader should be cruel to a black child? Because of his blackness this child became, in the insane mind of this civilization, and in the mind of this captain, a symbol of natural power. And the infancy of the boy would remind this man of his own infancy, of his own memory of vulnerability, of his own naturalness. Thus, at one and the same time, he could show his power over Nature, and punish his own vulnerable child, the child within him who was still part of Nature. Underneath his hatred and his cruelty existed a profound self-hatred.

Each time that the child refused to do as he ordered, he was, in an undiscovered region of his own soul, terrified. For this could only mean that he was losing his power, and therefore that his whole existence was being threatened. In this way, the captain could believe that he murdered a nine-month-old child in defense of himself. And if a part of him suffered with that child, he could punish his own compassion, and compassion itself, by forcing the child's mother to throw the child overboard. For such a compassion is also dangerous to this mind, since compassion brings us back to our own capacity to feel.

The same blend of economic and symbolic motivation inspired the Holocaust. At the time of Hitler's rise to power, Germany suffered from a terrible economic depression. And at the same time the old paradigmatic view of man at the center of the universe was again being threatened by scientific discovery. The Nazi Party identified the Jew as responsible for the economic privation. But what is the emotional experience of economic poverty? It is not simply the absence of money that is felt, but the absence of food, or shelter, or safety. Poverty, or even economic insecurity, places us at the mercy of Nature. We become afraid of loss, of suffering, of death. In its delusion of power over Nature, the European mind had made the Jew the symbol of Nature. Frightened by economic insecurity and by a changing worldview, the Nazi stripped the Jew of civil rights and of the right to own possessions, and the Holocaust began.

We can recognize in Hitler's madness a self-portrait of this civilization that has shaped our minds. Today modern science makes the same attempt to control procreation through genetic engineering. And in an article by Rosalie Bertell (in *Reclaim the Earth*), one reads that radiation causes genetic mutation and sterility. Thus civilization continues to rage at procreation. And today we also share with the Nazi mind a plan for a final solution to the problem of Nature. This solution is to destroy Nature and replace Nature with a record of her destruction. One sees this pattern again and again in history. Despite the fact that the Third Reich attempted to hide the existence of concentration camps from international scrutiny, the atrocities committed in them were carefully documented by the SS (*Schutzstaffel*, a quasi military unit of the Nazi party). Hitler used to watch films in his private rooms of men and women being murdered and tortured.

Today US military strategists have developed a new plan for winning a nuclear war. They argue that the winner of a nuclear war will be the side that has kept the best record of destruction, the side that knows the most about what has taken place. Hence intelligence-gathering devices are being prepared for launching into space, where these machines will not be destroyed. These men have actually confused their own physical survival with the survival of information.

It is in the nature of the deluded mind to choose to preserve its delusion over its own life. When the German armies were faltering on the Russian Front, Hitler diverted troop and supply trains from that crucial battle in order to carry women, men and children to Auschwitz to their deaths. He imagined his war against the Jew to be more important. And this was the real war in which his mind was engaged—a war, in fact, with himself. For Hitler's personal hatred for the Jew was a covert hatred of a part of himself.

This is also true of our civilization as a whole. We do not know ourselves. We try to deny what we know. We try to break the heart and the spirit of Nature, which is our own heart and our own spirit. We are possessed by an illness created by our minds, an illness that resembles sado-masochism, schizophrenia, paranoia—all the forms of the troubled soul. We are divided from our selves. We punish ourselves. We are terrified of what we know and who we are. And finally, we belong to a civilization bent upon suicide, secretly committed to destroying Nature and destroying the self that is Nature.

But we each have another secret too, a secret knowledge of wholeness. The schemata of memory exclude our memory of childhood. We do not think we still know what it was to be a child, untaught by culture to be divided from ourselves. Yet within each of us, in our bodies, that memory still exists. Our own breath reminds us of that knowledge, of a time when we were curious, when we let Nature speak to us and in us.

There exists a culture that is not alienated from Nature but expresses Nature. The mind is a physical place. The mind is made up of tissue and blood, of cells and atoms, and possesses all the knowledge of the cell, all the balance of the atom. Human language is shaped to the human mouth, made by and for the tongue, made up of sounds that can be heard by the ear. And there is to the earth and the structure of matter a kind of resonance. We were meant to hear one another, to feel. Our sexual feelings, our capacity for joy and pleasure, our love of beauty, move us toward a love that binds us to an existence. If there is a sound wave anywhere on this earth, if there is the sound of weeping or of laughter, this reaches my ears, reaches your ears. We are connected not only by the fact of our dependency on this biosphere and our participation in one field of matter and energy, in which no boundary exists between my skin and the air and you, but also by what we know and what we feel. Our own knowledge, if we can once again possess it, is as vast as existence.

I am a woman born in and shaped by this civilization, with the mind of this civilization, but also with the mind and body of a woman, with human experience. Suffering grief in my own life, I have felt all the impulses that are part of my culture in my own soul. In my resistance to pain and change, I have felt the will toward self-annihilation. And still the singing in my body daily returns me to a love of this earth. I know that by a slow practice, if I am to survive, I must learn to listen to this song.

2

The Ecology of Feminism and the Feminism of Ecology

Ynestra King

> [Woman] became the embodiment of the biological function, the image of nature, the subjugation of which constituted that civilization's title to fame. For millenia men dreamed of acquiring absolute mastery over nature, of converting the cosmos into one immense hunting ground. It was to this that the idea of man was geared in a male-dominated society. This was the significance of reason, his prouded boast.
> —Horkheimer and Adorno, *Dialectic of Enlightenment*[1]

All human beings are natural beings. That may seem like an obvious fact, yet we live in a culture that is founded on the repudiation and domination of nature. This has a special significance for women because, in patriarchal thought, women are believed to be closer to nature than men. This gives women a particular stake in ending the domination of nature—in healing the alienation between human and nonhuman nature. This is also the ultimate goal of the ecology movement, but the ecology movement is not necessarily feminist.

For the most part, ecologists, with their concern for nonhuman nature, have yet to understand that they have a particular stake in ending the domination of women. They do not understand that a central reason for woman's oppression is her association with the despised nature they are so concerned about. The hatred of women and the hatred of nature are intimately connected and mutually reinforcing. Starting with this premise, this article explores why feminism and ecology need each other, and suggests the beginnings of a theory of ecological feminism: ecofeminism.

What Is Ecology?

Ecological science concerns itself with the interrelationships among all forms of life. It aims to harmonize nature, human and nonhuman. It

18

is an integrative science in an age of fragmentation and specialization. It is also a critical science which grounds and necessitates a critique of our existing society. It is a reconstructive science in that it suggests directions for reconstructing human society in harmony with the natural environment.

Social ecologists are asking how we might survive on the planet and develop systems of food and energy production, architecture, and ways of life that will allow human beings to fulfill our material needs and live in harmony with nonhuman nature. This work has led to a social critique by biologists and to an exploration of biology and ecology by social thinkers. The perspective that self-consciously attempts to integrate both biological and social aspects of the relationship between human beings and their environment is known as *social ecology*. This perspective, developed primarily by Murray Bookchin,[2] to whom I am indebted for my understanding of social ecology, has embodied the anarchist critique that links domination and hierarchy in human society to the despoilation of nonhuman nature. While this analysis is useful, social ecology without feminism is incomplete.

Feminism grounds this critique of domination by identifying the prototype of other forms of domination: that of man over woman. Potentially, feminism creates a concrete global community of interests among particularly life-oriented people of the world: women. Feminist analysis supplies the theory, program, and process without which the radical potential of social ecology remains blunted. Ecofeminism develops the connections between ecology and feminism that social ecology needs in order to reach its own avowed goal of creating a free and ecological way of life.

What are these connections? Social ecology challenges the dualistic belief that nature and culture are separate and opposed. Ecofeminism finds misogyny at the root of that opposition. Ecofeminist principles are based on the following beliefs:

1. The building of Western industrial civilization in opposition to nature interacts dialectically with and reinforces the subjugation of women, because women are believed to be closer to nature. Therefore, ecofeminists take on the life-struggles of all of nature as our own.

2. Life on earth is an interconnected web, not a hierarchy. There is no natural hierarchy; human hierarchy is projected onto nature and then used to justify social domination. Therefore, ecofeminist theory seeks to show the connections between all forms of domination, including the domination of nonhuman nature, and ecofeminist practice is necessarily antihierarchical.

3. A healthy, balanced ecosystem, including human and nonhuman inhabitants, must maintain diversity. Ecologically, environmental simplification is as significant a problem as environmental pollution. Biological simplification, i.e., the wiping out of whole species, corresponds to reducing human diversity into faceless workers, or to the homogenization of taste and culture through mass consumer markets. Social life and natural life are literally simplified to the inorganic for the convenience of market society. Therefore we need a decentralized global movement that is founded on common interests yet celebrates diversity and opposes all forms of domination and violence. Potentially, ecofeminism is such a movement.

4. The survival of the species necessitates a renewed understanding of our relationship to nature, of our own bodily nature, and of nonhuman nature around us; it necessitates a challenging of the nature-culture dualism and a corresponding radical restructuring of human society according to feminist and ecological principles. Adrienne Rich says, "When we speak of transformation we speak more accurately out of the vision of a process which will leave neither surfaces nor depths unchanged, which enters society at the most essential level of the subjugation of women and nature by men. . . . "[3]

The ecology movement, in theory and practice, attempts to speak for nature—the "other" that has no voice and is not conceived of subjectively in our civilization. Feminism represents the refusal of the original "other" in patriarchal human society to remain silent or to be the "other" any longer. Its challenge of social domination extends beyond sex to social domination of all kinds, because the domination of sex, race, and class and the domination of nature are mutually reinforcing. Women are the "others" in human society, who have been silent in public and who now speak through the feminist movement.

Women, Nature and Culture: The Ecofeminist Position

In the project of building Western industrial civilization, nature became something to be dominated, overcome, made to serve the needs of men. She was stripped of her magical powers and properties and was reduced to "natural resources" to be exploited by human beings to fulfill human needs and purposes which were defined in opposition to nature (see Merchant, who interprets the scientific revolution as the death of nature, and argues that it had a particularly detrimental effect on women.)[4] A dualistic Christianity had become ascendant with the earlier demise of old goddess religions, paganism, and animistic belief systems.[5] With the disenchantment of nature came the conditions for unchecked scientific exploration and technological exploitation.[6] We bear the consequences today of beliefs in unlimited control over nature and in science's ability to solve any problem, as nuclear power plants are built without provisions for waste disposal, and satellites are sent into space without provision for retrieval.

In this way, nature became "other," something essentially different from the dominant, to be objectified and subordinated. Women, who are identified with nature, have been similarly objectified and subordinated in patriarchal society. Women and nature, in this sense, are the original "others." Simone de Beauvoir has clarified this connection. For de Beauvoir, "transcendence" is the work of culture, it is the work of men. It is the process of overcoming immanence, a process of culture-building that is based on the increasing domination of nature. It is enterprise. "Immanence," symbolized by women, is that which calls men back, that which reminds man of what he wants to forget. It is his own link to nature that he must forget and overcome to achieve manhood and transcendence:

> Man seeks in woman the Other as Nature and as his fellow being. But we know what ambivalent feelings Nature inspires in man. He exploits her, but she crushes him, he is born of her and dies in her; she is the source of his being and the realm that he subjugates to his will; Nature is a vein of gross material in which the soul is imprisoned, and she is the supreme reality; she is contingence and Idea, the finite and the whole; she is what opposes the Spirit, and the Spirit itself. Now ally, now enemy, she appears as the dark chaos from whence life wells up, as this life itself, and as the over-yonder toward which life tends. Woman sums up Nature as Mother, Wife, and Idea; these forms now mingle and now conflict, and each of them wears a double visage.[7]

For de Beauvoir, patriarchal civilization is about the denial of men's mortality—of which women and nature are incessant reminders. Women's powers of procreation are distinguished from the powers of creation—the accomplishments through the vehicles of culture by which men achieve immortality. And yet this transcendence over women and nature can never be total: thus the ambivalence, the lack of self without other, the dependence of the self on the other both materially and emotionally. Thus develops a love-hate fetishization of women's bodies, which finds its ultimate manifestation in the sado-masochistic, pornographic displays of women as objects to be subdued, humiliated, and raped—the visual enactment of these fears and desires. (See Griffin, *Pornography and Silence*, for a full development of the relationship between nature-hating, women-hating, and pornography.)[8]

An important contribution of de Beauvoir's work is to show that men seek to dominate women and nature for reasons that are not simply economic. They do so as well for psychological reasons that involve a denial of a part of themselves, as do other male culture-making activities. The process begins with beating the tenderness and empathy out of small boys and directing their natural human curiosity and joy in affecting the world around them into arrogant attitudes and destructive paths.

For men raised in woman-hating cultures, the fact that they are born of women and are dependent upon nonhuman nature for existence is frightening. The process of objectification, of the making of women and nature into "others" to be appropriated and dominated, is based on a profound forgetting by men. They forget that they were born of women, were dependent on women in their early helpless years, and are dependent on nonhuman nature all their lives, which allows first for objectification and then for domination. "The loss of memory is a transcendental condition for science. All objectification is a forgetting."[9]

But the denied part of men is never fully obliterated. The memory remains in the knowledge of mortality and the fear of women's power. A basic fragility of gender identity exists that surfaces when received truths about women and men are challenged and the sexes depart from their "natural" roles. Opposition to the not-very-radical Equal Rights Amendment can be partially explained on these grounds. More threatening are homosexuality and the gay liberation movement, because they name a more radical truth—that sexual orientation is not indelible, nor is it naturally heterosexual. Lesbianism, particularly, which suggests that women who possess this repudiated primordial power can be self-sufficient, reminds men that they may not be needed. Men are forced into remembering their own dependence on women to support and mediate the construction of their private reality and their public civilization. Again there is the need to repress memory and oppress women.

The recognition of the connections between women and nature and of woman's bridge-like position between nature and culture poses three possible directions for feminism. One direction is the integration of women into the world of culture and production by severing the woman-nature connection. Writes anthropologist Sherry Ortner, "Ultimately, both men and women can and must be equally involved in projects of creativity and transcendence. Only then will women be seen as aligned with culture, in culture's ongoing dialectic with nature."[10] This position does not question nature-culture dualism itself, and it is the position taken by most socialist-feminists (see King, "Feminism and the Revolt of Nature")[11] and by de Beauvoir and Ortner, despite their insights into the connections between women and nature. They see the severance of the woman-nature connection as a condition of women's liberation.

Other feminists have reinforced the woman-nature connection: woman and nature, the spiritual and intuitive, versus man and the culture of patriarchal rationality.[12] This position also does not necessarily question nature-culture dualism or recognize that women's ecological sensitivity and life orientation is a socialized perspective that could be socialized right out of us depending on our day-to-day lives. There is no reason to believe that women placed in positions of patriarchal power will act any differently from men, or that we can bring about a feminist revolution without consciously understanding history and without confronting the existing economic and political power structures.

Ecofeminism suggests a third direction: a recognition that although the nature-culture dualism is a product of culture, we can nonetheless *consciously choose* not to sever the woman-nature connection by joining male culture. Rather, we can use it as a vantage point for creating a different kind of culture and politics that would integrate intuitive, spiritual, and rational forms of knowledge, embracing both science and magic insofar as they enable us to transform the nature-culture distinction and to envision and create a free, ecological society.

Ecofeminism and the Intersection of Feminism and Ecology

The implications of a culture based on the devaluation of life-giving and the celebration of life-taking are profound for ecology and for women. This fact about our culture links the theories and politics of the ecology movement with those of the feminist movement. Adrienne Rich has written:

> We have been perceived for too many centuries as pure Nature, exploited and raped like the earth and the solar system; small wonder if we now long to become Culture: pure spirit, mind. Yet it is precisely this culture and its political institutions which have split us off from itself. In so doing it has also split itself off from life, becoming the death culture of quantification, abstraction, and the will to power which has reached its most refined destructiveness in this century. It is this culture and politics of abstraction which women are talking of changing, of bringing into accountability in human terms.[13]

The way to ground a feminist critique of "this culture and politics of abstraction" is with a self-conscious ecological perspective that we apply to all theories and strategies, in the way that we are learning to apply race and class factors to every phase of feminist analysis.

Similarly, ecology requires a feminist perspective. Without a thorough feminist analysis of social domination that reveals the interconnected roots of misogyny and hatred of nature, ecology remains an abstraction: it is incomplete. If male ecological scientists and social ecologists fail to deal with misogyny—the deepest manifestation of nature-hating in their own lives—they are not living the ecological lives or creating the ecological society they claim.

The goals of harmonizing humanity and nonhuman nature, at both the experiential and theoretical levels, cannot be attained without the radical vision and understanding available from feminism. The twin concerns of ecofeminism—human liberation and our relationship to nonhuman nature—open the way to developing a set of ethics required for decision-making about technology. Technology signifies the tools that human beings use to interact with nature, including everything from the digging stick to nuclear bombs.

Ecofeminism also contributes an understanding of the connections between the domination of persons and the domination of nonhuman nature. Ecological science tells us that there is no hierarchy in nature itself, but rather a hierarchy in human society that is projected onto nature. Ecofeminism draws on feminist theory which asserts that the domination of woman was the original domination in human society, from which all other hierarchies—of rank, class, and political power—flow. Building on this unmasking of the ideology of a natural hierarchy of persons, ecofeminism uses its ecological perspective to develop the position that there is no hierarchy in nature: among persons, between persons and the rest of the natural world, or among the many forms of nonhuman nature. We live on the earth with millions of species, only one of which is the human species. Yet the human species in its patriarchal form is the only species which holds a conscious belief that it is entitled to dominion over the other species, and over the planet. Paradoxically, the human species is utterly dependent on nonhuman nature. We could not live without the rest of nature; it *could* live without us.

Ecofeminism draws on another basic principle of ecological science—unity in diversity—and develops it politically. Diversity in nature is necessary, and enriching. One of the major effects of industrial technology, capitalist or socialist, is environmental simplification. Many species are simply being wiped out, never to be seen on the earth again. In human society, commodity capitalism is intentionally simplifying human community and culture so that the same products can be marketed anywhere to anyone. The prospect is for all of us to be alike, with identical needs and desires, around the globe: Coca Cola in China, blue jeans in Russia, and American rock music virtually everywhere.

Few peoples of the earth have not had their lives touched and changed to some degree by the technology of industrialization. Ecofeminism as a social movement resists this social simplification through supporting the rich diversity of women the world over, and seeking a oneness in that diversity. Politically, ecofeminism opposes the ways that differences can separate women from each other, through the oppressions of class, privilege, sexuality, and race.

The special message of ecofeminism is that when women suffer through both social domination and the domination of nature, most of life on this planet suffers and is threatened as well. It is significant that feminism and ecology as social movements have emerged now, as nature's revolt against domination plays itself out in human history and in nonhuman nature at the same time. As we face slow environmental poisoning and the resulting environmental simplification, or the possible unleashing of our nuclear arsenals, we can hope that the prospect of the extinction of life on the planet will provide a universal impetus to social change. Ecofeminism supports utopian visions of harmonious, diverse, decentralized communities, using only those technologies based on ecological principles, as the only practical solution for the continuation of life on earth.

Visions and politics are joined as an ecofeminist culture and politics begin to emerge. Ecofeminists are taking direct action to effect changes that are immediate and personal as well as long-term and structural. Direct actions include learning holistic health and alternate ecological technologies, living in communities that explore old and new forms of spirituality which celebrate all life as diverse expressions of nature, considering the ecological consequences of our lifestyles and personal habits, and participating in creative public forms of resistance, including nonviolent civil disobedience.

Toward an Ecofeminist Praxis: Feminist Antimilitarism

Theory never converts simply or easily into practice: in fact, theory often lags behind practice, attempting to articulate the understanding behind things people are already doing. *Praxis* is the unity of thought and action, or theory and practice. Many of the women who founded the feminist antimilitarist movement in Europe and the United States share the ecofeminist perspective I have articulated. I believe that the movement as I will briefly describe it here grows out of such an understanding. For the last three years I have been personally involved in the ecofeminist antimilitarist movement, so the following is a first-hand account of one example of our praxis.

The connections between violence against women, a militarized culture, and the development and deployment of nuclear weapons have long been evident to pacifist feminists.[14] Ecofeminists like myself, whose concerns with all of life stem from an understanding of the connections between misogyny and the destruction of nature, began to see militarism and the death-courting weapons industry as the most immediate threat to continued life on the planet, while the ecological effects of other modern technologies pose a more long-term threat. In this manner militarism has become a central issue for most ecofeminists. Along with this development, many of us accepted the analysis of violence made by pacifist feminists and, therefore, began to see nonviolent direct action and resistance as the basis of our political practice.

The ecofeminist analysis of militarism is concerned with the militarization of culture and the economic priorities reflected by our enormous "defense" budgets and dwindling social services budgets. The level of weaponry and the militaristic economic priorities are products of patriarchal culture that speaks violence at every level. Our freedom and our lives are threatened, even if there is no war and none of the nuclear weapons are ever used. We have tried to make clear the particular ways that women suffer from war-making—as spoils to victorious armies, as refugees, as disabled and older women and single mothers who are dependent on dwindling social services. We connect the fear of nuclear annihilation with women's fear of male violence in our everyday lives.

For ecofeminists, military technology reflects a pervasive cultural and political situation. It is connected with rape, genocide, and imperialism, with starvation and homelessness, with the poisoning of the environment, and with the fearful lives of the world's peoples— especially those of women. Military and state power hierarchies join and reinforce each other through military technology. Particularly as shaped by ecofeminism, the feminist anti-militarist movement in the United States and Europe is a movement against a monstrously destructive technology and set of power relationships embodied in militarism.

Actions have been organized at the Pentagon in the United States and at military installations in Europe. The Women's Pentagon Action, originally conceived at an ecofeminist conference which I and others organized, has taken place at the Pentagon twice so far, on November 16 and 17, 1980, and November 15 and 16, 1981. It included about two thousand women the first year, and more than twice that the second. I took part in planning both actions and we took care to make the actions reflect *all* aspects of our politics. Intentionally there were no speakers, no leaders; the action sought to emphasize the connections between the military issue and other ecofeminist issues.

The themes of the Women's Pentagon Action have carried over into other actions our group has participated in, including those organized by others. At the June 12-14, 1982 disarmament demonstrations in New York City, the group's march contingent proclaimed the theme: "A feminist world is a nuclear free zone," the slogan hanging beneath a huge globe held aloft. Other banners told of visions for a feminist future, and members wore bibs that read "War is man-made," "Stop the violence in our lives," and "Disarm the patriarchy." There have been similar actions, drawing inspiration from the original Women's Pentagon Actions, elsewhere in the United States and in Europe. In California, the Bohemian Club, a male-only playground for corporate, government, and military elite, was the site of a demonstration by women who surrounded the club, enacting a life-affirming protest ritual (see Starhawk). [15] In England on December 12, 1982, thirty thousand women surrounded a US military installation, weaving into the fence baby clothes, scarves, poems and other personal-life symbols. At one point, spontaneously, the word *freedom* rose from the lips of the women and was heard round and round the base. Three thousand women nonviolently blocked the entrances to the base on December 13 (see Fisher). [16]

The politics being created by these actions draw on women's culture: embodying what is best in women's life-oriented socialization, building on women's difference, organizing antihierarchically in small groups in visually and emotionally imaginative ways, and seeking an integration of issues.

These actions exemplify ecofeminism. While technocratic experts (including feminists) argue the merits and demerits of weapons systems, ecofeminism approaches the disarmament issues on an intimate and moral level. Ecofeminism holds that a personalized, decentralized life-affirming culture and politics of direct action are crucially needed to stop the arms race and transform the world's priorities. Because such weaponry does not exist apart from a contempt for women and all of nature, the issue of disarmament and threat of nuclear war is a feminist issue. It is the ultimate human issue, and the ultimate ecological issue. And so ecology, feminism, and liberation for all of nature, including ourselves, are joined.

Endnotes

1. Max Horkheimer and Theodor W. Adorno, *Dialectic of Enlightenment*, Seabury Press, New York, 1972, p. 248.
2. Murray Bookchin, *The Ecology of Freedom: The Emergence and Dissolution of Hierarchy*, Cheshire Books, Palo Alto, 1982.
3. Adrienne Rich, *On Lies, Secrets, and Silence*, W. W. Norton, New York, 1979, p. 248.

4. Carolyn Merchant, *The Death of Nature: Women, Ecology, and the Scientific Revolution*, Harper & Row, New York, 1980.
5. Rosemary Radford Reuther, *New Woman/New Earth: Sexist Ideologies and Human Liberation*. Seabury Press, New York, 1975.
6. Merchant, op.cit.
7. Simone de Beauvoir, *The Second Sex*, Modern Library, Random House, New York, 1968, p. 144.
8. Susan Griffin, *Pornography and Silence: "Culture's" Revenge against Nature*, Harper & Row, New York, 1981.
9. Horkheimer, op.cit., p. 230.
10. Sherry B. Ortner, "Is Female to Male as Nature is to Culture?" *Woman, Culture and Society*, Michele Zimbalist Rosaldo and Louis Lamphere, eds., Stanford University Press, Stanford, 1974, p. 87.
11. Ynestra King, "Feminism and The Revolt of Nature," *Heresies* 13: 12-16, Fall 1981.
12. Many such feminists call themselves ecofeminists. Some of them cite Susan Griffin's *Woman and Nature* (Harper & Row, San Francisco, 1978) as the source of their understanding of the deep connections between women and nature, and their politics. *Woman and Nature* is an inspirational poetic work with political implications. It explores the terrain of our deepest naturalness, but I do not read it as a delineation of a set of politics. To use Griffin's work in this way is to make it into something it was not intended to be. In personal conversation and in her more politically explicit works such as *Pornography and Silence* (1981), Griffin is antidualistic, struggling to bridge the false oppositions of nature and culture, passion and reason. Both science and poetry are deeply intuitive processes. Another work often cited by ecofeminists is Mary Daly's *Gyn/ecology* (1978). Daly, a theologian/philosopher, is also an inspirational thinker, but she is a genuinely dualistic thinker, reversing the "truths" of patriarchal theology. While I have learned a great deal from Daly, my perspective differs from hers in that I believe that any truly ecological politics, including ecological feminism, must be ultimately antidualistic.
13. Adrienne Rich, *Of Woman Born*, W. W. Norton, New York, 1976, p. 285.
14. Barbara Deming, *We Cannot Live Without Our Lives*, Grossman, New York, 1974.
15. Starhawk, *Dreaming the Dark: Magic, Sex and Politics*, Beacon Press, Boston, 1982, p. 168.
16. Berenice Fisher, "Women Ignite English Movement," *Womanews*, Feb. 1983.

Other Sources

Daly, Mary. *Gyn/ecology: The Metaethics of Radical Feminism*. Boston: Beacon Press, 1978.
Griffin, Susan. *Woman and Nature*. New York: Harper & Row, 1978.
King, Ynestra. "All is Connectedness: Scenes from the Women's Pentagon Action USA." In *Keeping the Peace: A Women's Peace Handbook*, Lynne Johnes, ed., London: The Women's Press, 1983.

3
A New Movement, A New Hope: East Wind, West Wind, and the Wind from the South

Corinne Kumar D'Souza

The Universal Mode

The Third World has, for too long, accepted as its rubric of reference a worldview that has hegemonized its cultures, its civilizations, decided its development model, its aesthetic categories, outlined its military physiognomy, determined its science and technology, its nuclear options. It is a cosmology constructed of what has come to be known as "universal" values: a universal worldview that has subsumed the civilizations of the Third World in its Eurocentric mode; a universal world order that has subjugated women in its androcentric matrix; a universal cosmology that is both imperialist and patriarchal.

This concept of "universalism" has its foundations in the political creed and philosophy of European liberal thought which proclaimed the ushering in of the industrial mode of production. The political philosophers emphasized the importance of private endeavor, private interests, private profits: competition and utilitarianism were its cornerstones. A philosophy based on the concept of possessive individualism generated an image of an individual who owed nothing to society. The individual was a product of the machinations of the market economy, and human labor—like every other commodity, could be bought and sold, beaten and used. A philosophy whose ideological and political roots were embedded in the specific historical context of the culture of the West: what qualified it then to be termed "universal"?

This reductionist vision of the world in which the center of the world was Europe and, later, North America (the West) encapsulated all civilizations into its own western frames, submerging them, erasing them. It made universal the specific historical experiences and cultural exigencies of the West; it announced that what was relevant to the West had to be the model for the rest of the world; what was good for the center had to be meaningful for the periphery. All that was western then simply became universal; every other civilization, every other system of knowledge.

The "other" in this cosmology was the civilizations of Asia, Africa, Latin America. Scarcely twenty years were enough to make two billion people define themselves as underdeveloped. It reduced all social totalities to one single model: all systems of science to one megascience, all indigenous medicine to one imperial medicine, all development to growth, to gross national product, to progress, to the "western self-image of homo economicus with all needs commodity *defined*," as Illich says. Concepts of gender have been deeply interwoven into the fabric of this cosmology. The "other" in this universal paradigm is woman, the nonmale, the nonpowerful, the nonhuman. In its construction of knowledge of the world, this paradigm left out the women; it has rendered the existence and experience of women mute and invisible. An androcentric perspective which, in its universal applicability, has "rendered" women not only unknown, but virtually unknowable.[1] For it not only marginalizes and excludes woman but denies her very existence, defining what it sees of her as what she is not. Woman is the "other," the deviant, the aberration. Woman is not man. This, in essence, is part of the universal patriarchal construct, whatever the cultural ethos, whatever the civilized idiom. The universal mode has determined the patterns of the world, indicating the scientific signs, giving it the development symbols, generating the military psyche, defining knowledge, truth: universal truths which have been gender blind. It recognizes poverty but refuses the feminization of poverty; science, but denies the genderization of science; development, but is blind to sexual economics.

The Scientific Worldview and the Genderization of Science

There exists in this universal mode a deep commitment to a conception of the world that is "scientific." Underlying its fundamental categories is a construction of knowledge that is "scientific"—rational, objective, neutral, linear, and also patriarchal. Cosmologies that do not fit into the framework whose basis was the certainty of scientific knowledge are dismissed and ridiculed: the cosmologies of "other" civilizations are submerged; the knowledge of "other" peoples, of "women," destroyed. The one, monolithic scientific paradigm in all its rationality and objectivity that dominates all civilizations, in all its patriarchalism, denies women.

The founding fathers of modern science (from the seventeenth century onward) described the universe as a well-organized machine; their paradigm defined the world in mathematical terms. Galileo, for whom nature spoke in quantifiables; Newton, who could explain all in fundamental measurables; Descartes' philosophy, which was mathematical in its essential nature. Societal parameters must be analyzed according to definite laws, measured by different scientific methods. The laws of the physical sciences were extended to developing the laws of society and only that which could be quantified, measured, and empirically determined was of any value and consequence. By adopting this Cartesian framework, the social sciences reduced complex phenomena into collectable, manageable, and—more important— controllable data, developing a "whole vocabulary of power, purposes, values and identity . . . ," which would be "rammed into measurable forms."[2] What happened then to facts that would not adjust into the existing methods? What became of the unmeasurable phenomena? What happened to work that could not be priced? All that is scientific, we are told, is certain, evident knowledge; all else, rejected.

By separating and then eliminating all the qualities of life from the quantities of which they are a part, the architects of the machine worldview were left with a cold, inert universe made up entirely of dead matter. This cosmology laid the basis for a thorough "desacralization of all forms of life during the ensuing industrial age."[3] The power and privileges of the powerful, the elimination of the weak and powerless, could be rationalized by appealing to the universal laws of nature. Marx and Engels and all the other "fathers" shared the same cosmology; they acknowledged the same theory of nature as the basic premise of the industrial mode. Utilitarianism was its idiom; they were convinced that the universe worked according to definite laws; and so too society. A cosmology that exalted "competition, power and violence over convention, ethics and religion. Thus it has become a portmanteau of nationalism, imperialism, militarism and dictatorship, of the cults of the hero, the superman and the master race."[4] A scientific worldview that has become the universal: a scientific worldview that also heralded the "masculine birth" of time.

Modern science evolved in a particular historical conjuncture—the rise of industrial capital and the market economy, the philosophy of possessive individualism and utilitarianism, the politics of the nation state. But if "modern science evolved in and helped to shape a particular social and political context, by the same token it evolved in conjunction with and helped to shape a particular ideology of gender. . . . gender ideology was a crucial mediator between the birth of modern science and the economic and political changes of the time."[5] Bacon often used metaphors of gender to describe the new science as power, "a force virile enough to penetrate and subdue nature, to bind nature to man's service and make her his slave" and thus achieve "the dominion of man over the universe." Bacon's purpose was not to know nature but to control, to gain power over "her." Nature was mysterious, passive, inert, female, and the task of the new scientists was to dominate her, to manipulate her, to transform her. Earlier worldviews, according to the modern scientists, could only "catch and grasp at nature," never "seize or detain her." The new worldview abounded in sexual metaphor and patriarchal imagery. Bacon sought a hasty and lawful marriage between Mind (masculine) and Nature (feminine): a marriage that was not a union of mind and matter but one that established the "empire of man over nature." "Masculine philosophers either conceived of nature as an alluring female, virgin, mysterious and challenging," or in their minds killed off nature entirely, writing of it as "mere matter, lifeless, barren, unmysterious, above all unthreatening, but still female."[6] The maleness of Mind and the femaleness of Matter has been significant in the construction of gender in relation to the dominant ideals of knowledge. This construction of knowledge brought its own meanings to the world.

Science and its worldview may, through its laws, explain the appearance, even the structure of phenomena, using its tools of quantification and objectification, but does not and cannot, capture their essence. It reduces the history of whole peoples into frames of "poverty line," "development," "progress." It writes the history of whole epochs, leaving out the women who are half of human experience, and in so doing can never penetrate the depths of the different rhythms of cultures, never grasp the meaning of the different idioms of civilizations or of peoples' spaces, never understand the different cosmologies of the women, the blacks, the marginalized, the silenced.

The modern scientific worldview is linear and in its linearity it characterizes whole cultures as uncivilized, undeveloped, unprogressive. Progress is the universal measuring stick of modernity, underlying which is a substratum of intolerance and violence. It reduces the cultures of the Third World to a single monoculture, a uniformity. The concept of progress in its linear movement is intrinsic to the typology of the evolutionary scientists who describe society in stages: a hunting culture is more primitive and therefore less civilized than an agrarian one, and that in turn more primitive than one committed to the industrial mode. The industrialized society is the peak of progress—the "other" civilizations must catch up. The dominant mode must become the universal.

This linear mode of thought determines not only civilizations but also consciousness: it becomes the norm by which "other" consciousness is measured. Other, meaning Third World; other, meaning women. Consciousness in this paradigm is stratified into higher and lower states, where higher is the rational, objective, scientific, the masculine; and the lower strata of "false consciousness" are populated by women and other oppressed people.

And it is this "false consciousness" of the masses that must be inculcated with a "scientific temper," so that the ultimate goal is attained—"people becoming rational and objective . . . favouring . . . a universalist outlook" (from a "Statement on Scientific Temper," October 25, 1980, signed by a group of scientists and social scientists in India). This "scientific establishment" goes on to describe the "scientific temper" that must permeate our society as "neither a collection of knowledge or facts, although it promotes such knowledge; nor is it rationalism, although it promotes rational thinking. It is something more. It is an attitude of mind which calls for a particular outlook and pattern of behaviour. It is of *universal* applicability and has to permeate through our society as the dominant value system, powerfully influencing the way we think. . . . " Ashis Nandy in the M. N. Roy Memorial address, 1980, titled "Science, Authoritarianism, Culture," analyzes how modern science is deeply structured isolation: "Our future, as we all know in this society, is being conceptualized and shaped by the modern witchcraft called the science of economics. If we do not love such a future, scientific child-rearing and scientific psychology are waiting to cure us of such false values and the various schools of psychotherapy are ready to certify us as dangerous neurotics. Another set of modern witch doctors has taken over the responsibility of making even the revolutionaries among us scientific."

But what if this worldview, which has depended on a logic of timelines, is also erroneous? What if the most fundamental error is the search for monocausation? What if the world is really a field of interconnecting events arranged in patterns of multiple meaning?[7] What if the scientific worldview is only one of the worldviews? What would happen to science and social science, which have become mega-industries? Scientists and social scientists who need their power and privileges are part of an ideological status quo which in turn needs the universality of the social sciences, in all their value-neutrality, their rationality and their objectivity, to legitimize and reproduce a violent social order, nationally and internationally.

Science explains the world by drawing a clear line between who is subject and what is object; the object could be Third World, machines, drugs, blacks, weapons, women—objects that can be measured, managed, manipulated. It then proceeds to collect and collate data, to fragment, to arrange, to analyze, to fit the object into categories and concepts and explain it in a language so confusing that it has nothing to do with reality. For instance, it may analyze the "facts" of poverty with its percentages and statistics; it could explain the structure of poverty vis-a-vis scientism, technological determinism and yet, in its knowledge and construction of poverty, actually leave the poor out. It dichotomizes the subject from the object, distancing the observer from the observed. How else will observer bias be avoided, how else its value-neutrality preserved? And it does more. It fractures the human being, separating the human self from human knowledge, the professional from the personal. It not only rends the "subjective social world from the objective one, idealism from materialism," but also "involvement and emotion from reason and analysis."[8]

Women and "Development"

We are all hostages of the universal mode.

A universal mode of knowledge that has made the Third World dispensable: a patriarchal worldview that has made women unknowable, invisible. This silence and invisibility took different forms in different cultures: in Iran, Pakistan, they hid us behind the chador (veil), in Egypt they mutilated our genitals, in Europe they burnt us as witches at the stake, in India, as brides, we are still for burning. . . . in China they bound our feet and still today in different cultures the "mind binding and spirit binding" continues.

It is a way of seeing; it is a way of not seeing.

And we cannot see women through the existing universal, patriarchal paradigms. In the existing construction of knowledge, concepts, and categories, to define women's place is shadow; women's work, shadow work; women's lives, shadow.

But we must see what is there: we must lift "the enormous weight of patriarchal thought, valuations and the thousands of years of institutionalized disadvantaging of women."[9] For women are, no matter how we draw the lines of caste, class, or race, the poorest of the poor. Almost everywhere women are pushed into low-paid, low-skilled jobs; almost everywhere women work longer hours, under more difficult conditions; almost everywhere lack nutrition, health care, maternity benefits; almost everywhere are used, abused. This is the women's face of poverty, the hidden face. In this paradigm woman has no place, she is excluded, denied, negated; it pretends she does not exist. Its definition of life "excludes the experience, denies the expression and negates the work of the non-powerful, the non-white, the non-western, the non-male!"[10]

In this mode of knowledge, the dominant view has consistently weighted competition over cooperation, exploitation over conservation, rationality over intuition, the yang over the yin. Capra, in *The Turning Point*, lists the associations of yin and yang, the two archetypal poles in the Chinese worldview, in which yin is associated with the "feminine, as responsive, co-operative, intuitive, sympathizing; the yang with the masculine, demanding, aggressive, competitive, rational, analytic."[11] In the existing worldview the duality paradigm favoring the masculine qualities creates a society in which the male mode of aggression, violence and control becomes the dominant mode, generating the militaristic mindset, the nuclear mentality, the war culture.

But the rational and the intuitive are two modes of perception, two ways of knowing. They are "not independent of each other." They are "two modes of consciousness which have been recognized as characteristic properties of the human mind."[12] In the eastern worldview (meaning oriental) these two seeming opposites do not belong to different opposing categories but are rather "two points of a single whole."

Nothing is only yin or only yang.

What is needed is to rediscover both the subjective and objective modes of knowing, creating newer and richer perceptions of knowledge that are more complex, creative. In weaving together these new knowledges, we will find new words, invent new meanings, envision new patterns, regenerate new cultural and "people's spaces," creating a new world order.

This could be the beginning of a new cosmology.

The South Wind

"I can tell the wind is rising, leaves trembling in the trees."

It is not difficult to see that we are at the end of an epoch, "when every old category begins to have a hollow sound, and when we are groping in the dusk to discover the new."[13] Can we find new words, envision new ways, "create out of the material of the human spirit" possibilities to transform the existing exploitative social order, to discern a greater human potential? What we need in the world today, is a new universalism; not a universalist cosmology, but a universalism that can combine dialectically the different cultural and civilizational idioms in the world. A universalism that will not deny the accumulated experience and knowledge of all the past generations; one that will not accept the imposition of any monolithic, "universal" structures under which, it is presumed, all other peoples must be subsumed. A new universalism that will respect the plurality of the different societies—of their philosophy, of their ideology, their traditions and cultures, one which will develop in the context of the dialectics of different civilizations, birthing a new cosmology.

The South Wind "rises in all its grandeur" bringing much to this cosmology. The South as movements for change in the Third Worlds; the South as the women's movements, wherever the movements exist; the South as the development of new frameworks, seeking a new language to describe what it perceives, rupturing the existing theoretical categories, breaking the mind constructs, challenging the one, real, objective reality. The South Wind must reclaim both the subjective and the objective modes of knowing, creating a wider and deeper structure of knowledge in which the observer is not distanced from the observed, the researcher from the researched, the dancer from the dance. The new cosmology will move away from Eurocentric and androcentric methodologies which only observe and describe, methodologies which quantify, percentify, classify, completely indifferent to phenomena which cannot be contained or explained through its frames. The South Wind invites us to create a new spectrum of methods which depart from the linear mode of thought and perception to one that is more complex, holistic. It urges us to discover more qualitative methodologies—oral history, experiencial analysis, action-research, poetry metaphor—which perhaps would reveal the complexities of reality more critically, more creatively, to place together the fragments, to discern the essence, to move into another space, another time, recapturing submerged knowledge, generating new spaces.

The movements for change need, today more than ever, to move toward developing conceptual paradigms born of a praxis that is rooted in the specificity of its social, cultural and political processes and able to relate the particular to the universal. No finished parameters of other revolutions of other days, born as they are of specific social ferments, can be applied mechanistically to its reality. For the peoples of the South, this alternative will develop a form of socialism, a new socialism, that will be embedded in the cultural methods of the three continents; a socialism that will not confine itself only to changing the objective reality, the material conditions of life, but which would seek a qualitative change in individuals, in social institutions, in gender relations, in political processes. It is extremely difficult to think of the need for qualitative changes to be included in the perspectives and visions for change in the national liberation movements, for the immediate needs in the Third World are expressed in quantitative terms: more food, better shelters, sufficient wages. Yet, history has shown us and continues to indicate through the phenomena of the "leftist" military juntas and the palace coups in the Third World, that the revolution to change the objective reality without addressing itself to the subjective factors has often only meant the replacement of one system of repression by another: the dehumanization, the brutalization takes other forms. What we need is a vision that would not only encompass the creation of better material conditions of life, but one that would go further; a new kind of socialism, that could, for the people's movements of the South at least, signify one historical choice.

These movements for an alternative social order are, as yet, only beginning within the different social formations, with no definite patterns but firm roots in the struggles and methods of the people. They express not only rejection of the present society, but the need to envision a new political world order and the determination to create it. These movements must seek a profound social change which would lead not merely to the replacement of one oppressive system by another within the old rubric, but a transformation that would lead to a qualitatively more human social order, a new consciousness. This demands not mere slogans, but a new politics, a new political praxis, a new political culture. This political praxis recognizes that the struggle for a different political order cannot be confined only to changes in the production process—in that a change in the ownership of the means of production or in material conditions will automatically bring a more equal social order—but finds its expression in a diversity of social movements. The women's movements unfolding in the different civilizations of the world could be a new point of coalescence of other movements for change—movements for peace in the West, for civil rights in the socialist countries, movements of blacks, national liberation movements. These autonomous, self-determining movements have a great significance in themselves and in relation to one another; and represent, perhaps, the beginning of a general awakening to that new phase of our evolution which alone can promise us any future. It is in the recognition of the relatedness of these movements which confront the structures of social control that the movements in the South will produce a form of politics and a new political culture that will depart from the existing dominant political and patriarchal modes and bring onto the historical stage plurality of the struggles of the people and the pluralism of civilizations.

The dominant political culture expressed through the increasing armament complex and military mindset pervades every dimension of life in society. Inherent within this political mode is a concept of power that is used to hegemonize, to repress, to violate; a political culture of terror. The new political praxis of the women's movements and other social movements in the South and the movements within other social systems, must move beyond this culture of power politics and develop a praxis that consciously refuses to mirror the existing political forms of power (as is understood within existing world political paradigms to maintain the balance of power). Instead, it must develop a concept of power that facilitates and encourages the creative potential in each one and in social movements, and in this process develops new political practices, a different code of ethics. What we need now is "the maturity to value freedom and tradition, the individual and community, science and nature, men and women."[14] The movements for change in different societies will not be identical, each bringing its own emphasis, its own ethos; its own politics, its own praxis. What is significant is that changes in the microcosm can, in their totality, produce a larger change in the global macrocosm, creating new spaces. Hopefully then, "the armourers and the police will begin to lose their authority. The ideologists will lose their lines. A new space for politics will open up."[15]

For the rest, it is not difficult to see that our epoch is a birth time and a period of transition; a time for deeper, creative investigation, and concrete struggles; a time for cultural rejuvenation, and the transformation of the entire fabric of social relationships; a time to develop a new universalism, and for the Third World, a new socialism; a time for new ventures, new visions.

And this is possible if we are willing to unearth the truth in all our "universals"—science, technology, development. Will we find a new understanding if instead of assessing what constitutes progress, we look at the victims of progress? Do we need new concepts to define work, the hierarchy of work, the monopoly of wage work over all kinds of work? Perhaps too a redefinition of needs; a redefinition of skills (man's work skilled, women's work unskilled), a reconceptualizing of wealth in an ecological framework of security in a peace paradigm, of development in a human rights perspective. Do we need to develop a new construction of knowledge, searching for "knowledge" that is not included in the universal, scientific body of knowledge, "knowledge" that is nonscientific? Perhaps it will only be the "insurrection of the submerged knowledges"[16] that will birth a new cosmology, a new social order. In all this, what is essential is not to develop new doctrines or dogmas, or "to define a new, coherent political schema . . . but to suggest a new, imaginative attitude, one that can be radical and subversive, by which alone we will be able to change the logic of our development."[17] What is essential is to go beyond the politics of terror of today's world and to search for a vision to create an alternative political order, a new pattern of civilization, bringing *to human consciousness a thought it thought unthinkable, making another consciousness afraid.*[18]

And to begin to move outside the universal, Eurocentric, patriarchal patterns, to search for new concepts that would touch and explain women's lives and experiences, that is to find fresh spaces, to find new historical possibilities for our time; and the women's movements signify one such possibility. It has the potential to fundamentally alter the nature of all knowledge, it has the promise to change the quality of life. Feminism is, to the social sciences, a distinct paradigm shift, to the social movements, a distinct rupture.

It brings to the world new meanings, new hope.

Endnotes

1. Barbara Du Bois, *Passionate Scholarship, Theories of Women's Studies*, Gloria Bowles and Renate Duelli Klein, eds., Routledge and Kegan Paul, London, 1983.
2. Mike Hales, *Science or Society, The Politics of the Work of Scientists*, Pan Books Ltd., 1982.
3. Jeremy Rifkin, *Algeny*, Penquin Books, 1987.
4. Gertrude Himmelfarb, *Darwin and the Darwinian Revolution*, W. W. Norton, New York, 1959.
5. Evelyn Fox Keller, *Gender and Science*, Yale University Press, 1985.
6. Brian Easlea, *Fathering the Unthinkable: Masculinity, Science and the Nuclear Arms Race*, Pluto Press, 1983.
7. Joan Robert, ed., *Beyond Intellectual Sexism*, David McKay, New York, 1976.
8. Lis Stanley and Sue Wise, *Back into the Personal: Or Our Attempt to Construct Feminist Research Theories of Women's Studies*, Gloria Bowles and Renate Duelli Klein, eds., Routledge and Kegan Paul, 1983.
9. Gerder Lerner, "Placing Women in History: A Theoretical Approach," paper presented at Organization of American Histories, San Francisco, 1980.
10. Bari Watkins, *Feminism: A Last Chance for the Humanities, Theories of Women's Studies*, Gloria Bowles and Renate Duelli Klein, eds., Routledge and Kegan Paul, 1983.
11. Fritjof Capra, *The Turning Point*, Simon and Schuster, USA, 1982.
12. Ibid.
13. E. P. Thompson, *Exterminism and the Cold War*, Verso Books, London, 1982.
14. Charlene Spretnak and Fritjof Capra, *Green Politics*, Paladin, Grafton Books, 1984.
15. Thompson, op.cit.
16. Gustavo Esteva, "Regenerating People's Spaces," *Alternatives*, Vol. XII, No. 1.
17. Andre Gorz, *Ecology as Politics*, South End Press, Boston, 1980.
18. W. H. Auden, *New Year Letter*, Faber and Faber, 1941. These lines referred specially to Karl Marx.

4
Mama Coyote Talks to the Boys*
Sharon Doubiago

The deep ecology movement is shockingly sexist. Shocking because deep ecology consciousness is feminist consciousness or—to put it in less loaded terms—ecology consciousness is traditional woman consciousness.

But nowhere is this acknowledgment made. Instead, papers, books, and repeated efforts are made to establish a tradition to show the similarity of deep ecology consciousness with "intuitionists, mystics and transcendentalists," with "the New Physicists," with Buddhism and traditional American Indian philosophies toward nature—all fields of study which are exotic, removed and masculine. In fact, as you, male ecologists, will have to admit upon any reflection, your bed partners and the person who most likely dominated your childhood have been sharing this consciousness with you all your lives.

Deep ecologists "are willing to listen to their inner voices," Warwick Fox declares. As everyone knows (and as many have deplored), Woman traditionally listens to her inner voice. The habit is considered symptomatic; indeed, hormonal, anatomic. Out of the vision that we are otherwise doomed, deep ecologists are attempting to articulate a paradigm of consciousness, relatedness, nonhierarchical thinking and "structuring" for the human being in Nature.

Feminist Rage and the Failure of New Left Men

As I have explored in my essay, "Where Is The Female On The Bearshit Trail?" and as Dorothy Dinnerstein does so brilliantly and concisely in the last chapter of *The Mermaid and the Minotaur: Sexual Arrangements and Human Malaise*, the antiwar, antiestablishment, ecological, back-to-the-land movement of the sixties and seventies was a movement in large part of young males taking on traditional female values and consciousness. Dinnerstein shows how this phenomenon evolved

*Excerpted from a longer, unpublished essay, "Mama Coyote Talks to the Boys."

directly, not rebelliously, from the values of our parents. Severely domesticated by three psychic shocks of World War II—our dropping the bomb on Japan; the full revelations of the German extermination camps; the bitter disillusionment of the American Left with Stalin—the generation of the thirties and forties turned then from the world and idealistic notions of bettering it, to the home, the job, the nuclear family, to the small private world where it might be possible to effect meaningful work.

Dinnerstein describes how and why the patriarchy through all history has been, more or less begrudgingly, supported by women. Women have had the role of, have been loved and valued for being, the Other— that is, the Voice of the heart, love, conscience, unconsciousness, compassion, sensitivity, sensuality, nature, nonlinear intuitive perception—the Other that men have demanded and greatly needed to turn back to, to return home to, from their ruthless world-making, their bloody battlefields.

There have been attempts by women throughout history to make their consciousness, their reality, a part of formal history. But when this finally began to occur in the sixties, the effect for women was that their traditional realm, for which they had always been valued, was co-opted by the men, who in turn demanded that women remain in the lesser aspects of the realm—as menial servants, as custodial mothers only, as loving supporters when they returned home from doing this new battle in the world. In other words, women lost their main value to the guys who no longer fulfilled their traditional role of provider, of respecter and lover of that which had been so unique in women. "The special rage in young contemporary feminism," Dinnerstein says, "has to do with men's failure (loss of nerve? inability? unwillingness?) to carry through the overt integrative effort they at last began: the integrative effort which in its own sudden and surprising way started to come forward to fuse with what women have tried to do in every foray into history they have attempted. . . . "

Nowhere in the present is the male failure more apparent than in the exclusion of feminism from the ecology movement. "What each sex knows best," Dinnerstein says, "has been distorted by a neurotically motivated sealing off from what the other knows best." Experience has given women "more intimate knowledge of these counter-considerations just as it has given men more intimate knowledge of formal world-making."

Women Have Always Thought Like Mountains

And so we have the male ecology movement, with all *you guys* (The True Traditional Separatists) trying to newly articulate a consciousness that women have always articulated (to you especially): that women, in Dinnerstein's words, "know best." Women have always thought like mountains, to allude to Aldo Leopold's paradigm for ecological thinking. (There's nothing like the experience of one's belly growing into a mountain to teach you this.) It is embarrassing to read some of your dissertations. For example, the way your traditional male philosophy defines a concept like "ethic": "An ethic, ecologically, is a limitation on freedom of action in the struggle for existence" (Aldo Leopold). That's hardly the way I'd define "ethic," nor can I imagine many women defining it thus—nor, for that matter, an American Indian, or a Buddhist mystic.

Starhawk's essays on Immanence—with her differentiations between "power-over" and "power-within"—are a good antidote to this kind of mechanical, linear, rights-and-duties thinking, "uncritically embedded," to use your words, "in the old paradigm." This definition of "ethic" is the reversal of "power-over"; it is, alas, power-loss. And here we are, at your oldest paradigm again, the one separatism evolves from: dualism. Dualism without that wonderfully feminine tool which that wonderful guy (Karl Marx) introduced mid-nineteenth century: synthesism.

Misogyny: The Ultimate Hatred of Nature

And so I want to ask you—I want you to ask yourselves—are you really deep ecologists? (The term reminds me of those bumperstickers: "Well-diggers Go Deeper, Divers Stay Down Longer!") Are you serious when you state repeatedly the need for a "fundamental change in thinking," for paradigm shifting, for "the man capable of transforming himself," when you recognize "there will be no revolution without a revolution in perception"? If so, why then are you not feminists? Some of you claim in your papers not to be afraid of mysticism and metaphysics. Are you afraid of women? Why is the ecology movement so utterly bereft of any and all knowledge of the vast work that has been done in the past 15 years on the irrefutable connection between mysogyny and hatred of nature? Ynestra King writes:

> Ecology requires a feminist perspective. Without a thorough analysis of social domination that reveals the interconnected roots of misogyny and hatred of nature, ecology remains an abstraction: it is incomplete. If male ecological scientists and social ecologists fail to deal with misogyny, the deepest manifestation of nature-hating in their own lives, they are not living the ecological lives or creating the ecological society they claim.

One wonders how serious you are as scholars, even? How you can maintain the notion of scholarly objectivity and research while blatantly ignoring the large field of study that exactly parallels yours, that in fact, is your field? Feminism and ecology are inseparable. They are the same subject, far more so than your favorite examples of Buddhism and Indian concepts. "One fears," George Sessions says, "that many western philosophers and other intellectuals are so thoroughly entrenched in their modern western academic training and methodologies and narrow specialties that they are going to be of very little help toward, and might actually constitute a reactionary hindrance to, the development of an ecological paradigm, or alternative worldview." The danger of this for deep ecologists is nowhere more apparant than in its separation from ecofeminism.

Ecofeminism. And your field, ecomasculinism. And to think ecology is supposed to be about connections, "unbroken wholeness which denies the classical idea of analyzability of the world into separately and independently existing parts" (David Bohm)! Like the figure of Coyote, that skinny, immoral, overly masculine cartoon trickster figure who, for many ecopoets, represents the Spirit of Earth, the deep ecology movement is tragicomically whacked out of balance, off the axis in its omission and exclusion of ecofeminist scholarship.

The Killing Split Between Male and Female Sensibilities

Deep ecologists and ecofeminists share a core vision: we are doomed if we do not change and change fast. We also share the terrible despair at times that the work is hopeless. The understanding of who and what is to blame for this outrageous predicament is the same in both: feminists call it The Patriarchy; ecologists evading the gender issue call it Western Culture, Science and Technology, Capitalism, Materialism, etc. Because of sexism, because of the psychotic avoidance of the issue at all costs, ecologists have failed to grasp the fact that at the core of our suicidal mission is the psychological issue of gender, the oldest war, the war of the sexes. This is the work that has been done so brilliantly by ecofeminists.

Truly profound, superior works have been produced by ecofeminists, superior because the women, typically, have made use of your work while you have remained ignorant of theirs. For this reason and perhaps because women have always thought like mountains, the ecofeminists are leaving you behind. I say this, admittedly, in an effort to stir your famous, competitive spirits, to goad you into going to this work.

Feminist theory of the past five years has moved into extraordinary, essential, but previously unexplored realms. No longer are feminist theorists afraid to really look at the issues of male/female anatomy and biology, for example, or issues like rape fantasies or sadomasochism, or the issue of dominance and submission that some maintain is at the core of the sex act. In the separate disciplines of philosophy, psychology, sociology, political science, ecology, and biology, there is nothing as profoundly new or as newly essential as what is occurring in the all-encompassing field of feminism. Real thinking is occurring, not science fiction projections like some of yours, but real analysis of ourselves that sexism has always prevented in the past, stemming from the core understanding that we are on the brink due to "the killing split—the split between male and female sensibilities" (Dinnerstein).

And so the paradigm change I am presenting to you: *Ecologists must become feminists.* If you don't, you are doomed to remain outside the real work of saving Earth. That is, you will remain the enemy you yourselves have identified. If in fact your visions have been authentic, if you mean the terms by which you define yourselves (which include the perception that it is dangerous work for the psyche), then it is time for ecophilosophers to embrace feminism.

5
Women/Wilderness*
Ursula K. LeGuin

What Freud mistook for her lack of civilisation is woman's lack of *loyalty* to civilisation.

—Lillian Smith

Civilized Man says: I am Self, I am Master, all the rest is Other—outside, below, underneath, subservient. I own, I use, I explore, I exploit, I control. What I do is what matters. What I want is what matter is for. I am that I am, and the rest is women and the wilderness, to be used as I see fit.

To this, Civilized Woman, in 1978 in the voice of Susan Griffin replies as follows:

We say there is no way to see his dying as separate from her living, or what he had done to her, or what part of her he had used. We say if you change the course of this river you change the shape of the whole place. And we say that what she did then could not be separated from what she held sacred in herself, what she had felt when he did that to her, what we hold sacred to ourselves, what we feel we could not go on without, and we say if this river leaves this place, nothing will grow and the mountain will crumble away, and we say what he did to her could not be separated from the way that he looked at her, and what he felt was right to do to her, and what they do to us, we say, shapes how they see us. That once the trees are cut down, the water will wash the mountain away and the river be heavy with mud, and there will be a flood. And we say that what he did to her he did to all of us. And that one act cannot be separated from another. And had he seen more clearly, we say, he might have predicted his own death. How if the trees grew on the hillside there would be no flood. And you cannot divert this river. We say look how the water flows from this place and returns as rainfall, everything returns, we say,

---

*In June 1986, Gary Snyder invited me to come talk to his class in Wilderness at the University of California at Davis. I told him I would say a little about women and wilderness and read some poetry, mostly from my book *Always Coming Home*. "Women/Wilderness" is what I said before getting into the reading. Highly tendentious, it was meant to, and did, provoke lively discussion.

and one thing follows another, there are limits, we say, on what can
be done and everything moves. We are all part of this motion, we
say, and the way of the river is sacred, and this grove of trees is sacred,
and we ourselves, we tell you, are sacred.
—Susan Griffin, *Woman and Nature*

What is happening here is that the wilderness is answering. This
has never happened before. We who live at this time are hearing news
that has never been heard before. A new thing is happening.

Daughters, the women are speaking.
They arrive
over the wise distances
on perfect feet.

The women are speaking: so says Linda Hogan of the Chickasaw
people. The women are speaking. Those who were identified as having
nothing to say, as sweet silence or monkey chatterers, those who were
identified with Nature, which listens, as against Man, who speaks—
those people are speaking. They speak for themselves and for the other
people, the others who have been silent, or silenced, or unheard, the
animals, the trees, the rivers, the rocks. And what they say is: We
are sacred.

Listen: they do not say "Nature is sacred." Because they distrust
that word, Nature. Nature as not including humanity, Nature as what
is not human, that Nature is a construct made by Man, not a real
thing; just as most of what Man says and knows about women is mere
myth and construct. Where I live as a woman is to men a wilderness.
But to me it is home.

The anthropologists Shirley and Edwin Ardener, talking about an
African village culture, made a useful and interesting mental shape.
They laid down two circles largely but not completely overlapping,
so that the center of the figure is the tall oval of interlap, and on each
side of it are facing crescents of non-overlap. One of the two circles is
the dominant element of the culture, that is, Men. The other is the
Muted element of the culture, that is, Women. As Elaine Showalter
explains the figure, "All male consciousness is within the dominant
circle, accessible to or structured by language." Both the crescent that
belongs to men only, and the crescent that belongs to women only,
outside the shared, central, civilized area of overlap, may be called
"the wilderness." The men's wilderness is real, it is where men can go
hunting and exploring and having all-male adventures, away from the
village, the shared center, and it is accessible to and structured by
language. "In terms of cultural anthropology, women know what the
male crescent is like, even if they have never seen it, because it becomes

the subject of legend . . . But men do not know what is in the wild," that is, the no-man's-land, the crescent that belongs to the muted group, the silent group, the group within the culture that *is not spoken*, whose experience is not considered to be part of human experience, that is, the women.

Men live their whole lives within the Dominant area. When they go off hunting bears, they come back with bear stories, and these are listened to by all, they become the history or the mythology of that culture. So the men's "wilderness" becomes "Nature," considered as the property of "Man."

But the experience of women as women, their experience unshared with men, that experience is the wilderness or the wildness that is utterly other—that is in fact, to Man, unnatural. That is what civilization has left out, what culture excludes, what the Dominants call animal, bestial, primitive, undeveloped, unauthentic . . . what has not been spoken, and when spoken, has not been heard . . . what we are just beginning to find words for, our words, not their words: the experience of women. For dominance-identified men and women both, that is true wildness. Their fear of it is ancient, profound, and violent. The misogyny that shapes every aspect of our civilization is the institutionalized form of male fear and hatred of what they have denied, and therefore cannot know, cannot share: that wild country, the being of women.

All we can do is try to speak it, try to say it, try to save it. Look, we say, this land is where your mother lived and where your daughter will live. This is your sister's country. You lived there as a child, boy or girl, you lived there—have you forgotten? All children are wild. You lived in the wild country. Why are you afraid of it?

PART TWO
HEALING
ALL OUR RELATIONS:
ECOFEMINIST POLITICS

> We all have a right to live on this Earth. We have the right to be free and to live in balance with nature, a part of nature, not apart from nature. We have the right not to be separated from our Mother, and we have the duty and obligation not to have our Mother destroyed by patristic stupidity.
> —Anne Cameron, "First Mother and the Rainbow Children"

The essence of feminism, that the personal is the political, is the driving force behind all ecofeminist political action. For we know that when we resist the rape of the earth, we are fighting the same mentality that allows the rape of women. We know, too, that insisting on healthy relationships with each other lays the foundation for healthy relations with the natural world. The existence of humanity and, without doubt, other species as well, is literally at stake. In our desire to save the earth, we, as ecofeminists, believe that it is folly to overlook the interconnectedness of the war on nature and the daily, often hidden war on "others"—whole cultures, women, children, and animals.

This section begins with a feminist creation myth by Anne Cameron followed by a discussion of the connections between the personal, political, and spiritual. She believes that feminists have always been concerned with the environment and that ecofeminism is an apology to the boys. Certainly the Chipko movement, from the heart of the Himalayas, where women have stood before the axes of the woodcutters time and again, shows how the spirit of ecofeminism has been practiced long before the term was ever coined. Pamela Philipose traces the spread of the spirit of the Chipko movement in a discussion of environmental activism throughout the rest of India. What is being defended is a 'right' relationship with the earth and this is beautifully shared by Gwaganad, a Haida woman, in her story of how her body tells her, every year, that it is time to harvest the herring roe. The destruction of place and cultures is the *real* story of development, as told by Vandana Shiva as she reveals how it has created real poverty. Coming to terms with our own processes of "othering" is the subject of Rachel Bagby's moving account of how feminist environmentalists in the United States are realizing their need to become color-wise in the defense of the earth. Finally, Marti Kheel writes about how western medicine, a recent phenomenon, is the real "alternative healing" and, in contrast to holistic practices, it represents the "greatest deviation in healing the world has ever known."

Tampons

Ellen Bass

My periods have changed. It is years
since I have swallowed pink and gray darvons, round
chalky midols from the bottle with the smiling girl.
Now I plan a quiet space,
protect myself those first few days when my uterus lets
go and I am an open anemone. I know
when my flow will come. I watch my mucous pace
changes like a dancer, follow the fall
and rise of my body heat. All this
and yet I never questioned them, those slim white handies.

It took me years to learn to use them
starting with pursettes and a jar of vaseline.
I didn't know where the hole was.
I didn't even know enough
to try to find one. I pushed until
only a little stuck out and hoped
that was far enough.
I tried every month through high school.

And now that I can change it in a moving car—
like Audrey Hepburn changing dresses in the taxi
in the last scene of Breakfast at Tiffany's—
I've got to give them up.

Tampons, I read, are
bleached, are
chemically treated to
compress better,
contain asbestos.
Good old asbestos. Once we learned not to shake it—
Johnson & Johnson's—on our babies or diaphragms,
we thought we had it licked.

So what do we do? They're universal.
Even macrobiotics and lesbian separatists are hooked on them.

Go back to sanitary napkins?
    Junior high, double napkins
    on the heavy days, walking home damp underpants
    chafing thighs. It's been a full twelve years
    since I have worn one, since Spain when Marjorie pierced my ears
    and I unloaded half a suitcase of the big gauze pads in the hotel trash.

Someone in my workshop suggested tassaways, little
cups that catch the flow.
                They've stopped making them,
                we're told. Women found they could reuse them
                and the company couldn't make enough
                money that way. Besides,
                the suction pulled the cervix out of shape.

Then diaphragms.
        It presses on me, one woman says.
        So swollen these days. Too tender.

Menstrual extraction, a young woman says.
I heard about that. Ten minutes
and it's done.
      But I do not trust putting tubes into my uterus each month.
      We're told everything is safe
      in the beginning.

Mosses.
The Indians used mosses.
        I live in Aptos. We grow
        succulents and pine.
        I will buy mosses
        when they sell them at the co-op.

Okay. It's like the whole birth control schmeer.
There just isn't a good way. Women bleed.
We bleed.
The blood flows out of us. So we will bleed.
Blood paintings on our thighs, patterns
like river beds, blood on the chairs in
insurance offices, blood on Greyhound buses
and 747's, blood blots, flower forms
on the blue skirts of the stewardesses.

Blood on restaurant floors, supermarket aisles, the steps of government
buildings. Sidewalks
                                                    Gretel's bread
                      will have
                                              like
                      blood trails,

crumbs. We can always find our way.

We will ease into rhythm together, it happens
when women live closely—African tribes, college sororities—
our blood flowing on the same days. The first day
of our heaviest flow we will gather in Palmer, Massachusetts
on the steps of Tampax, Inc. We'll have a bleed-in.
We'll smear the blood on our faces. Max Factor
will join OB in Bankruptcy. The perfume industry
will collapse, who needs
whale sperm, turtle oil, when we have free blood?
For a little while cleaning products will boom,
409, Lysol, Windex. But
the executives will give up. The cleaning woman is leaving a
red wet rivulet, as she scrubs down the previous stains.
It's no use. The men would have to
do it themselves, and that will never come up
for a vote at the Board. Women's clothing manufacturers, fancy
furniture, plush carpet, all will phase out. It's just not
practical. We will live the old ways.

Simple floors, dirt or concrete, can be hosed down
or straw, can be cycled through the compost.
Simple clothes, none in summer. No more swimming pools.
Swim in the river. Yes, swim in the river.
Dogs will fall in love with us.
We'll feed the fish with our blood. Our blood
will neutralize the chemicals and dissolve the old car parts.
Our blood will detoxify the phosphates and the
PCB's. Our blood will feed the depleted soils.
Our blood will water the dry, tired surface of the earth.
We will bleed. We will bleed. We will
bleed until we bathe her in our blood and she turns
slippery new like a baby birthing.

6
First Mother
and the Rainbow Children

Anne Cameron

First there was the Great Egg and, inside it, the promise of all life. That promise of life began to stir, to swell, to grow, and the shell holding the promise began to stretch. The shell cracked and, from inside the egg, the water of life began to flow: a single river of hope and commitment.

The River of Life brought with it the seeds of grass and tree, of flower and vine, of fruit and vegetable, of all those things which grow on or in the earth and reach for the sky. When these wonders were growing, spreading across the surface of the egg, the fish and fowl emerged, and took their places in the streams and the lakes, in the branches of the trees and in the skies above them. Then the animals came from within the egg, and moved along the river of life, emerging from the water and taking their place in the creation of all things. Every animal, every bird, every fish and every mammal who lives in the water, every snake and turtle, every one of the bugs and insects, every marvel of creation had its place and took it.

The Creator, the Voice Which Must Be Obeyed, then made First Woman. Her body was made of the dirt of the earth, this very earth on which we stand, this land, our home, and that was no accident. Her bones and teeth were made of the shells of the creatures of the sea, and the minerals in the rocks, and this was no accident. Her hair was made of the grass and moss, the same grass, the same moss that still grows all around us, and this was no accident. The light in her eyes, the light of life and knowing, was the light of the sun, the moon, the stars, and this was no accident.

First Mother did not come here from somewhere else. She did not come from the sky, she did not come from another star, she did not travel here from another planet, she was created here, on this, our home, of this very soil and her blood is the water of the sea, salty and life sustaining.

First Mother did not yet have the gift of speech, but she had the gift of understanding and of empathy. And she had within her body the gift of life. From her, from her body, from her body made of the soil and minerals of the earth and the water and salts of the sea, came children, many children, and they were all sisters and brothers, they all had the same mother, First Mother. And, as with flowers, these children did not all come in the same color; some were brown as the earth, some were black as the night, some were red and some were pale, some saffron, and it pleased and amused them that they were not all identical. In time, these children grew to be adults, and had children of their own but, like their mother, they did not yet have the gift of speech.

They all followed the Dream, the Dream of harmony and love, of responsibility and commitment, of honor and respect, and they gave thanks for the bounty of the earth they shared.

And the Voice Which Must Be Obeyed gave them the gift of speech. They were at the fires, at night, with First Mother, who was by now many times a grandmother and great-grandmother, giving their Thanks, and the sparks which come from the cedar as it burns danced in the night darkness, upward, taking with them the prayers of the Children of the Rainbow family. The Creator blessed the prayer and accepted it, sent the sparks back downward, as blessing, and the throats of the Rainbow Family swelled with sound, language burst forth from them, floating on lip-kissed breath, rising with emotion, and words were formed, and the first of the words were those words which mean Mother.

The River of Life divided that night, and formed four rivers which flowed off in four directions, and the Rainbow family divided, to follow the rivers. Some of the cousins, with black skin, moved along one river, to find a homeland and fill their corner of the earth, some of the cousins, with yellow skin, moved along another river to find a homeland, some of the cousins with white skin, followed the third river to find their homeland, and the cousins with red skin stayed here and spread over this land, their homeland. Each of the family of cousins took with them the knowledge of the Great Egg, the knowledge of First Mother, the knowledge of the Dream, and the knowledge that the Earth, which formed the body of First Mother, was Mother of the First Mother and thus Grandmother to all of us.

And they all promised that if ever the day came when Mother Earth needed their protection, they would return to aid her, would re-form the Rainbow Family, would stand together as one people again, and give of their strength to protect Grandmother Earth, mother of First Mother, mother of us all.

And First Mother knew that her time had come, her purpose was fulfilled, her tasks finished. She left her shell of meat and bones and became something other than what she had been. She became part of the totality of creation, and each time the sun touches our skin, that is her touch, each time the rain moistens the earth, she is with us, when the breeze ruffles our hair, that is her hand, touching us as a mother touches her child, and when we sleep, she watches over us. Her meat and bones went back into the earth, returning to the mother-of-all, as will our meat and bones when our days here are finished, and yet she is with us all the time whether we remember her or not.

We are all her children and we all have the right to walk freely on the face of the Grandmother. We have the right and responsibility to live our lives fully, with dignity and with pride. And we have the obligation to First Mother, and to the earth from which she was made, to protect and honor the Old Grandmother, the Earth who has always nourished us and provided for us.

Some of the far-roaming Rainbow Children lost their Dream, some of us had the Dream wrenched from us, some of us had the Dream stolen from us, but the Dream is alive. Some of us have fragments of the Dream, some of us have pieces which others of us have lost. Together, we can re-form and relearn the Dream. We can use the precious gift of speech, which came to us from the sparks of the fire, to warm the hearts of all our cousins, all our children and, with love and reponsibility, we can heal ourselves of the sorrows and of the mistakes we have all made, we can once again know ourselves, and our parents, our grandparents, First Mother, and we can protect the Old Grandmother, this earth on which we live and to which we will all one day return.

When I was eight or nine, or maybe ten or eleven, I don't remember for sure now, Klopinum would share her stories with me. She taught me without me knowing I was being taught. She taught me the friendship and peace of solitude and the joy and laughter of companionship. She taught me to go to a freshwater source, to strip and to pray, to bathe and strengthen myself, to give thanks for everything I had and to recommit myself to all that is good and proper. She taught me there is only one way to do something, and that is the right way. If a thing is not done the right way, it is not done at all. She taught me you do not put garbage or waste in your drinking water, she taught me you do not heedlessly cut every tree and leave the earth to erode, unprotected and insulted. She taught me you do not foul the air you breathe, and she taught me you do not move on this earth disrespectfully and cruelly.

She taught me so much, and then suddenly she was gone. And now her great-grandson is like family to me and we call each other cousin. His daughter is my apprentice, because it is only proper that we give to the young what the elders have given to us; and if a thing is not done properly, it is not done. She gave me what I needed to stay sane in an insane world and, when I was older, and no longer a child, and needed to find my own spirit grandmothers, I knew how to recognize them because of what one very old woman had taught me. And for those of us whose Dream has been attacked and altered, made to appear to be untrue or irrelevent, the truth Klopinum guarded so well with her every breath and action is a rock which stands between us and the cold wind which could otherwise destroy us. We seek our Dream, we seek our Grandmother spirits, we seek what is true, and when we see, or hear, or are told, or learn of something, we can check it against what we see protected by old women like Klopinum; and always, if it is true, it is the same as what she knew. If someone tells me something and it contradicts what Klopinum taught, I know at least enough to have faith in her teaching because time will prove that the other thing is not true.

I am Celtic, and the Celts were the people of the horse, the people of the dog, the people of the bear, the people of the stag, the people of the wolf, the people of the salmon. We called ourselves the Pagans, the People Of The Earth, and our colors were red, black, yellow, and white. Our skill was weaving and the tying of knots, and we fished the rivers and the ocean. We honored The Mother, and inherited through her, and we honored oak, alder, cedar, and hawthorne. We measured our lives by the phases of the moon and built circles of stones to aid us in mathematics and to help us draw ourselves closer to that other world we cannot see but always feel. We had the medicine wheel and the sweat house, we had puberty training and ritual, and we learned the secrets of boat-building and navigation from the salmon and the seal.

People unlike us came from somewhere else, and our children were taken from us, educated in the ways and beliefs of the newcomer, made strangers to us. Our language was forbidden, our religion destroyed, our culture altered for all time and, in time, we became lost and confused, and identified with the strangers more than with our own people. We became like those who had come into our land, and we perpetrated against ourselves the same crimes, perpetuated the same sins, and began to hate ourselves for it.

We even came here and began to do to others what had already been done to us. But in the coming here we touched something that stirred a memory in our hearts and souls. And the Dream we had almost forgotten, the Dream we had ourselves almost destroyed, stirred. Some of us met old women like Klopinum and were shown a better way and, in the showing, we remembered things for which we had no explanation. Our Dream was never lost, it was only waiting for the day we would begin to assume our responsibilities.

With the awakening of the Dream we began to turn to the old women, and they introduced us to Old Woman, and what we learned, we called "feminism." Feminism taught us that the personal is political and spiritual. Every decision a person makes in her life is a personal, political, and spiritual decision. If you decide you will never live as a slave to drugs or alcohol, you have made a personal decision, but you have made a political decision and you have made a spiritual choice. That decision can only be made with the help and teachings of the ones who have defended and protected the Dream; the elders of the Rainbow People, children of First Mother.

We all have a right to live on this Earth. We have the right to be free and to live in balance with nature, a part of nature, not apart from nature. We have the right not to be separated from our Mother, and we have the duty and obligation not to have our Mother destroyed by patristic stupidity.

The feminist movement has long believed and lived "the personal is political, the political is personal," and now we have learned that the spiritual is an integral part of both personal and political. There can be no separation of spirituality, it is not something you do for an hour on Sunday afternoon, you live your belief or you demonstrate that you do not have a belief.

The feminist movement has also given us all a wonderful tool for developing and honing a personal analysis of the world around us; ask yourself "is it an accident?" then ask yourself "who benefits?" If that doesn't help you analyze what is happening, ask yourself "who benefits?" then ask yourself "is it an accident?"

They would like us all to believe that the answer to world hunger lies in a drastically reduced birth rate. Without analyzing or even thinking very much about it, we accept this idea, use contraceptive devices, and limit population growth. We do not always realize that many of the contraceptive devices are sure to shorten our lives. We believe unquestioningly that the experts are telling the truth when they say there are too many people for the earth's food resources.

Bullshit. The earth is easily producing enough food to provide every living human with a 3500–4000 calories-a-day diet. Anyone who eats that many calories for very long is going to wind up FAT. (Obesity is a major health concern in some areas of the world.) This food is sold to those who can afford it, and the "excess" food is destroyed. How can there be "excess" food when children die of malnutrition, starvation, and the diseases which opportunistically attack the underfed? Every time a child dies of hunger, it is OUR FAULT. The Earth did what she has always done, she provided the food. Our own greed and our timidity in challenging those who hoard and destroy food, helped kill the dead children.

Food has become available mainly to those with "money," and if you don't have it, you starve. But "money" is bullshit, too! Dow Jones, New York Stock Exchange, Toronto Stock Exchange, World Bank . . . does anybody really understand any of that? If "money" was what it was all about, you could print some in your basement and it would be "worth" something.

Resources is what we're talking. That money is worthless if it isn't backed by something, if it doesn't represent something. Resources. Every ten minutes, day and night, week in and week out, the United States expends enough resources in the development and continuation of the arms, nuclear, and space races to feed, clothe and educate every person on the face of the globe for 20 years.

Think on that. Try the logic of feminism. "Who benefits?" "Is it an accident?" Who benefits? Well, the generals, admirals, and other crazed professional killers benefit. They keep their highly paid jobs and get promoted to higher paid jobs, and then retire with very generous pensions. The makers of bulldozers and front-end loaders and trucks and mining equipment benefit, the owners of mines, the . . . "Is it an accident?" What accident? when those with more money than they know what to do with wind up getting more, and children die because we "cannot afford" to give them the food we are using bulldozers to bury, the food we are burning with all that napalm they didn't manage to use in one war zone or another.

Have you ever really looked at those dying children? Have you ever dared allow yourself to wonder why it is most of them have dark skin, dark hair, dark eyes and parents who are also dark? "Who benefits?" "Is It An Accident?"

Most of the wealth in the world, whether measured in money or in resources, is controlled by men. And the men who control those men are not dark-skinned. Is that an accident? Who benefits?

But we are ALL "native people." We are native to this earth.

After the opening of the egg, when there was the world and her beauty, when there were fish in the water and birds in the air, when there were mountains rich with trees, and clean water to nourish them, the Creator, the Voice Which Must Be Obeyed, took soil from this land, this very land, here, the land on which we stand, and made First Mother. Her bones are made of the shells of the creatures who live in the sea and the minerals in the earth, her blood is the ocean, her hair is the grass and the moss. She did not come from some other world, she did not fall from space, she was not delivered in a flying saucer, she was made here, and she was made of this Earth, of our Mother, who has always cared for us. And First Mother lived more years than we can imagine, and had children (she is Mother Of All People) and when she died, she went back to the Earth, who is our Mother and our Grandmother. When we have lived our lives and died, we too will return to the Earth, return to our Mother, return to our Grandmother, who will accept us as we have never been accepted here, and she will heal us.

We owe her our love, we owe her our allegiance, we owe her at least our energy and our protection. At the very least we owe her protection.

At the Stein Festival* in the late summer of 1987 a well-meaning woman stood up and talked about how all we really needed was love. If we just learned to love each other, the problems would no longer exist. I have been hearing this "love" theory for so long I am just about ready to spit up on my sneakers. While we're sitting in a circle loving each other, the corporations are hosing us in the ear and the military is testing new and more fantastic ways to blow us to hell.

Another woman stood up and said it was all up to the native Indians: they alone could save us from destruction. While we sit around talking about love? Does she realize how much of an insult it is to some of us to be erased as people with free will, to be left waiting for someone else to save us?

A man stood up and talked of how the native Indians should use public relations more effectively. They should send representatives to Asia to explain to those people, the ones who buy our logs, what logging is doing to the forests, to the mountains, rivers, meadows, and people.

Native North American people have the lowest per capita income in both Canada and the United States. They have the lowest life expectancy, the highest infant mortality rate. . . . Where is the money coming from to send people to Asia? Where is the money for effective public relations? The American utilities lobby can spend more than THREE BILLION DOLLARS fighting legislation to put an end to acid rain. Where do native people get that kind of money?

What is this bullshit in the environmental movement? There we were, in one of the most beautiful places I have ever seen, some of us there for native rights, some for ecology. I was not there for ecology. The ones who were true environmentalists were noticeable in the crowd; they had worn clothing, much-used, comfortable, durable, probably available in any WorkWear World store. Then there were the others in their specialty gear; highly processed fibers, almost all of them

*An intentional gathering in the alpine meadows of the Stein River in British Columbia, held to celebrate the value of this wilderness in the face of industry and government plans to log it.

artificial or "man-made" fibers, guaranteed to keep you warm when the weather is cold, keep you cool when the weather is warm, from the waist up they were wearing a thousand dollars worth of gear. Their tents came in all colors; burgundy and silver, blue and white, green and white, and in all shapes and sizes. The gear they had was obviously new, and could have kept them alive on a trip to the polar cap. They spoke of love, and of feeling lucky to be able to see such a beautiful place, they spoke in almost sing-song voices and asked repeatedly, "What can we do when we leave this wonderful place?," "Tell us what to do . . ."

Money. Send money to the tribal council, send money to the organizations already on the line to stop the patriarchy from destroying us all. If you can think of nothing else, send money.

It's better than nothing. And yet I really wonder what can come of a bunch of people who can unabashedly fork over that kind of money for that kind of gear, then sit asking other people to do their thinking for them!!

The feminist movement has always insisted that we take personal responsibility for our own thoughts, actions, and our situations in life. Nobody can help how she feels, but we can all make sure we DO something about the feelings, and do something constructive and positive.

In the province of British Columbia, at least, designation as "parkland" is no protection for natural treasures. Our provincial experts have decided it is possible to allow both logging and mining in "recreational" areas. Apart from the obvious desecration done by logging and mining, there are other detriments, the most readily remarkable being roads which are an invitation to all-terrain vehicles, dirt bikes, motorcycles, four-wheel-drive vehicles, and such. You always know where they've been by the litter of beer cans and broken bottles they leave in their noisy, stinking wake.

Making places like the Stein into "parkland" is no protection at all. A person has only to look at the commercialization of most parks to see what happens. Then look at untouched wilderness, and think that for ten million years the native people of North America have been the guardians and stewards of that land. They have gone there for vision quest, they have gone hunting and fishing, they have gone to pick berries and to show their children the face of the Dream. After ten million years and ample evidence of constant use in the past, the wilderness is undamaged.

When someone claims to be an environmentalist and yet does not actively support the land claims of the native North American people, I do not believe I am talking to a real environmentalist. I think I am talking to a fool. Yes, land claims are a "political" matter. That makes them a personal matter, by feminist definition. And if it is political and personal, it is spiritual.

Having apologistic and spineless parrots on our side is like having no help at all. They are the ones who insist on pretending to believe it is possible to enter into some kind of informed dialogue with the corporations. The corporations are not interested in any kind of dialogue; for them it's a case of "mind over matter": they don't mind WHAT they do and they think you don't matter.

I don't want "nice" people thinking I'm a wonderful person. I don't like "nice" people. "Nice" people have been sitting around condoning the most bestial kind of crap for hundreds of years. So busy being "nice" and "non-confrontative" and "socially acceptable," so busy trying to "change the system from within" and "raise the awareness of the board of directors" that they have accomplished absolutely nothing at all.

You don't need to pay a thousand dollars to go sit at the foot of a volcano in Hawaii to "get in touch" with your Mother. Go sit on your front lawn if you have one. If you don't, go to the closest city or municipal park. Find a tree. Sit with your spine against the tree. Concentrate on ignoring the dogs, kids, peanut vendors and air pollution. Think about that tree. Feel her bark against your back. Think what she has seen. Think.

I just saved you a thousand dollars. Send it to the Lytton-Mount Currie band who are trying to stop the logging of the Stein River valley. Send it to Greenpeace. Send it to an antinuclear group. Give it to your local Rape Relief Center. Give it to your Indian Center.

You don't need to chase after every charlatan who comes down the pike promising redemption of one sort or another. Your redemption, if you need it, is inside yourself. You have a RIGHT to be angry! Use your eyes. Look around. Believe the evidence of your own eyes. LOOK AT WHAT THEY HAVE DONE AND ARE STILL DOING! That is your MOTHER they are ganging up on, that is your MOTHER they are trying to kill. Of course you have the right to be angry. You're a disgrace to your mother if you aren't angry.

Now take that anger, and use it as energy. Commit yourself to a certain amount of money out of your pay check every month. What do you pay for cablevision or for videos you rent, or for beer, or . . . and send that money to the group of your choice.

Start looking around at the dying streams and rivers. Wake up. Smell the exhaust, the fumes from the factories. Find out what they're putting in your food!

Stop being like driftwood; it's often very decorative, it is sometimes quite beautiful, but in the final analysis it is only good for fuel. Don't ride around on every tide and fad. This is no rehearsal, you know, this is IT: your life. There's no rewrite, no "cut, try again."

I would be less than honest with you if I were to leave you with the idea that I am at all interested in "the Green Party" as a political alternative. I find them as patriarchal and as hung-up on unimportant crap as any other political party. By me, the system stinks and it will do no good to try to "fix" it. By me, politics is a day-to-day personal and spiritual commitment, not something you go out and vote for once every now and again. I do not believe any party in the system will ever do anything except continue the system. Put all politicians in a sack of flour, shake it, and they come out looking, sounding, and stinking the same. As soon as they become "the party in power," they become the party In Power, and they do what they used to criticize the other guys for doing. As long as we think "they" will run things for us, "they" will run things for the perpetuation of the system which allowed them to get into the driver's seat in the first place.

I also have very little faith in the men who purport to have espoused feminism. I'd believe them more if they stayed home and looked after the kids, did the cooking and housework, and made it easier for the women to do what the men have never been able to do since Rome pulled together the first full-time standing army and set out to invade the known world, most of which was binarchic and woman-centered.

Feminism makes most men uncomfortable because feminism demands that we all, men included, examine and question the basic tenets of our culture. Examination forces us all to realize that men—all men, but especially middle-class white men and their bosses—are privileged. They have a better chance at education, a better chance at meaningful employment, and a much higher economic expectation and possibility than anyone else. Many of these men think they have "climbed" a ladder of success because of their own abilities; many of these men think they have, by their own unique talents, managed to wrest for themselves a good income; they do not want to have to face the fact that much of what they have was made possible to them because of their color and gender. They do not want to admit they have benefited because others have been exploited and oppressed. They do not want to have to give up any of what they have and they do not want to admit they support a system which actively damages other people and this Earth.

And suddenly "feminism" is being avoided as a term. We have "post-feminism," and we have "womanism" and we have "new age-ism" and we have "ecofeminism." The term "ecofeminism" suggests that the old "feminism" was not at all concerned with ecology, could not have cared less about the environment, had no analysis of industrial exploitation, and ignored the need for peace.

Why would women suggest that "feminism" needs to be put aside in favor of "ecofeminism"? I suggest it is because some of the boys have been expressing discomfort or disapproval or negativism toward feminism. I suggest it is because some of the boys have said hard-nosed feminists make them feel "unwelcome" (which often means we aren't obviously impressed and grateful to be given the attention and possibly even approval of these men).

So to have the participation, cooperation and approval of the man, a new term must be found. However, that term must not in any way ignore feminism or cut people off from the writings and teaching of the women who have been, in large part, responsible for the raising of consciousness of the very ones looking for a new label. Without the feminists we'd be back in the fifties, where Father Knows Best and the future belongs to Leave It To Beaver and The Fonz! So keep part of it, keep the part that is your link to sanity, but water it down so it will be acceptable to the boys.

The term "ecofeminism" is an insult to the women who put themselves on the line, risked public disapproval, risked even violence, and jail. It is an insult to the women who made rape openly and publicly unacceptable, it is an insult to the women who encouraged and challenged us to first talk about, then do something to stop, sexual abuse of women and children, and the horror of incest.

Feminism has always been actively involved in the peace movement, in the antinuclear movement, and in the environmental protection movement. Feminism is what helped teach us all that the link between political and industrial included the military and was a danger to all life on this planet. To separate ecology from feminism is to try to separate the heart from the head.

I am not an ecofeminist. I am a feminist. Feminism demands that I be as realistic as possible. Feminism encourages me to have dreams, to be idealistic, and to find ways to do more than sit around wishing and dreaming, to find ways to put into practice what I have had the good fortune to learn from the Guardians of the Dream.

It isn't always comfortable. It isn't always easy. Often people are offended when their unthinking and supposedly well-meaning overtures are not welcomed. Two weeks after the three-day Stein festival, I got a telephone call at 5:45 P.M., as I was making supper for my family. The caller, a soft-voiced woman with the vocabulary of a middle-class lady, said she had attended the Stein festival and thought a lot about what she had learned. She now wanted to "get involved in some environmental issues," and wanted to come over and spend a few days or a week talking to me and "discuss various options." She wanted to know how I "felt about that." I told her I didn't feel very open to it at all. I also told her the time for talking is long past. We know what needs to be done. We know what is being done to our Grandmother Earth. We have pinpointed the hot spots, and we can see with our own eyes the damage already done. We don't need to talk about it any more!

I told this woman to stop wasting her time and mine. To stop dithering and get involved. Write letters to editors and talk it up with people you know. Find out which organizations are moving to defend our homeland, and lend your support, give your energy, and contribute money because it costs incredibly to publish newsletters, distribute them and pay the postage.

I know this woman was offended and her feelings were hurt by my flat rejection of her idea to visit me and discuss yet again what is absolutely obvious. I was upset when I finally pried the phone off my ear some fifteen minutes later!

I had told this woman I was making supper. That didn't mean anything to her, she felt her own agenda was more important. Making supper is not just some damn thing we do because we have to do it! Making supper is preparing food for the people we must love. Making supper is a way of nourishing more than the body, it is a sacrament. It is something that has been done for millenia, mostly by women, and for most of that time very little thanks or recognition was given to the work or the one doing it. In a world where four out of five children go to bed painfully hungry every night, making supper is a gift. Just having the food to make supper with is a gift! A gift provided by this Earth, our Homeland, our Mother, our Old Grandmother.

I live here. This small piece of land nourishes me physically and spiritually. The massive cedars on this land are safe for as long as my love and I live here, because we are not going to sell them to the loggers. The fir, alder, and wild cherry will not become something to cut down and drag away, leaving tortured earth. The world will have to do without the Pampers plastic-lined diapers which could be made from the trees on this property.

I am very jealously protective of this place and it matters very much to me who comes here and who doesn't. I don't want ineffectual and crappy energy turned loose here, I don't want energy-draining black holes coming here because they have decided they would like to come for whatever their personal reasons are, to talk about something that does *not* need endless discussion and *does* need immediate action.

I am not the Big Mother figure. I refuse to accept that responsibility. Nobody needs to come here to discuss what should be done to help stop the heartless assault against the Old Grandmother. The Voice Which Must Be Obeyed gave us all the intelligence we need. We are the ones who have chosen not to use our innate ability to reason. Someone with the benefits of a middle-class vocabulary and education does not need to spend forever wondering about what she might decide to do (or not do!). All she has to do is start DOING. Anything else

is bullshit. And I don't want to have bullshit on this piece of land. I
          stop it from happening to other pieces of land, but
          . The people who are welcome here are people who

          ing things like following the profits of the new age
          tainments purporting to be of a spiritual nature.
(And no, I did not make a spelling error! These are not prophets, they
are profits.) If we want to truly learn from the Guardians of the Dream
we must listen to them, not to every fake and phony mouthing things
which are soothing and comfortable. If we truly want to learn any of
the spiritual things we say we want to learn, we have to give respect
to the people who have guarded the Dream for all these long, cold,
and lone years.

The Circle of Elders of the Lakota Nation has expressed its disapproval
of the profits of the new age, and either we listen to the Elders and
respect what they are saying or we choose to ignore the Dream
Guardians. Ignore the Dream Guardians and you ignore the Dream.
Ignore the Dream and you help those who move against the Dream.
Then . . . who benefits? Then . . . is it an accident?

The meek and mealy-mouthed are helping the patriarchy as it spreads
like a mad sickness, infecting the Earth and threatening us all with
extinction. The black holes who suck energy are deflecting too many
of us from what really needs to be done. While they are still talking,
while they are apologizing, while they are asking us to put our energy
into their ineffectual time-wasting foolishness, our mother is being
attacked. I know the feminists are standing, working, moving to
protect the Earth.

7
Women Act:
Women and Environmental
Protection in India
Pamela Philipose

May plants, the waters and the sky
Preserve us, and the woods and mountains
With their trees for tresses
                    —*Rig Veda* (ancient Indian religious text)

It is now a universally established fact that it is the woman who is the worst victim of environmental destruction. And the poorer she is, the greater is her burden. What may spell prosperity for some, spells disaster for her.

Industrialization, the phenomenal growth of cities, the proliferation of a cash economy, all these factors have played havoc with the earth's vast stores of natural wealth—its forests, its rivers, its very air.

What has all this meant for the women of the developing world? In simple terms, it has meant longer hours spent doing back-breaking household tasks, like collecting water, foraging for fodder and fuel. A ceaseless cycle that goes on in good health or bad, in pregnancy or old age, in all kinds of weather. According to one Indian study, women spent 90 percent of their time cooking, and nearly 80 percent of that fetching water and firewood. It has also meant industrial disasters which have snuffed out thousands of human lives in the course of a few hours. It has meant that whole communities suddenly find themselves face to face with starvation.

I would now like to take you on a guided tour of India. We'll be making three important halts. The first, which I have called "Earth," is a case study from the northernmost villages of Uttar Pradesh (U.P., a northern state) which lie in the lap of the Himalayas. This region has witnessed a remarkable nonviolent ecological movement, popularly known as the *Chipko andolan* (the hug-the-trees movement).

The second section, which is entitled "Air," deals with the great Bhopal tragedy. Bhopal is a city of approximately 800,000 people in Madhya Pradesh (a state which forms the heartland of India).

For the third section, we'll travel down to the coastal villages on the southern tip of the subcontinent, in the state of Kerala, which have witnessed a thirty-four–year fisherfolk agitation. This section goes under the heading "Water."

Earth

The Chipko movement clearly demonstrated, as no other movement did before it, that women have a deep commitment to preserving their environment, since it is directly connected to their household needs. It also shows how nonviolent methods can sometimes "move mountains."

The first incident that heralded this new movement took place at Gopeshwar village, in the Chamoli district of U.P. Three hundred ash trees in the region had been allotted to a sports goods manufacturer by forest officials.

In March 1973, the agents of the company arrived at Gopeshwar to oversee the felling of the trees. Meanwhile, the villagers met and decided together that they would not allow a single tree to be cut down by the company.

With the support of Sarvodaya activists (Sarvodaya workers believe in the nonviolent ideology of Gandhi), they walked in a procession, beating drums and singing traditional songs. They had decided to hug the trees that the laborers, hired by the company, were to axe. The agents of the sports company had to retreat in the face of this unexpected onslaught.

The Gopeshwar incident was only the first of a long line of similar actions, but already the enthusiastic participation of the women was very evident.

Actually, flooding had helped to dramatize the issue, when the Alaknanda River, which runs through the region, breached its banks in 1970. Hundreds of homes were swept away. Sarvodaya workers, notably a young man called C. P. Bhatt (who has since won one of Asia's most prestigious awards—the Magsaysay) succeeded in explaining the links between the flooding and the consistent tree-felling by lumber companies, which had resulted in tremendous soil erosion. In 1973, when the floods occurred again, the villagers were quite conscious of the deforestation problem.

A year had gone by since Gopeshwar village had managed to retain its trees. The Forest Department announced an auction of almost 2,500 trees in the Reni forest, overlooking the Alaknanda River. This time it was the women who acted.

It so happened that the men of the village were away collecting compensation for some land taken from them when the employees of the lumber company appeared on the scene. One little girl spotted them and ran to inform Gaura Devi about it. Gaura Devi, a widow in her fifties, was a natural leader, and organized a group of about thirty women and children who went to talk to the contractor's men.

Gaura Devi is said to have pushed her way forward and stood before a gun carried by one of the laborers. She defied him to shoot her first, before touching the trees. "Brother, this forest is our *maika* (mother's home). Do not axe it. Landslides will ruin our homes and fields." She and her companions were successful in forcing the angry contractor and his men to return without their logs. That night, the women of the village stood guard over their beloved trees.

Soon after this incident the U.P. government set up an official committee to inquire into the validity of the Chipko activists' demands. After two years, the committee reported that the Reni forest belt was a sensitive area and that no trees should be felled there. The government banned tree-felling in the area for ten years.

News of the Reni victory soon spread. The real importance of the Chipko movement was that it did not fizzle out. Its message was taken by committed activists from village to village. A prominent Sarvodaya leader, Sunderlal Bahuguna, participated in a 120-day march on foot, propagating the importance of preserving the forests.

But what was really remarkable was the initiative shown by the women. They agitated in novel ways. In one instance, in November 1977, the women of Advani village in Tehri Garwhal tied sacred threads around trees marked for felling, determined to save the trees, even at the cost of their lives. (According to Hindu custom, tying a sacred thread on somebody establishes the relationship of the protector and the protected.) The forest officer who had visited the village on that occasion to persuade the women to relent finally lost his temper and shouted, "You foolish women. Do you know what the forests bear? Resin, timber, foreign exchange." One woman responded in the same tone, "Yes, we know what forests bear. Soil, water and pure air."

Then, in August 1980 a curious thing happened, at another village in Dangori Pantoli. The all-male village council had made an agreement with the Horticultural Department under which a nearby oak forest was to be felled in exchange for a cemented road, a higher secondary school, a hospital, and electricity for the village.

On hearing about this deal, the Sarvodaya activists working there tried to persuade the council to change its stand. The men did not agree, but the women in the village decided they would protect the oak forest at any cost. The men were so incensed by this that they warned the women they would be killed if they defied the council's decision. Undeterred, a large number of women went ahead, held a Chipko demonstration, and saved the forest. The government soon banned tree-felling in this region as well.

The incident showed just how far the women had progressed. They had new confidence. They now demanded to be members of village councils; they formed *Mahila Mandals* (women's committees) to ensure the protection of forests; they appointed watch-women who received regular wages to supervise the extraction of forest products; they planted saplings.

Today, there is a woman leader in the Gopeshwar (local government) that was unheard of earlier. Little wonder, then, that the image the Chipko movement brings to mind is that of a group of toil-worn women hugging a tree to save it.

Similar movements are taking place in other regions of India too—like the Appiko Movement in the western Ghatts region of Karnataka; the Girnar Movement in Gujarat and Goa. The bad news is that, according to the latest satellite data, India is losing 1.3 million hectares of forest per year. The Indian government's ambitious social forestry programmes seem to cater more to the needs of paper and other wood-based industries than to the fuel and fodder requirements of the people who are being robbed of their forests. So unless more and more Chipko-type movements take place, the harvest will be a bitter one.

Air

"Bhopal" is now synonymous with mass death through industrial pollution. It has become the sharpest indictment yet of the duplicitous and hypocritical policies of multinationals that have one set of safety considerations and criteria for plant and equipment design in the West, and quite another set for their Third World subsidiaries.

Spread over an area of forty square kilometers, the Union Carbide complex of Bhopal manufactured MIC-based pesticides. (MIC is Methyl Isocyanate). On the night of December 23, 1984, the highly toxic MIC escaped from the factory, converting a quarter of the sleeping city into a gas chamber.

Consider this: at Bhopal's Hamidia Hospital, the first patient reported at 1:15 A.M. with eye trouble. In just five minutes 1,000 suffering men, women, and children with serious respiratory and eye problems pleaded for medical help. By 2:30 A.M. there were 4,000. The next morning hundreds lay dead on the streets.

No one knows how many people really died that night. While the official figure is 2,347, an unofficial UNICEF assessment put it at 10,000. About 30,000 to 40,000 people were seriously injured, and another 200,000 badly affected, of which 75 percent were slum dwellers, 40 percent children, 15 to 20 percent women in the reproductive age group, and 10 percent elderly women. The worst affected by far were the poorest of the poor. Their patched dwellings offered them very little protection against the gas.

Autopsy findings done on the bodies revealed massive destruction of lung tissue, damaged livers and kidneys, and circulatory systems completely drained of blood. Cyanide was found in the blood and viscera of the victims.

For those who survived, it was almost a living death. Men and women were completely or partially blinded, with continual watering and burning of the eyes, incessant headaches, vomiting, breathlessness, racking coughs. Psychologically, they were anxious and depressed, many had lost their loved ones, many were reduced to penury because they couldn't work any more.

The manner in which the government conducted relief work was singularly ineffective and chaotic—a confusion compounded by controversy over the right line of treatment. Union Carbide did not help matters by its attempts to feed the public with disinformation. Relief funds very often did not reach the hands they were meant for. And the victims, with women figuring prominently among them, began to heckle medical teams. They also held demonstrations outside the residence of the chief minister of the state.

Voluntary agencies did some of the best relief work. For instance, the women of the *Nagrik Rahat aur Punarwas Samiti* discovered for the first time that women exposed to MIC were suffering from severe disorders of the reproductive system, in addition to other complications. Many women experienced up to five menstrual discharges during the first six weeks of the incident. Most women complained of abdominal pain and highly acidic vaginal secretions which caused burning.

It was left to two committed women doctors—Dr. Rani Bang and Dr. Mira Sadgopal—to systematically document their findings after examining fifty-five gas-affected women, three months after the disaster. Their study confirmed that, since the gas exposure, an extremely high percentage of women had developed gynecological diseases like leucorrhea (94 percent), pelvic inflammatory diseases (79 percent), excessive menstrual bleeding (46 percent), retroverted uteri (64 percent) and cervical erosion (67 percent).

Those women who were pregnant at the time of the disaster were in a pathetic state. Quite apart from the effects of the poisonous gas itself, hypoxia—or lack of oxygen resulting from lung damage in the mother—is known to cause fetal distress. Most of the victims were given high doses of coricosteroids and tetracycline—both of which could have caused fetal damage. All this was known at the time, but no effort was made to educate the women about the possibilities of the ill-effects and offer safe facilities for abortion to those who didn't want to take chances.

Somehow, the women's movement in India was not able to make a deep impact on a situation that warranted much more sustained campaigning and relief work. But there have been a few exceptions. Members of *Saheli*, a Delhi-based women's group which works toward providing a social support structure to women in distress, camped in Bhopal for months together, helping to run a clinic which offered medical relief to victims. SEWA (Self Employed Women's Association) of Bhopal, helped give employment and rehabilitation to affected people. The *Chattisgarth Jagruti Sanghatana*, the Women's Centre, Bombay, and the *Sahiar*, Baroda, sent women activists to conduct surveys and highlight the problem in the media.

Today, the gas victims of Bhopal receive very little media attention. They remain locked in their own private hells, face-to-face with the prospect of adverse carcinogenic and mutagenic effects visiting not just the generation of children conceived around the time of the tragedy, but future generations as well. Today, about two years after the incident, mental illnesses proliferate. Surveys revealed that 22 percent of the screened population suffered from mental disorders. Of these, 37.3 percent had neurotic depression, 24.9 percent had anxiety syndrome, and 35.2 percent were afflicted by adjustment reaction.

The damage the Union Carbide complex did to the people of Bhopal cannot be measured in monetary terms. Yet, as the case for compensation comes up in the Bhopal district court, the company has launched an aggressive counter-claim, shifting the onus for the disaster to the government of India, and quibbling over the amount of compensation. Regardless of the ensuing court battle, the real losers are the victims themselves.

Water

The struggle to obtain clean drinking water is written into the lives of so many of my countrywomen that a former member of our Planning Commission once wryly remarked, "If men had to fetch drinking water, then two hundred thirty thousand villages would not have remained without the provision of drinking water after thirty years of planned development."

By and large, Indian women have not organized enough to fight for their right to clear drinking water. There have been, however, some remarkable mass actions initiated or supported by women.

Noted political activist and sociologist Gail Omvedt reported on how a rural women's group, the *Mukti Sangarsh*, tackled the drought situation, aggravated by the failure of the rains for the fourth successive year in the Sangli district of Maharashtra (ironically enough, the wealthiest state of India, where Bombay is capital). Their crops were drying up, their cattle were dying of starvation, there was an acute shortage of drinking water, so the peasant women came out in large numbers for the first time and joined the men in organizing a road-blocking agitation on July 30, 1984. They drove their bullock carts and cattle on the road and held up traffic for several hours. The authorities were forced to sit up, and promised organized relief. In the same state there is a unique body called the *Pani Panchayat* (Water Committee), also dominated by women. The women here corner politicians at public meetings, organize sit-ins and rallies—all on one issue—water.

In Ambur Town, Tamil Nadu (a southern state which has had to face alarmingly frequent droughts), men, women, and children protested against the polluted drinking water caused by tannery effluents released directly into the Palar River. They carried pitchers of the contaminated water and broke them in front of the municipal offices. But most of these actions are desperate measures taking place in the face of acute hardship.

A more sustained ecological movement is taking place in an adjoining state—Kerala. The fisherfolk of this state are locked in a thirty-four-year-old struggle with the trawler owners. They are agitating against the government's blind policy of adopting various foreign fishing techniques without taking into consideration local circumstances and needs.

For generations, traditional fisherfolk have caught fish in shallow coastal waters. In the fifties, mechanized trawlers were introduced, in a bid to exploit the rich marine life of the coastal waters. These trawlers use nets that sweep the depths of the sea, disturbing the ecology of the sea basin, gobbling up fish stocks far in excess of their specific requirements. All this, in turn, has drastically affected the yields of the traditional fisherfolk.

To take just one example, there are about one hundred trawlers equipped with purse-seiners in Kerala's waters today. Purse-seiners are purse-like nets which have the capacity to hold vast fish stocks at one sweep. Not many know that these very nets have had disastrous consequences in Peru, as their very efficiency resulted in a sudden depletion of "whitebait" fish there. These nets, in fact, were banned in Peru.

One of the main demands of the agitating fisherfolk is a ban on inshore fishing by trawlers during the three month breeding season, so that marine life in these waters is not threatened. But now the scene is riven with a new class of middlemen and investors—some of whom happen to be powerful politicians in their own right—who have a vested interest in seeing that the trawlers hold undisputed sway over the fishing waters.

Women have been both in the ranks and in the forefront of this struggle. I met some of these women activists, and heard the powerfully moving songs they sang. They are extremely articulate—Kerala having the highest levels of female literacy in India.

But an unusual element in this particular campaign is the involvement of socially conscious clergymen and women. In 1984, Sister Alice, a crusading nun of the Order of Assumption Sisters, held a fifteen-day fast in the heart of Calicut Town over the issue. She stated clearly, "I do not believe in charity (as exmplified by people like Mother Teresa) which does not tackle issues of social justice." Nuns like Sister Alice and priests, inspired by radical theology, defied the Roman Catholic Church in Kerala, and have involved themselves in this issue since 1980. Today they, along with the fisherfolk of Kerala, are gearing themselves for yet another phase in the long-drawn-out battle—a nationwide agitation, to be launched next March.

One of the biggest challenges facing the Indian women's movement today is to forge links between some of these disparate and scattered struggles, between rural and urban women's groups, and bring about a wider, more broad-based women's liberation movement.

There are some very real problems. The most obvious, of course, are the practical difficulties of keeping in touch and in tune with each other's aspirations and involvements in a sustained manner. India is a large country, and while it may make a very powerful symbol to have a Chipko activist extend a hand of support to a Kerala fisherwoman, there are over four thousand miles separating them.

There is also the great urban-rural divide. Most of the urban women activists come from backgrounds that are far removed from that of their sisters in the countryside. Their experiences as women and as activists in the city are, in many areas, totally different and so, too, not surprisingly, their preoccupations. But there are areas of commonality.

The image of a group of women hugging a tree to save it has inspired many a city activist to document the Chipko struggle through books, newspapers, articles, videos, and films. It has brought many city activists into the forefront of the campaign against environmental destruction. In the same way, "urban issues" like bride-burning, personal law reform, and issues of health are now increasingly relevant in the countryside as capitalist relations of production become more and more manifest here.

On an international level, too, there is tremendous scope for extending hands of support. Each and every one of the case studies I have cited here have international parallels. To cite a few examples: tree-felling in the Amazon basin; a major industrial disaster in Seveso, Italy, when deadly gases escaped from a chemical plant; drought in Ethiopia; severe fish depletion in Peru; mercury poisoning in Minamata, Japan; the recent accident near Basel in Switzerland involving the pharmaceutical multinational Sandoz, which has led to the Rhine being poisoned right up to the North Sea; and, of course, Chernobyl. The list is endless.

I would like to improvise on a phrase from the feminist poet, Marge Piercy. All the women around the world who take part in movements like the ones I've described are working to make part of the same quilt to keep us from freezing to death in a world that grows harsher and bleaker. More power to their work-worn hands!

8

Speaking for the Earth:
The Haida Way
Gwaganad

The human connection with the land is often eloquently stated by the native people. Here, Gwaganad of Haada Gwaii (the Queen Charlotte Islands), shares her experience of what it is to live with nature. Her statement was made before Justice Harry McKay (here called Kilsli) in British Columbia's Supreme Court on November 6, 1985, in the matter of the application by Frank Beban Logging and Western Forest Products Ltd. for an injunction to prohibit Haida picketing of logging roads on Lyell Island, South Moresby.

Kilsli, Kilsligana, Kiljadgana, Taaxwilaas. Your Honour, chiefs, ladies held in high esteem, friends. I thank you for this opportunity to speak today. I was aware that I could get a lawyer, but I feel you lose if you go through another person.

My first language is Haida. I feel through another person, a lawyer, they also speak another language, and I would have lost what I hope to help Kilsli understand and feel.

Since the beginning of time—I have been told this through our oral stories—since the beginning of time the Haidas have been on the Queen Charlotte Islands.

That was our place, given to us.

We were put on the islands as caretakers of this land.

Approximately two hundred years ago foreigners came to that land. The Haida are very hospitable people. The people came. They were welcomed. We shared. They told us that perhaps there is a better way to live, a different religion, education in schools. The Haida tried this way. The potlatches were outlawed. In many schools my father attended in Kokalitza, the Haida language was not allowed to be spoken. He was punished if he used his language. To this day, Watson Price, my father, understands every word of the Haida language, but he doesn't speak it.

76

So the people came. We tried their way. Their language. Their education. Their way of worship. It is clear to me that they are not managing our lands well. If this continues, there will be nothing left for my children and my grandchildren to come. I feel that the people governing us should give us a chance to manage the land the way we know how it should be.

It seems that the other cultures don't see trees. They see money. It's take and take and take from the earth. That's not the way it is in my mind.

On Lyell Island—I want to address Lyell Island and South Moresby, the injunction being served on us. I want to say why that concerns me. To me it is a home of our ancestors. As Lily stated, our ancestors are still there. It is my childhood. Every spring come March my father and mother would take me down to Burnaby Narrows. We stayed there till June. It's wonderful memories I had. I am thankful to my parents for bringing me up the traditional way. There was concern on the Indian agent's part that I missed too much school. But how can you tell them that I was at school?

Because of that upbringing, because I was brought down to Lyell Island area, Burnaby Narrows and living off the land—that's why I feel the way I do about my culture and the land.

In those early years the first lesson in my life that I remember is respect. I was taught to respect the land. I was taught to respect the food that comes from the land. I was taught that everything had a meaning. Every insect had a meaning and none of those things were to be held lightly. The food was never to be taken for granted. In gathering the food—the nearest I can translate—I can say to gather food is a spiritual experience for me.

We are a nation of people at risk today. They say that to make a culture the language is important. I am proud to say I speak my language, but not too many more people in my age do. So you can say in a sense, if this keeps up, the language is going fast. In the past the culture was in very much jeopardy when the potlatching was outlawed. We almost lost ourselves as a people. That culture has been revived in the past few years. There is pride in being a Haida, pride in being a native. The only thing we can hold onto to maintain that pride and dignity as a people is the land. It's from the land we get our food, it's from the land we get our strength. From the sea we get our energy. If this land such as Lyell Island is logged off as they want to log it off—and they will go on logging. We have watched this for many years. I have read records that our forefathers fought in 1913. It's been an ongoing fight. But no one is really hearing us. They said they wouldn't log Lyell Island at first and now I hear they are going to go ahead. So today I am here because pretty soon all we are going to be fighting for is stumps. When Frank Beban and his crew are through and there are stumps left on Lyell Island, they got a place to go. We, the Haida people, will be on the Island. I don't want my children and my future grandchildren to inherit stumps. They say, "Don't be concerned, we're planting trees again. Wait for the second growth. It will be just like before." I travel all around the Island a lot with my family. I see lots of things. This summer I got to see second growth and it pained me a great deal, because I kept hearing there is second growth coming. I saw twenty-year-old second growth around Salt Lagoon. They were planted so close that the trees couldn't grow big. They were small and there was no light getting into them. They couldn't grow. You could see and you could feel that they could not grow. Therefore, I don't feel too hopeful when I hear second growth.

I want to touch now on another very important area in my life as a food gatherer. It is my job, my purpose, to insure that I gather certain food for my husband and my children, and I want to share one part. It's called *gkow*. That's herring roe on kelp. In the spring the herring come and they spawn on kelp. For many years now I have been harvesting that and putting it away for the winter. But so far I haven't heard what—why is food gathering spiritual?

It's a spiritual thing that happens. It doesn't just happen every year. You can't take that for granted. We can't take that for granted because everything in the environment has to be perfect. The climate has to be perfect, the water temperature, the kelp have to be ready and the herring have to want to spawn.

But I want to share what goes on in my spiritual self, in my body, come February. And I feel it's an important point. That's what makes me as a Haida different from you, Kilsli. My body feels that it's time to spawn. It gets ready in February. I get a longing to be on the sea. I constantly watch the ocean surrounding the island where the herring spawn. My body is kind of on edge in anticipation.

Finally the day comes when it spawns. The water gets all milky around it. I know I am supposed to speak for myself, but I share this experience with all the friends, the lady friends, that we pick together this wonderful feeling on the day that it happens, the excitement, the relief that the herring did indeed come this year. And you don't quite feel complete until you are right out on the ocean with your hands in the water harvesting the kelp, the roe on kelp, and then your body feels right. That cycle is complete.

And it's not quite perfect until you eat your first batch of herring roe on kelp. I don't know how to say it well, but your body almost rejoices in that first feed. It feels right. If you listen to your body it tells you a lot of things. If you put something wrong in it, your body feels it. If you put something right in it, your body feels it. Your spiritual self feels it. In order to make me complete I need the right food from the land. I also need to prepare it myself. I have to harvest it myself. The same thing goes for fish, the fish that we gather for the winter. But I wanted to elaborate on the harvesting of kelp to give you an idea of how it feels as Haida to harvest food.

So I want to stress that it's the land that helps us maintain our culture. It is an important, important part of our culture. Without that land, I fear very much for the future of the Haida nation. Like I said before, I don't want my children to inherit stumps. I want my children and my grandchildren to grow up with pride and dignity as a member of the Haida nation. I fear that if we take that land, we may lose the dignity and the pride of being a Haida. Without that there is no—there is no way that I can see that we could carry on with pride and dignity. I feel very strongly—that's why I came down to express my concern for my children and grandchildren.

So today, if that injunction goes through and the logging continues—and there is a saying up there, they say, "Log it to the beach." Then what? What will be left and who will be left? We can't go anywhere else but the Island.

I study a lot about our brothers on the mainland, the North American Plains Indians in their history. They moved a lot because they were forced to. Some moved north, south, east, west, back up against the mountains and back again.

We as Haida people can't move anymore west. We can go over into the ocean is all. So when the logging is gone, is done, if it goes through and there is stumps left, the loggers will have gone and we will be there as we have been since the beginning of time. Left with very little to work with as a people.

Again I want to thank you, Kilsli, for this opportunity to speak and share my culture. Thank you very much.

9
Development, Ecology, and Women
Vandana Shiva

Development As a New Project of Western Patriarchy

"Development" was to have been a postcolonial project, a choice for accepting a model of progress in which the entire world remade itself on the model of the colonizing modern West, without having to undergo the subjugation and exploitation that colonialism entailed. The assumption was that western style progress was possible for all. Development, as the improved well-being of all, was thus equated with the westernization of economic categories—of needs, of productivity, of growth. Concepts and categories about economic development and natural resource utilization that had emerged in the specific context of industrialization and capitalist growth in a center of colonial power were raised to the level of universal assumptions and applicability in the entirely different context of basic needs satisfaction for the people of the newly independent Third World countries.

Yet, as Rosa Luxemberg has pointed out, early industrial development in western Europe necessitated the permanent occupation of the colonies by the colonial powers and the destruction of the local "natural economy".[1] According to her, colonialism is a constant necessary condition for capitalist growth: without colonies, capital accumulation would grind to a halt. "Development"—as capital accumulation and the commercialization of the economy for the generation of "surplus" and profits—thus involved the reproduction not merely of a particular form of creation of wealth, but also of the associated creation of poverty and dispossession. A replication of economic development based on commercialization of resource use for commodity production in the newly independent countries created the internal colonies.[2]

Development was thus reduced to a continuation of the process of colonization. It became an extension of the project of wealth creation

80

in modern western patriarchy's economic vision, which was based on the exploitation or exclusion of women (of the West and non-West), on the exploitation and degradation of nature, and on the exploitation and erosion of other cultures. "Development" could not but entail destruction for women, nature, and subjugated cultures, which is why, throughout the Third World, women, peasants, and tribals are struggling for liberation from "development" just as they earlier struggled for liberation from colonialism.

The United Nations Decade for Women (1975–1985) was based on the assumption that the improvement of women's economic position would automatically flow from an expansion and diffusion of the development process. Yet, by the end of the Decade, it was becoming clear that development itself was the problem. Insufficient and inadequate "participation" in "development" was not the cause of women's increasing underdevelopment. It was, rather, their enforced but asymmetric participation in it, by which they bore the costs but were excluded from the benefits, that was responsible. Development exclusivity and dispossession aggravated and deepened the colonial processes of ecological degradation and the loss of political control over nature's sustenance base. Economic growth was a new colonialism, draining resources away from those who needed them most. The discontinuity lay in the fact that it was now new national elites, not colonial powers, that masterminded the exploitation on grounds of "national interest" and growing GNPs, and it was accomplished with more powerful technologies of appropriation and destruction.

Ester Boserup[3] has documented how women's impoverishment increased during colonial rule, pointing out those rulers who spent centuries subjugating and crippling their own women into de-skilled, de-intellectualized appendages, disfavored the women of the colonies on matters of access to land, technology, and employment. The economic and political processes of colonial underdevelopment bore the clear mark of modern western patriarchy, and while large numbers of women and men were impoverished by these processes, women tended to lose more. The privatization of land for revenue generation displaced women more critically, eroding their traditional land-use rights. The expansion of cash crops undermined food production, and women were often left with meager resources to feed and care for children, the aged, and the infirm, when men migrated or were conscripted into forced labor by the colonizers. As a collective document by women activists, organizers and researchers stated at the end of the UN Decade for Women, "The almost uniform conclusion of the Decade's research is that, with a few exceptions, women's relative access to economic resources, incomes and employment has worsened, their burden of work has increased, and their relative and even absolute health, nutritional and educational status has declined."[4]

Women's displacement from productive activity by the expansion of development was rooted largely in the manner in which development projects appropriated or destroyed the natural resource base used for sustenance and survival. It destroyed women's productivity both by removing land, water, and forests from their management and control, as well as through the ecological destruction of these resources, impairing nature's productivity and renewability. While gender subordination and patriarchy are the oldest of oppressions, they have taken on new and more violent forms through the project of development. Patriarchal categories which understand destruction as "production" and regeneration of life as "passivity" have generated a crisis of survival. Passivity, as an assumed category of the "nature" of nature and women, denies the activity of nature and life. Fragmentation and uniformity as assumed categories of progress and development destroy the living forces which arise from relationships within the "web of life" and the diversity in the elements and patterns of these relationships.

The economic biases and values against nature, women, and indigenous peoples are captured in this typical analysis of the "unproductiveness" of traditional natural societies:

> Production is achieved through human and animal, rather than mechanical, power. Most agriculture is unproductive; human or animal manure may be used but chemical fertilisers and pesticides are unknown. . . . For the masses, these conditions mean poverty.[5]

The assumptions are evident: nature is unproductive; organic agriculture based on nature's cycles of renewability spells poverty; women and tribal and peasant societies embedded in nature are similarly unproductive, not because it has been demonstrated that in cooperation they produce *less* goods and services for needs, but because it is assumed that "production" takes place only when mediated by technologies for commodity production, even when such technologies destroy life. A stable and clean river is not a productive resource in this view: it needs to be "developed" with dams in order to become so. Women, sharing the river as a commons to satisfy the water needs of their families and society are not involved in productive labor; when substituted by the engineering man, water management and water use become productive activities. Natural forests remain unproductive until they are developed into monoculture plantations of commercial species. Development is thus equivalent to maldevelopment, a development bereft of the feminine, the conservation, the ecological principle. The neglect of nature's work in renewing herself, and women's work in producing sustenance in the form of basic, vital needs is an essential part of the paradigm of maldevelopment, which sees all work that does not produce profits and capital as non- or unproductive work. As Maria Mies has pointed out, this concept of surplus has a patriarchal bias because, from the point of view of nature and women, it is not based on material surplus produced *over and above* the requirements of the community: it is stolen and appropriated through violent modes from nature (who needs a share of her produce to reproduce herself) and from women (who need a share of nature's produce to produce sustenance and ensure survival).[6]

From the perspective of Third World women, productivity is a measure of producing life and sustenance; that this kind of productivity has been rendered invisible does not reduce its centrality to survival—it merely reflects the domination of modern patriarchal economic categories which see only profits, not life.

Maldevelopment As the Death of the Feminine Principle

In this analysis, maldevelopment becomes a new source of male-female inequality. 'Modernization' has been associated with the introduction of new forms of dominance. Alice Schlegel has shown that under conditions of subsistence, the interdependence and complementarity of the separate male and female domains of work is the characteristic mode, based on diversity, not inequality.[7] Maldevelopment militates against this equality in diversity, and superimposes the ideologically constructed category of western technological man as a uniform measure of the worth of classes, cultures, and genders. Dominant modes of perception based on reductionism, duality, and linearity are unable to cope with equality in diversity, with forms and activities that are significant and valid, even though different. The reductionist mind superimposes the roles and forms of power of western male-oriented concepts on women, all nonwestern peoples, and even on nature, rendering all three "deficient," and in need of "development." Diversity, and unity and harmony in diversity, become epistemologically unattainable in the context of maldevelopment, which then becomes synonymous with women's underdevelopment (increasing sexist domination), and nature's depletion (deepening ecological crises). Commodities have grown, but nature has shrunk. The poverty crisis of the South arises from the growing scarcity of water, food, fodder, and fuel, associated with increasing maldevelopment and ecological destruction. This poverty crisis touches women most severely, first because they are the poorest among the poor, and then because, with nature, they are the primary sustainers of society.

Maldevelopment is the violation of the integrity of organic, interconnected, interdependent systems, that sets in motion a process of exploitation, inequality, injustice, and violence. It is blind to the fact that a recognition of nature's harmony and action to maintain it are preconditions for distributive justice. This is why Mahatma Gandhi said, "There is enough in the world for everyone's need, but not for some people's greed."

Maldevelopment is maldevelopment in thought and action. In practice, this fragmented, reductionist, dualist perspective violates the integrity and harmony of humankind in nature, and the harmony between men and women. It ruptures the cooperative unity of masculine and feminine, and places man, shorn of the feminine principle, above nature and women, and separated from both. The violence to nature as symptomatized by the ecological crisis, and the violence to women, as symptomatized by their subjugation and exploitation, arise from this subjugation of the feminine principle. I want to argue that what is currently called development is essentially maldevelopment, based on the introduction or accentuation of the domination of man over nature and women. In it, both are viewed as the "other," the passive nonself. Activity, productivity, and creativity which were associated with the feminine principle, are expropriated as qualities of nature and women, and transformed into the exclusive qualities of man. Nature and women are turned into passive objects, to be used and exploited for the uncontrolled and uncontrollable desires of alienated man. From being the creators and sustainers of life, nature and women are reduced to being "resources" in the fragmented, antilife model of maldevelopment.

Two Kinds of Growth, Two Kinds of Productivity

Maldevelopment is usually called "economic growth," measured by the Gross National Product. Porritt, a leading ecologist, has this to say of GNP:

> *Gross* National Product—for once a word is being used correctly. Even conventional economists admit that the hey-day of GNP is over, for the simple reason that as a measure of progress, it's more or less useless. GNP measures the lot, all the goods and services produced in the money economy. Many of these goods and services are not beneficial to people, but rather a measure of just how much is going wrong; increased spending on crime, on pollution, on the many human casualties of our society, increased spending because of waste or planned obsolescence, increased spending because of growing bureaucracies: it's all counted.[8]

The problem with GNP is that it measures some costs as benefits (e.g., pollution control) and fails to measure other costs completely. Among these hidden costs are the new burdens created by ecological devastation, costs that are invariably heavier for women, both in the North and South. It is hardly surprising, therefore, that as GNP rises, it does not necessarily mean that either wealth or welfare increase proportionately. I would argue that GNP is increasingly becoming a measure of how real wealth—the wealth of nature and that produced by women for sustaining life—is rapidly decreasing. When commodity production as the prime economic activity is introduced as development, it destroys the potential of nature and women to produce life and goods and services for basic needs. More commodities and more cash mean less life—in nature (through ecological destruction) and in society (through denial of basic needs). Women are devalued, first, because their work cooperates with nature's processes and, second, because work which satisfies needs and ensures sustenance is devalued in general. Precisely because more growth in maldevelopment has meant less sustenance of life-support systems, it is now imperative to recover the feminine principle as the basis for development which conserves and is ecological. Feminism as ecology, and ecology as the revival of *Prakriti*—the source of all life—become the decentered powers of political and economic transformation and restructuring.

This involves, first, a recognition that categories of "productivity" and growth which have been taken to be positive, progressive and universal are, in reality, restricted patriarchal categories. When viewed from the point of view of nature's productivity and growth, and women's production of sustenence, they are found to be ecologically destructive and a source of gender inequality. It is no accident that the modern, efficient, productive technologies created within the context of growth in market economic terms are associated with heavy ecological costs, borne largely by women. The resource and energy-intensive production processes they give rise to demand ever-increasing withdrawals from the ecosystem. These withdrawals disrupt essential ecological processes and convert renewable resources into nonrenewable ones. A forest, for example, provides inexhaustible supplies of diverse biomass over time if its capital stock is maintained and it is harvested on a sustained yield basis. The heavy and uncontrolled demand for industrial and commercial wood, however, requires the continuous overfelling of trees which exceeds the regenerative capacity of the forest ecosystem, and eventually converts the forests into nonrenewable resources. Women's work in the collection of water, fodder, and fuel is thus rendered more energy- and time-consuming. (In Garhwal, for example, I have seen women who originally collected fodder and fuel in a few hours, now traveling long distances by truck to collect grass and leaves in a task that might take up to two days.) Sometimes the damage to nature's intrinsic regenerative capacity is impaired not by overexploitation of a particular resource but, indirectly, by damage caused to other related natural resources through ecological processes. Thus the excessive overfelling of trees in the catchment areas of streams and rivers destroys not only forest resources, but also renewable supplies of water, through hydrological destabilization. Resource intensive industries disrupt essential ecological processes not only by their excessive demands for raw material, but by their pollution of air and water and soil. Often such destruction is caused by the resource demands of nonvital industrial products.

In spite of severe ecological crises, this paradigm continues to operate because, for the North and for the elites of the South, resources continue to be available, even now. The lack of recognition of nature's processes for survival *as factors in the process of economic development* shrouds the political issues arising from resource transfer and resource destruction, and creates an ideological weapon for increased control over natural resources in the conventionally employed notion of productivity. All other costs of the economic process consequently become invisible. The forces which contribute to the increased "productivity" of a modern farmer or factory worker, for instance, come from the increased use of natural resources. Lovins has described this as the amount of "slave" labor presently at work in the world.[9] According to him, each person on earth, on an average, possesses the equivalent of about 50 slaves, each working a 40-hour week. Humankind's global energy conversion from all sources (wood, fossil fuel, hydroelectric power, nuclear) is currently more than 20 times the energy content of the food necessary to feed the present world population at the FAO (Food and Agriculture Organization of the United Nations) standard diet of 3,600 calories per day. The "productivity" of the western male compared to women or Third World peasants is not intrinsically superior; it is based on inequalities in the distribution of this "slave" labor. The average inhabitant of the United States, for example, has 250 times more "slaves" than the average Nigerian. If Americans were short of 249 of those 250 "slaves," one wonders how efficient they would prove themselves to be?

It is these resource and energy intensive processes of production which divert resources away from survival, and hence from women. What patriarchy sees as productive work is, in ecological terms, highly destructive production. The second law of thermodynamics predicts that resource intensive and resource wasteful economic development must become a threat to the survival of the human species in the long run. Political struggles based on ecology in industrially advanced countries are rooted in this conflict between *long term survival options* and *short term over-production and over-consumption*. Political struggles of women, peasants, and tribals based on ecology in countries like India are far more acute and urgent since they are rooted in the *immediate threat to the options for survival* for the vast majority of the people, *posed by resource intensive and resource wasteful economic growth* for the benefit of a minority.

In the market economy, the organizing principle for natural resource use is the maximization of profits and capital accumulation. Nature and human needs are managed through market mechanisms. Demands for natural resources are restricted to those demands registering on the market; the ideology of development is in large part based on a vision of bringing all natural resources into the market economy for commodity production. When these resources are already being used by nature to maintain her production of renewable resources and by women for sustenance and livelihood, their diversion to the market economy generates a scarcity condition for ecological stability and creates new forms of poverty for women.

Two Kinds of Poverty

In a book entitled *Poverty: the Wealth of the People,* an African writer draws a distinction between poverty as subsistence, and misery as deprivation. It is useful to separate a cultural conception of subsistence living as poverty from the material experience of poverty that is a result of dispossession and deprivation.

Culturally perceived poverty need not be real material poverty: subsistence economies which satisfy basic needs through self-provisioning are not poor in the sense of being deprived. Yet the ideology of development declares them so because they do not participate overwhelmingly in the market economy, and do not consume commodities produced for and distributed through the market *even though they might be satisfying those needs through self-provisioning mechanisms*. People are perceived as poor if they eat millet (grown by women) rather than commercially produced and distributed processed foods sold by global agribusiness. They are seen as poor if they live in self-built housing made from natural material like bamboo and mud rather than in cement houses. They are seen as poor if they wear handmade garments of natural fiber rather than synthetics. Subsistence, as culturally perceived poverty, does not necessarily imply a low physical quality of life. On the contrary, millet is nutritionally far superior to processed foods; houses built with local materials are far superior, being better adapted to the local climate and ecology; natural fibers are preferable to manufactured fibres in most cases, and certainly more affordable.

This cultural perception of prudent subsistence living as poverty has provided the legitimization for the development process as removing poverty. As a culturally biased project, it destroys wholesome and sustainable lifestyles and creates real material poverty, or misery, by the denial of survival needs themselves, through the diversion of resources to resource intensive commodity production. Cash crop production and food processing take land and water resources away from sustenance needs, and exclude increasingly large numbers of people from their entitlements to food. At no point has the global marketing of agricultural commodities been assessed against the background of the new conditions of scarcity and poverty that it has induced. This new poverty, moreover, is no longer cultural and relative: it is absolute, threatening the very survival of millions on this planet.

The economic system based on the patriarchal concept of productivity was created for the very specific historical and political phenomenon of colonialism. In it, the input for which efficiency of use had to be maximized in the production centers of Europe, was industrial labor. For colonial interest, therefore, it was rational to improve the labor resource *even at the cost of wasteful use of nature's wealth*. This rationalization has, however, been illegitimately universalized to all contexts and interest groups. And, on the plea of increasing productivity, labor-reducing technologies have been introduced in situations where labor is abundant and cheap, and resource-demanding technologies have been introduced where resources are scarce and already fully utilized for the production of sustenance. Traditional economies with a stable ecology have shared with industrially advanced affluent economies the ability to use natural resources to satisfy basic vital needs. The former differ from the latter in two essential ways. First, the same needs are satisfied in industrial societies through longer technological chains requiring higher energy and resource inputs and excluding large numbers without purchasing power. And second, affluence generates new and artificial needs requiring the increased production of industrial goods and services. Traditional economies are not advanced in the matter of nonvital needs satisfaction, but as far as the satisfaction of basic and vital needs is concerned, they are often what Marshall Sahlins has called "the original affluent society." The needs of the Amazonian tribes are more than satisfied by the rich rainforest; their poverty begins with its destruction. The story is the same for the Gonds of Bastar in India or the Penans of Sarawak in Malaysia.

Thus economies based on indigenous technologies are viewed as "backward" and "unproductive." Poverty, as the denial of basic needs, is not necessarily associated with the existence of traditional technologies, and its removal is not necessarily an outcome of the growth of modern ones. On the contrary, the destruction of ecologically sound traditional technologies, often created and used by women, along with the destruction of their material base is generally believed to be responsible for the "feminization" of poverty in societies which have had to bear the costs of resource destruction.

The contemporary poverty of the Afar nomad is not rooted in the inadequacies of traditional nomadic life, but in the *diversion of the productive pastureland of the Awash Valley*. The erosion of the resource base for survival is increasingly being caused by the demand for resources by the market economy, dominated by global forces. The creation of inequality through economic activity which is ecologically disruptive arises in two ways. First, inequalities in the distribution of privileges make for unequal access to natural resources—these include privileges of both a political and economic nature. Second, resource intensive production processes have access to subsidized raw material on which a substantial number of people, especially from the less privileged economic groups, depend for their survival. The consumption of such industrial raw material is determined purely by market forces, and not by considerations of the social or ecological requirements placed on them. The costs of resource destruction are externalized and unequally divided among various economic groups in society, but are borne largely by women and those who satisfy their basic material needs directly from nature, simply because they have no purchasing power to register their demands on the goods and services provided by the modern production system. Gustavo Esteva has called development a permanent war waged by its promoters and suffered by its victims.[10]

The paradox and crisis of development arises from the mistaken identification of culturally perceived poverty with real material poverty, and the mistaken identification of the growth of commodity production as better satisfation of basic needs. In actual fact, there is less water, less fertile soil, less genetic wealth as a result of the development process. Since these natural resources are the basis of nature's economy and women's survival economy, their scarcity is impoverishing women and marginalized peoples in an unprecedented manner. Their new impoverishment lies in the fact that resources which supported their survival were absorbed into the market economy while they themselves were excluded and displaced by it.

The old assumption that, with the development process, the availability of goods and services will automatically be increased and poverty will be removed, is now under serious challenge from women's ecology movements in the Third World, even while it continues to guide development thinking in centers of patriarchal power. Survival is based on the assumption of the sanctity of life; maldevelopment is

based on the assumption of the sacredness of "development." Gustavo
Esteva asserts that the sacredness of development has to be refuted
because it threatens survival itself. "My people are tired of
development," he says, "they just want to live."[11]

The recovery of the feminine principle allows a transcendence and
transformation of these patriarchal foundations of maldevelopment. It
allows a redefinition of growth and productivity as categories linked
to the production, not the destruction, of life. It is thus simultaneously
an ecological and a feminist political project which legitimizes the way
of knowing and being that creates wealth by enhancing life and
diversity, and which delegitimizes the knowledge and practice of a
culture of death as the basis for capital accumulation.

Endnotes

1. Rosa Luxemberg, *The Accumulation of Capital*, Routledge and Kegan Paul, London,
1951.
2. An elaboration of how "development" transfers resources from the poor to the
well-endowed is contained in J. Bandyopadhyay and V. Shiva, "Political Economy of
Technological Polarisations" in *Economic and Political Weekly*, Vol. XVIII, 1982, pp.
1827-32; and J. Bandyopadyay and V. Shiva, "Political Economy of Ecology
Movements," in *Economic and Political Weekly*.
3. Ester Boserup, *Women's Role in Economic Development*, Allen and Unwin, London,
1970.
4. DAWN, *Development Crisis and Alternative Visions: Third World Women's Perspective*,
Christian Michelsen Institute, Bergen, 1985, p. 21.
5. M. George Foster, *Traditional Societies and Technological Change*, Allied Publishers,
Delhi, 1973.
6. Maria Mies, *Patriarchy and Accumulation on a World Scale*, Zed Books, London, 1986.
7. Alice Schlegel, ed., *Sexual Stratification: A Cross-Cultural Study*, Columbia University
Press, New York, 1977.
8. Jonathan Porritt, *Seeing Green*, Blackwell, Oxford, 1984.
9. A. Lovins, cited in S. R. Eyre, *The Real Wealth of Nations*, Edward Arnold, London,
1978.
10. Gustavo Esteva, "Regenerating People's Space," in *Towards a Just World Peace:
Perspective From Social Movements*, S. N. Mendlowitz and R. B. J. Walker, Butterworths
and Committee for a Just World Peace, London, 1987.
11. Esteva, op.cit.

10
A Power of Numbers
Rachel Bagby

Imagine. A room fulla women and nary a one in the minority or majority, if the measuring question is of-color or not of-color.

That's right. Imagine yourself in a gathering of committed, dynamic, earth-, self-, and other-loving women, where there, amidst many, many differences is parity; color-wise. No one can say "we don't do it that way" because there is no established *we*. Everyone is equally a guest and shaper of the party.

It only happens by design; and by design, only rarely. But when it happens . . . *girl* let me tell you! folks walk away a little bit changed. I know because I've been there. Twice. One event reached parity by conscious, painstaking effort, the other, with a deceptive ease. Both gatherings were sponsored by WomanEarth Institute.

A bit of background. WomanEarth is currently hubbed by a volunteer staff of two: Rachel Bagby—Black, attorney, writer, musician, organizer, workshop leader; and Gwyn Kirk—white, teacher, writer, "currently free to follow my interests through the generosity and support of others." *What* we hub is a growing network of women committed to helping each other and the earth thrive.

The women of WomanEarth are activists, grandmothers, carpenters, scholars, artists, scientists, healers . . . Whatever professional/sociopolitical-economic hats we wear, and most of us wear several, we share a commitment to create a world that reflects and nurtures our multi-dimensional and diverse interests. The issues on which WomanEarth focuses are ecology, feminism, spirituality, common differences, and public action.

While not all of us are actively involved in all of these issues—either as scholars or activists or both—some of us are. Whatever our issues, we are unified by the principles/processes underlying our work: challenging the dominant, destructive theories and practices of patriarchy with the wisdom of our analysis and lives; creating/refining intellectual, emotional, political, cultural and life-supporting tools of transformation; and a strong commitment to parity between women of color and white women in all aspects of WomanEarth's organization and activities; a most powerful way to put our lives where our mouths are.

These are our central commitments. Parity—Having parity shifts the power relations so that we begin to develop genuinely shared agendas and ways of working. None of us are tokens at someone else's party.

As we bond and build with the various themes of our various us(s), the fragmentary constructs of us/them begin to dissolve. Along the way, we continue to witness the evolving influence of class, economics, language, and emotional/racial history on the process. Thus, WomanEarth is a fertile ground for advancing the theories and practices involved in this woefully neglected (or persistently perplexing) aspect of the women's movement—how white women and women of color can join forces to advance our mutual interests.

Spirituality and Politics—How do we connect with our deepest, internal sense of power, evoke and place that power-from-within at the center of our political work?

Being a part of WomanEarth means acknowledging and actively entering into the mystery of our whole selves, that which is integrated with all that lives and supports life. It also means helping each other discover inclusive words and ways to describe and evoke that state of being.

Our first gathering in August 1986 at Hampshire College in Amherst, Massachusetts was a unique event. It was the first time any of us had been to a gathering where there was parity between women-of-color and white women, or where women decided to stop the planned program at points to spend time processing issues which separate us.

Not surprising, given our demographics. WomanEarth's first gathering brought women together from all over the world. Other than the fact that most of us were the kind of women people are unable to control and therefore call "uppity," it would be hard to be on the outside looking in and make generalizations about the group. Oral tradition has it that we owe that experience of parity between women-of-color and white women to Barbara Smith of Kitchen Table Press. See, Barbara was called in on early planning meetings by Ynestra King, story goes, because Barbara Deming told King the women's movement would go nowhere until white women learned how to work with women-of-color. Deming specifically mentioned Smith as someone King should make an effort to work with.

In one of the meetings between King, Smith, Gwyn Kirk, and perhaps other women, Smith threw out the challenge of creating parity at the first gathering. Story goes Smith said, "I'm tired of being on the fringes of white women's things." You got it Barbara. WomanEarth I was certainly not a white women's thing.

First, it was invitational; had to be if the goal of parity had any chance of being realized. The announcement reading in part:

> This summer, WomanEarth Feminist Peace Institute, an educational Institute formed in 1985 to provide resources and create educational settings where women from all racial and socio-economic backgrounds can meet to broaden their understanding of peace politics, is sponsoring an invitational meeting of women activists and scholars to work on "Reconstituting Feminist Peace Politics". . . .
>
> From our perspective, the established peace movement has an overly narrow focus. Discussion continues to be dominated by technicalities of weapons systems and the conception of peace often limited to disarmament. This movement has not been able to build on the mass mobilizations of 1982/83 and is still overwhelmingly white and middle class.

Story has it that responses to the controlled access to WomanEarth I from some white women active in the peace and ecology movements was fiery. "We don't *do* things that way," some said. Or, "that's a good idea, but, *of course, I'll be able to come no matter what,* right?" The women catching that fire, also white, also active in those movements, were both shocked and equal to the responses. Why this fear and anger in response to an experiment? What are you feeling as you read this paragraph?

And it took many calls, much coaxing from Papusa Molina, a Mexican woman who worked in the WomanEarth office for the summer, to convince the few women-of-color on *the list* to agree to come to Amherst that summer. Over and over came the questions. Why should we go there? Take a whole week off from work? Will it be worth it? What's the purpose?

Why did we come? Because we believed Molina's assurances. The possibility, the chance that YES! would have a place in the gathering. That we could and would embody the invitational possibility of *truly* working together. I was eager to meet other women-of-color who care about ideas and ways of being that I care about. I was eager to have my mother talk about her efforts to revitalize the North Philadelphia slum I called home; a place touched with her care in the form of community gardens, shared housing for elders and employment development for the young.

The invitation said we would "discuss how militarism affects ecological issues, world hunger, racism, the role of the US in the global economic and political power struggle, the movement of women in other countries for peace and equality, and the role of spirituality in working for peace. We seek to develop a broad-based feminist peace politics, to work together effectively across race and class lines, and to share ideas for imaginative, effective actions we can take locally, regionally, nationally and internationally."

It said nothing about the speak-out, however. We couldn't anticipate the scene of that Wednesday, white women on one side of the room, women-of-color on another. First the women-of-color then the white women answering two questions: What do you absolutely adore about being (Mexican, Black, Native American, Jewish, White Anglo-Saxon . . .)? What is it that you never, ever as long as you live want to hear from women who look like the women on the other side of the room?

With over forty of us speaking out, it took all night. Organically, the need to speak out was acknowledged as tensions rippled through this group of uppity women, women used to speaking our hearts and minds and guts. I missed the events leading up to its proposal and acceptance. My grandmother's death took me away from the first half of the gathering, kept my mother away for its entirety. When I returned, the program had been derailed a night and a day, catalyzed by a showing of *Broken Rainbow,* a film about Big Mountain atrocities of mining and relocation of Dine people.

Few of us had ever spoken out like we did at the speak-out. I hadn't. Mary Arnold, in introducing the process, said it would be empowering. Mary Arnold, a member of an ongoing multicultural network in Iowa that works on internalized and externalized racism, was right.

We entered the process with an oath of confidentiality. So the only story I can tell without breaking that oath is my own. I was shaken by the suggestion that we divide ourselves along color lines—in this corner, women-of-color . . . I heard a woman to my right say she was glad we were doing with our bodies what was going on in our minds and hearts. I didn't like it. Said so.

Then we celebrated. What is it that I absolutely love about my self? Clothed in a flowing outfit handmade by a friend, I strutted. Said nothing. My 5'9" cherrywood being spoke for itself, arms outstretched to show off my lines. Then I danced as I sang a celebration of life that brought the house *up!* "And I love alla that," I said. And the fact that I survived Stanford Law School and can still love alla that. And that I have a mutually nurturing relationship with a Black man. And recognize my mother as the wise elder that she is. There is more, much much more.

After we each celebrated our selves, we got up to say what we never, ever, as long as we lived, wanted to hear from a white women. With many colored sisters at my back, facing that crowd of white faces, some familiar, some loved, some simply white. With every cell threatening to go its own way. Fast. (What was *my* fear?) I said, "Don't tell me you understand what it means to be Black just because you've had a Black lover." After we were all done, the white women said what they heard. It was empowering to say to twenty-some white women what I'd never said to any white woman before, but wanted to. It was empowering to know we were heard, as several white women got up to reflect back to us our words and feelings.

It was empowering to hear what the white women there liked about themselves. And rare. Especially so since this was, after all, a "gathering." All too often, my encounters with white women at ecology/ peace gatherings have been of a limited variety. Either they are so glad to see me there. Or they are so sorry there aren't more of me there. ("But," I never say, "there is only one of me on this entire planet.") Or they want to know the Black perspective on this or that. Or they want to tell me the trouble they've had convincing people-of-color that issues of ecology and peace are of the utmost importance.

To hear what the white women liked about themselves and what they never, ever, as long as they lived wanted to hear from a woman-of-color ever again—*that* was an education. One comment stuck in my heart and brought tears—that any woman would be denied the joy of learning another's dance because she had "white-skinned privileges . . . "

Something moved. This group of white women facing me became more human, more women with hopes and dreams and fears and pains that I could see and feel. I became more of myself, able to revel in it. Closer to telling folks who looked like folks who have a legacy of hurting folks who look like me to STOP IT. Something moved. Some little corner of consciousness was cleared out. Some possibility of trust, or at least of honesty, was created. Some ability to speak and listen to those we see as "other." All critical qualities and skills to develop as we work to create a world where environmental responsibility is as natural as breathing in a world controlled by folks who look and act like folks who have a legacy of hurting folks and plants and animals and entire ecosystems that share this planet with us.

Imagine. Attending an ecofeminist gathering where there is parity, no group being able to call it their thang to be done this way. No one or two bits of color there to be glad about, or wonder why they're there. As many different perspectives as there are people there, and the recognition of the need and eagerness to work at working together.

By design. Imagine how empowering it would be. Create it.

11

From Healing Herbs to Deadly Drugs: Western Medicine's War Against the Natural World

Marti Kheel

Most people in the western world conceive of "alternative healing" as a deviation from the norm. Modern western medicine, by contrast, is typically viewed as the culmination of a long, steady march toward progress and truth. Through a collective lapse of memory, our culture seems to have forgotten that modern western medicine is a relatively recent phenomenon and that most of what is now called "alternative healing" has been practiced for thousands of years throughout the world. Ironically, the true "alternative" is modern western medicine which represents the greatest deviation in healing the world has ever known. [1]

At the heart of this deviation lies a dramatic transformation in our society's attitude toward the natural world. Along with this change there has been a drastic alteration in our conception of animals and of their role in helping humans to attain health. Perhaps, nowhere can this change be more clearly illustrated than in the changeover from one of the most ancient forms of healing to one of the most common forms of medicine today—namely, the shift from the use of healing herbs to the use of deadly drugs.

Herbal healing is considered by many to be the earliest form of healing. [2] It has been practiced by lay women healers for thousands of years and still remains the chief form of healing in most parts of the world. Women, in fact, have been the primary healers throughout history. According to World Health Organization figures, they still provide 95 percent of the world's health care needs. [3] Their practices have grown out of a rich tradition of holistic healing. Sadly, this tradition has been destroyed throughout much of the western world.

Women "healers" now typically fill the ranks of the nursing profession where they play a role subordinate to the (male-dominated) "scientifically" trained medical elite. One of their chief functions is the dispensing of chemicals and drugs that only doctors are permitted to prescribe. Drugs—not herbs—have become the major treatment for the sick. And women have become the major consumers (and victims) of such drugs.[4]

In order to comprehend the transition from herbs to drugs and the transfer of power from women to men that accompanied it, we must understand the worldviews out of which both forms of healing evolved.[5] Herbal healing derives from a holistic worldview most fully expressed in matriarchal societies of the prehistoric world. These cultures regarded all parts of nature as interconnected aspects of a nurturing whole—the sacred Mother Earth. "Matter" (which derives from the same root word as "mother") was seen as a living being with a life force of her own. To use poultices, roots, and herbs was to trust in her healing energy and her vital force.

Women and nature were revered in these cultures and were seen as closely allied. Plants and animals were often depicted in close association with goddesses or seen as goddesses themselves. In every part of the world, a goddess was, at one time, invoked in time of sickness.[6] Alternately, she has taken the form of a plant, a snake, a cow, a lion, a female guardian spirit, and later on, the Virgin Mary. In numerous cultures, from the American Indians to the ancient Hebrews and the Greeks, the snake has been associated with deities of healing.[7] In the Judeo-Christian tradition, we see how far we have come from this earlier conception. Both a woman and an animal—Eve and the snake— are viewed as the source of all evil in the world.

The holistic philosophy of the early matriarchal cultures was reflected in a holistic attitude toward illness and health. The common premise of all holistic healing is the notion that the whole person, not simply their symptoms or their "disease," must be treated. Illness is not conceived as a single disease with a specific "cure" but, rather, as an expression of disharmony with the natural world. Both the inner "environment" of the body and the outer environment of the surrounding world are seen as an integrated whole.

The holistic tradition out of which herbal healing evolved honored not only the power of the body to heal, but that of the mind (or spirit) as well. Prayer, chants, incantations and other forms of ritual frequently accompanied both the preparation and the ingestion of herbs. Often, such ceremonies were seen as essential components of an herb's divine power, without which the healing process could not occur.

Healing was associated, in the early matriarchal cultures, with the life-giving capacities of women. The two main goddesses of healing,

Hygea and Panacea, were also the names of the Great Goddess's milk-giving breasts.[8] Our own word "nurse" carries this age-old association with women's life-giving, nurturing powers.

For most of human history, lay women healers have seen nature as their ally. Working with the substances of the earth and the body's own healing energy, they have sought to fortify health, not attack disease. Lay women healers have prepared ointments, poultices, herbal teas and baths to relieve pain and to help restore the body to health. They have provided contraceptive measures, performed abortions, and eased the pain of labor. They have washed sores, set bones, massaged painful joints, and performed rituals and prayers. For many women, knowledge of herbal preparations has been as common as is the knowledge of cooking today.[9]

Just as herbal healing rests upon a holistic world view, modern drug-oriented medicine derives from dualistic ideas. Whereas the holistic perspective honors the healing energy of the body and of the earth, modern western medicine is founded upon a distrust of nature and nature's power to heal. The history of western medicine is that of a long protracted struggle to conquer and subdue the vital force of nature; it is the attempt to render her inert. Significantly, in patriarchal cosmologies, it is the *logos* or the *nous* (the "word" or the "mind") which gives birth to the world, not nature or the Goddess herself, as was formerly believed. Increasingly, the vital force of life, including the power to heal, is no longer seen to rest in "mere matter," (the body or the Earth), but rather in the "rational," "scientific" (male) mind.

Two of the most important notions that contributed to the demise of the former worldview can be found in the philosophy of Francis Bacon and that of Rene Descartes. According to Bacon, nature could be viewed as a mysterious virgin whose secrets needed to be penetrated by the tools of science. Baconian science sought to discover "still laid up in the womb of nature many secrets of excellent use" that no man had reached before. The point was no longer just to know nature but to conquer and subdue her with the power of the "rational" (masculine) mind.

The Cartesian worldview carried the conquest of nature to its logical extreme—i.e., to the point of death. Nature, which was viewed as female, was relegated to an inferior and inactive realm, apart from "rational man." In contrast to the "vitalists," who believed there was an irreducible, vital aspect to all life, Descartes maintained that nature conformed to mechanical (chemical) laws. According to this view, nature was a machine, devoid of both rationality and soul. Animals, who were also machines, could experience no pain. Their cries of anguish upon being dissected were mere mechanical response.

The twin notions of conquering nature and of viewing nature as a machine have become the life-blood of modern western medicine. According to the modern, scientific viewpoint, disease reflects a failure in the body machinery. When disease strikes, it is the body's machinery that must be repaired. Whether the repair takes the form of surgery, a drug, or the replacement of "defective" body parts, such adjustments must be performed by those thought to have the necessary technology, expertise, and skill. The doctor and the doctor's tools alone can mend the failed machine.

Since the modern medical body is conceived as a machine, it is also thought to conform to Newtonian laws of cause and effect. Disease and ill health are thus seen to have a single, external "cause"—usually viruses, bacteria and other microorganisms. In order to restore health to the body, the offending agent need only be identified and rooted out. Typically, these enemy organisms are fought with chemical weapons forced from nature on another battlefront—the modern research laboratory.

This reductionistic view of the healing process has become so entrenched that it is difficult for many people to conceive of healing in any other way. And, yet, the concept of "one disease-one cure" (and one drug) is equally alien to the holistic view. [10] In the holistic tradition, only a single disease exists—namely, an imbalance or a lack of harmony with nature, whether within oneself or with the rest of the natural world.

Today, drugs have become the primary weapon employed by western medicine in its war against disease. Rather than trust in the healing power of nature—i.e., poultices, plants, and the body's own healing energy—western medicine prefers to respond to the "affront" of disease with an assault of its own. Just as Bacon sought to "storm the bastions" of nature with the tools of science, modern western medicine has declared a war of its own. It is a war waged against the body and all of the natural world. Unable to trust in the healing power of nature, western medicine prefers to "penetrate nature" in order to produce "cures" of its own. Plants are no longer valued in and of themselves. Rather, the most powerful properties of plants must be isolated, extracted and then synthesized into chemicals and drugs. Nature is seen as a resource which is useful only when transformed by men's rational mind.

The human body has become the central battlefield in western medicine's war against disease. Thus, two of the weapons used in the "war" against cancer are nitrogen mustard and radiation, both weapons used during the last world wars. The terminology of warfare permeates the modern, medical world. Thus, we hear of the "war on cancer" declared by presidential decree in 1971. We hear, too, of "bombarding" cells with an arsenal of drugs and of "magic bullets" that "target" cancerous sites. Conversely, we often hear of our alleged enemies described as cancerous growths or other forms of disease. Most of all, we hear that the war *will* be won, provided, of course, that biomedical research scientists are given sufficient funds.

It should come as no surprise, however, that the "war on cancer" (and other diseases) has produced more victims than cures.[11] Indeed, the warfare mentality of western medicine has made medical casualties a routine part of our world. In the United States, prescription drugs have become a major cause of iatrogenic (doctor-induced) disease, causing more deaths each year than accidents on the road.[12] "According to the FDA, 1.5 million Americans had to be hospitalized in 1978 as a consequence of taking drugs (which were supposed to 'cure' them of something or other). And some thirty percent of all hospitalized people get further damaged by the therapy that is imposed on them. The number of people killed in the U.S. by the intake of drugs has been estimated at some 140,000 each year."[13] Drug therapy has become so routine that 60 percent of American doctors prescribe antibiotics for the common cold.[14] Unfortunately, many drug "side effects" only appear after years of use, making it impossible to anticipate what such effects will be.

Meanwhile, the medical assault on our bodies is compounded by a chemical attack on another front—i.e., by the pesticides, additives and other chemicals and drugs that routinely pollute our water, food, and air. This massive chemical attack is wreaking untold damage on the "ecology" of our bodies and thus on our only genuine "defense" against disease—our body's natural immunological response.[15]

Faith in the medical profession has emerged largely unharmed by the prevalence of drug toxicity and drug abuse. On the contrary, most people now accord doctors the same reverence once reserved for priests delivering their sacraments to those who would be saved. And, yet, the veneration that today's doctors have come to expect as their due was only won through a long protracted struggle against all forms of healing that have not conformed to their own. The history of this battle takes us back many years.

Western medicine traces its scientific origins to the Hippocratic medicine of ancient Greece. Although this body of writing largely embraced sound holistic principles, it also contained the seeds of the dualistic mentality that later came to prevail. The theoretical conception of illness found in the notion of the four humors eventually led to the mechanistic notion of regulating disease and to the idea of forcibly driving (or draining) illness out. In Hippocratic medicine, the patient's symptoms were aggravated to the point of a healing crisis. Purgings, bleedings, induced vomitings and other "heroic" feats were some of the methods employed in this task. The notion of "aiding" nature had already led to the practice (by male physicians) of giving her a "helpful" shove. Meanwhile, witches and faith healers were branded by Hippocrates as charlatans and quacks.

It was not until the thirteenth century, however, that the attack on lay women healers became institutionalized. It was at this time that laws were passed requiring physicians to obtain licenses and medical training. Since universities were almost universally closed to women, lay women healers were, in effect, barred from the legal practice of medicine. There was, however, little in medical training or practice that we would recognize as "science." Medical students confined most of their studies to astrology, religion, and philosophy and read more of Plato, Aristotle, and Christian theology than medical theory. The heroic medicine espoused by the Hippocratic tradition had become the favored form of treatment for the sick. However, the purgatives used were no longer derived from plants alone but were also extracted from the far more toxic mineral world. The administration of mercury, lead and arsenic (along with blood-letting) had become routine practices. For centuries, physicians were too preoccupied with the correctness of their medical theories to notice that their treatments often caused more harm than good.[16]

Although it was the white, upper-class, male medical profession that, under the guise of science, ultimately wrested control from lay women healers, it was the church that initiated the first major blow. An estimated nine million people (mostly women) were executed or burned as witches between 1479 and 1735.[17] Interestingly, one of the titles for witches was "herberia," meaning "one who gathers herbs."[18] Often, the crime such women were accused of was literally their ability to heal. This attack by the church was, at once, directed against the Goddess-worshipping religion which embodied a reverence for all of the natural world and against the peasantry which lived by this tradition and passed its knowledge on.

In order to comprehend why healing should be considered a crime, it is necessary to understand the church's attitude toward women and all of the natural world. According to the church, the vital, healing force of nature resided not within the earth, but rather, within a male, sky God. Disease, illness, and even labor pains, were all expressions of God's will. Only church-approved individuals (mostly men with university training and the priests with whom they were obliged to consult) could work within "God's plan."

While the church was wielding its attack against lay women, the field of science was slowly developing ideas that would ultimately pose a far more serious challenge. The fields of physiology and chemistry, which evolved in part out of the herbal tradition, were subtly supplanting this tradition by subsuming it into a "science." The herbal tradition was not, however, fully usurped by science until many years later. Herbalism continued to be practiced throughout the countryside by lay women healers. Even up until the 1800s, most people consulted herbalists when sick. Drug preparations consisted primarily of "crude plants—i.e., ground up leaves, flowers and roots, or teas, extracts and tinctures of them. Medicine and botany were still intimately allied."[19] By the middle of the nineteenth century, at least in the United States and Europe, 80 percent of medicines used were still derived from plants. Today, less than 30 percent of the drugs used are plant-based.[20]

Only with the rise of the large pharmaceutical industries in the late nineteenth century and with the increased faith in science did the "regular" physicians successfully defeat the herbal, homeopathic, and other holistic traditions. The would-be medical profession saw in the rising pharmaceutical industry an opportunity to bolster its flagging reputation through an increased association with technology and science. To their good fortune, the pharmaceutical industry saw in the "regular" physicians an ideal vehicle for marketing their new drugs. The pharmaceutical industries, thus, began an all-out campaign (which has been continued to this day) to convince the "regulars" to prescribe their drugs. At the same time, the medical profession began an equally virulent drive to discredit the holistic practitioners (i.e., the "irregulars") for failing to fulfill the requirements of a "science." Thus, the fateful marriage between western medicine and science was sealed and the future course of western medicine was set.

The rise to prominence of the "regular" physicians went hand in hand with the rise of an elite, white class of men. In the United States, the attempt to legitimize this class of physicians was brought about through the complete restructuring of medical schools. The famous 1910 Flexner report, commissioned by the Carnegie Corporation, resulted in the closing of scores of medical schools for failing to meet the new "scientific" criteria. The new guidelines were based upon the mechanistic and mathematical ideas that had begun to dominate the field of science in Europe. Course requirements were to include a thorough immersion in anatomy, chemistry, pathology, and physics. Approved schools were also to provide full-time research faculty as well as a solid, technological base—the modern research laboratory. Many of the schools that were closed for failing to meet these criteria had been havens for women and blacks. The "regulars" thus successfully attained their current status as an elite profession, fully "legitimized" by the mystique of science.

Today's medical schools are living monuments to the victory of "science" over the earlier holistic worldview. Students now emerge from medical school with myriad courses in chemistry and physics but not a single course in the art of healing herbs. At most, the medical school graduate will have received one course in nutrition. He or she will enter the medical world with the faith of a true believer in the power of "science" (and drugs) to "cure."

The medical profession achieved ascendence over the holistic tradition largely because it was able to convince the public that their new drugs were the major factors in the elimination of infectious disease. The medical profession was, in fact, born of the germ/drug theory of disease on which it continues to thrive to this day. Although strong evidence suggests that most of the major infectious diseases declined most rapidly *before* the discovery of the much-touted vaccination programs and that there was no obvious change after the drugs were introduced,[21] the medical profession continues to proudly proclaim this "conquest" as its own. Careful studies, however, point to the decisive influence of environmental factors—improved nutrition and cleaner water and air.[22] Many of these improvements in health standards were the product of the Popular Health Movement of the 1830s and 1840s which was spearheaded by women.

Western medicine obstinately continues to deny the importance of environmental and lifestyle factors in the causation of disease. Even though it has been estimated that 80 percent or more of all cancers are attributable to environmental factors,[23] medical research continues to pour billions of dollars into finding magic (chemical) cures for this and other diseases. Approximately seventy thousand chemicals are presently in everyday use throughout the world with five hundred to one thousand new ones added to the list each year.[24] Our food is poisoned with pesticides and drugs and industries routinely pollute our water and our air. Research has also shown that meat-eating is a major cause of disease, not only due to the myriad chemicals and hormones that factory farm animals are forced to ingest, but also due to the high levels of protein, bacteria, cholesterol and fat that are found in meat.[25] And yet, the medical profession spends only a fraction of the health dollar on research into the prevention of disease.

One of the reasons for this skewed sense of priorities is that prevention is simply not a very dramatic thing to do. Western medicine is founded upon the notion of the heroic conquest of nature. To credit the environment or lifestyle with importance is letting nature steal the show. To concede that plants, exercise, food, and clean air may have more to do with healing than western medicine's arsenal of drugs is to remove the very foundation upon which western medicine is based.

Thus, industries continue to pollute our environment with toxic chemicals and drugs while medical scientists continue to refine increasingly potent drugs to "cure" us of the illnesses that our poisoned environment has produced; pharmaceutical industries bombard both our inner and outer "environment" with the equally toxic chemicals and drugs.

Western medicine's preference for the development and marketing of dangerous drugs over the earlier use of healing herbs is a direct product of its mechanistic beliefs. Rather than use the entire plant, western medicine prefers to isolate the plant's most active ingredients in order to develop a more potent force. However, in general, isolated and "refined" drugs are much more toxic than are the substances from which they are derived. (It is no coincidence that the word "pharmaceutical" derives from an ancient Greek word meaning "poison.") It appears that the combined properties of plants serve complementary functions providing safeguards that are missing when particular ingredients are refined and extracted from the whole plant. It would seem that the attempt to divide nature is a risky affair. To cite just one example: The foxglove leaf was used safely for thousands of years as an aid for those with heart problems. The drug "digitalis" was later isolated and refined and is now a standardized drug for heart disease. The problem, however, is that digitalis, unlike the foxglove leaf, is a deadly drug whose dosage needs to be carefully monitored. In its attempt to isolate the most powerful ingredient of the foxglove leaf, Western medicine replaced the earlier healing herb with a poisonous drug. [26]

Nowhere has the warfare model of modern western medicine had more tragic consequences than in its treatment of nonhuman animals. Nonhuman animals have become one of the major victims in western medicine's war against the natural world. They are the basic fodder used by the medical war machine.

Sadly, most of the current medical dollar is spent on zoological research which studies not how to help humans get well but, rather, how to make healthy animals sick. Day in and day out, animals are cut, burned, poisoned, starved, shocked, gassed, and frozen—all in the name of science.

In many of the earliest cultures, animals were viewed as the guardians of nature's secrets. Today, laboratory animals are literally pierced by the tools of science in hopes they will yield their secrets to the modern rational mind.

Throughout patriarchal cultures, animals have been sacrificed to the gods in the hopes of attaining fertility, abundance and renewed life. Today, we are told that the god of Progress requires the same sacrifice of animal life. Significantly, researchers do not "kill" animals in laboratories; the word "sacrifice" is still employed. Behind the sacrifice of animals at the altar of science lies the ancient and tragic belief that somehow, if animals are killed, human beings will be allowed to live.

Although animals had been "sacrificed," dissected, and experimented upon for thousands of years, it was only with the advent of the mechanistic worldview that such experimentation became an integral part of medical science. Since, according to the Cartesian worldview, animals were mere machines and could feel no pain, the ethical issues involved in animal experimentation were easily excised.

Thus, feeling, caring, and intuition were successfully banned from the laboratory with the advent of the mechanistic age. The true scientific spirit was decreed to follow the dictates of reason, not the feelings of the heart. Western medicine thus set out to conquer not only external nature but inner nature as well. Biomedical research on animals continues to follow this ideal. As today's medical student cuts into a laboratory animal, he simultaneously cuts himself off from his feelings of connection with other forms of life. He "conquers" all feelings of love and compassion with the power of the "rational" mind.

Whereas the church justified the abuse of animals (and women) by the claim that they were lacking in souls, today's biomedical research scientists attempt to justify laboratory experimentation by the contention that nonhuman animals are lacking in "rationality." Once again, "reason" is touted as the quality that elevates humans above the natural world. Why "reason" should be viewed as the most important trait that a being can possess is never "reasonably" explained.

The human capacity to "reason" is, indeed, unique, as a glance at the thinking of animal research scientists shows. Thus, while researchers attempt to justify animal experimentation by the claim that animals are *different* from human beings, they also seek to justify it scientifically by "reasoning" that animals are *similar* to human beings. But, although animals *are* similar to humans in the important aspects of life—i.e., they feel joy, sadness, loneliness, and fear—their physiologies differ significantly from our own. Each species has a unique constitution and develops diseases and responds to drugs in very different ways. Thus, "penicillin kills guinea pigs. But the same guinea pigs can safely eat strychnine, one of the deadliest poisons for humans—but not for monkeys"; opium is "harmless to dogs and chickens"; "morphine, which calms and anesthetizes humans, causes maniacal excitement in cats and mice"; thalidomide, though tested extensively and "proven" safe in several species, later caused birth defects in the ten thousand children born to pregnant mothers who took this drug.[27]

The stressful, artificial conditions in which laboratory animals are forced to live make generalization to the real life situation of humans an even greater leap of faith. Humans do not live in cages or germ-free environments; nor are their diseases induced by artificial means. A cancer or illness that grows organically follows a very different course from one that has been artificially induced.

The same faulty reasoning plagues not only medical research but product testing on animals as well. A large portion of animal experimentation cannot even claim to have lofty goals, consisting instead in the routine testing of consumer products including chemicals and drugs. None of these tests could be further removed from the actual conditions of the real world.

Of course, the ultimate experiment for every new drug occurs when it is ingested by human beings. A vicious cycle exists in which dangerous drugs are marketed because they "prove" safe in tests on animals; when such drugs then go on to produce illnesses and disease, animals are, once again, made the victims in science's search for elusive cures.

One of the major reasons that companies insist on using animal experimentation is the convenient legal alibi that animal research provides. When drug companies want to market a drug, they argue for the similarity between human and nonhuman animals. Conversely, when adverse reactions occur, they are quick to reply that animal studies cannot be applied with complete accuracy to human beings. The manufacturers of thalidomide were, in fact, acquitted on the grounds that research on animals could not reliably predict how a drug would affect human beings.[28]

When legal restraints are lifted, drug manufacturers show where their true priorities lie. Many chemicals and drugs that have been banned in the United States are actively promoted in Third World countries, where drug manufacturers can more easily ignore their disastrous results.[29]

Another reason for the continued existence of animal research and the drug industry is the profit motive. One of the perceived drawbacks of herbs is that they cannot be patented. Manufactured drugs, by contrast, produce billions of dollars every year. Likewise, animal experimentation is a multi-billion-dollar business providing enormous profits for the researchers, universities, breeders of animals, manufacturers of animal equipment, and pharmaceutical companies.

Since western medicine has left behind the tradition of healing herbs in preference for the development of toxic drugs, precise measurements and testing have taken on an importance that does not exist with herbs. Since, for the most part, herbs have a more gentle effect, there is no need for stringent testing. Herbs have, in fact, been tested for thousands of years, with the knowledge gained from such "tests" handed down through a rich folk tradition. Homeopathy, a close ally of herbal healing, provides an example of how different the concept of testing is within the holistic tradition. According to homeopathy, the best tests for the effect of a remedy are the ones that physicians perform on themselves.

Western medicine shows a preference for only those drugs that produce dramatic and visible effects. Due to its mechanistic and heroic orientation, it seeks a quick technological "fix" to restore the appearance of health. Even such emotional problems as grief, anxiety, and depression are now thought to have quick chemical "cures." This contrasts sharply with the basic principles of holistic healing in which the attempt is to improve health in a more profound and lasting way. Thus, in herbal healing, the best herbs are considered not those that produce an immediate, dramatic effect, but rather those that improve health gradually over a period of time.

Modern western medicine has sought to salvage disease from the untamed conditions of the natural world. Within the "controlled" setting of their laboratories, researchers have sought to replicate disease and to manufacture cures. But while medical scientists have been looking for "miracle" cures in their laboratories (apart from the natural world), the healing power of nature has continued to manifest itself throughout our lives. When we cut ourselves and our blood clots and our wound later heals with no outside help, we have seen its power at work. This regenerative life-force pervades every cell of our bodies. All of the various holistic or "alternative" practices attempt to affirm and work with this healing force. Different cultures have called it by a number of names. There is the *Prana* of India, the *Chi* of China and the *Ki* of Japan. The very word *physis*, from which our word "physician" derives, refers to both "Nature" and to this "vital force."

Although many of us have lost our connection to this healing power, it is one that nonhuman animals still retain. Animals *do*, ironically, have something to teach us, but it is not a knowledge that can be wrenched from their bodies behind laboratory walls. Many nonhuman animals know instinctively what to do when ill. For example, a "wild turkey during the rainy season force-feeds her young with leaves of the spice bush; a dog with a digestive problem chews upon the witch grass to produce vomiting; a bear feeds upon the fruit of rockberry with relish while fern roots become his healing agent; the wolf, bitten by a venomous snake, seeks out and chews snakeroot."[30] "Cats and dogs purge themselves with certain grasses and lie in wet mud (a source of natural 'antibiotic') in case of snake or insect bites or other irritations."[31] Wild animals will also naturally seek solitude and relaxation when ill.

Another example of "animal medicine" was discovered by a researcher in Africa. On certain days, he observed a group of chimpanzees traveling long distances in search of a shrub called *Aspilia pluriseta*. After carefully selecting particular leaves, the chimpanzees roll the leaves around one by one in their mouths, eventually swallowing them with a grimace. *Aspilia pluriseta* has since been found to contain a highly reactive red oil (thiarubin A) that is known to kill *Candida albicans* or *Staphylococcus albus.* In a nearby tribe it was found that the same species of leaf was consumed by humans to treat surface wounds, such as cuts and burns, and for stomach aches. People used the same three species used by the chimpanzees, but a species not used by chimpanzees was also not used by humans.[32]

Did these people learn their medicine through their observation of animals in the wild? Very possibly this is the case. A number of commentators believe, in fact, that many of the earliest herbal remedies used by humans were based on such observations of animals in the wild. The American Indians, who watched bears closely in order to learn what they would eat both for food and for medicine, are a case in point.

But how do animals distinguish plants and roots that are helpful from those that cause harm? Perhaps the best answer we can offer is that they are guided by instinct or natural knowing. Humans also have such instincts although we prefer to call them intuitions when referring to ourselves. In all probability, these instincts or intuitions guided humans as well as animals in their earliest forms of healing.[33]

Edward Bach, after whom "Bach Flower Essences" are named, provides a modern-day example of this phenomenon. Bach believed in using intuition as a guide to discovering the right plant medicine. These instincts or intuitions are our connection to the natural world and to the life energy that helps us to maintain health. In contrast to western, patriarchal medicine which aspires to be a science, such intuitive modes of healing resemble far more an art.

Unfortunately, most of this art has been lost to the modern world. Most of us have lost not only the actual knowledge of ancient healing practices but also the instincts and intuitions that formerly guided us toward health. We typically eat foods that are devoid of nutritional value and that contain numerous chemicals and additives that are harmful to our health. Similarly, we often fail to heed the subtle warnings that tell us to beware of dangerous pharmaceutical drugs.

Although western medicine's war against the body and against nature shows little sign of abating, significant signs of hope are also to be found. One source of hope can be seen in the growth of the animal liberation movement over the last ten years. Animal researchers compare the members of this growing movement to the Luddites who vainly smashed their machines in an attempt to forestall the modern, technological age. However, it is the very conception of animals as machines that the animal liberation movement seeks to destroy. The animal liberation movement, therefore, does pose one of the greatest challenges to the modern, technological age and to the mechanistic conception of life.

Other signs of promise can be found in the growth of the holistic health healing movement. This movement is encouraging not only because of the number of "alternative" health care practitioners who are emerging and the number of people who are now turning to such practitioners for their health care needs, but also because of the knowledge of holistic health care that has reached the public at large. More and more people are incorporating meditation, herbal supplements, yoga and other holistic practices into their daily lives; for the true role of a health care practitioner is not that of a mechanistic "curer" of disease, but rather that of a teacher who can guide us in working with the powers of the natural world.[34]

The wisdom of living in harmony with nature was possesed by our ancestors and is a heritage we would do well to reclaim. This wisdom embodies the principle of nonviolence so alien to modern western medicine in its war against the natural world. Holistic healing is a vital way in which we can honor this wisdom. By helping to integrate body, mind, instinct, and intuition, holistic healing enables us to live in harmony and ecological balance with all of the natural world. Along with the ecofeminist, environmental, and animal liberation movements, of which it is an integral part, holistic healing provides a formidable challenge to the violence perpetrated upon nature by the patriarchal mind. It is an antiwar protest of its own, helping to bring forth a world of peace and nonviolence for all living beings.

Endnotes

1. For convenience, I have used the term "western medicine" to refer to the practice of "allopathy" which has become the orthodoxy of the medical world today. However, as I hope to show, western medicine is also heir to a rich tradition of holistic healing which it has yet to honor.

2. Barbara Griggs, *Green Pharmacy: A History of Herbal Medicine*, Viking Press, New York, 1982, p. 6.

3. Quoted in Monicao Sjoo and Barbara Mor, *The Great Cosmic Mother: Rediscovering the Religion of the Earth*, Harper and Row, San Francisco, 1987, p. 35.

4. Women constitute a disproportionately large share of the consumer drug market, particularly for mood-modifying and hormonally based drugs. (Kahtleen McDonnel, ed., *Adverse Effects: Women and the Pharmaceutical Industry*, Women's Educational Press, Toronto, 1986, pp. 4-6).

5. For an in-depth history of women healers, see Dr. Kate Campbell Hurd-Mead, *A History of Women in Medicine from the Earliest Times to the Beginning of the Nineteenth Century*, The Haddam Press, Haddam, CT, 1938. Also see Barbara Ehrenreich and Deirdre English, *Witches, Midwives and Nurses: A History of Women Healers*, The Feminist Press, Old Westbury, NY, 1973, and Barbara Ehrenreich and Deirdre English, *For Her Own Good: 150 Years of Experts' Advice to Women*, Anchor Books, Garden City, NY, 1978.

6. Campbell Hurd-Mean, op.cit., p. 5.

7. Ibid.

8. Barbara Walker, *The Woman's Encyclopedia of Myths and Secrets*, Harper & Row, San Francisco, 1983, p. 420.

9. Griggs, op.cit., p. 89.

10. For an in-depth critique of western medicine's notion of specific aetiology, see Bernard Dixon, *Beyond the Magic Bullet*, Harper & Row, New York, 1978.

11. A recent comprehensive assessment of cancer research in the *New England Journal of Medicine* conceded that "we are losing the war on cancer." (John C. Bailes, III, and Elaine M. Smith, "Progress Against Cancer?," p. 314 (May 8, 1986: 1231).

12. E. W. Martin, Opening Statement, DIA/AMA/FDA/PMA Joint Symposium, "Drug information for patients," *Drug Information Journal*, II, Special Supplement, January 1977, 2S-3S.

13. Hans Reusch, *The Naked Empress*, Civis Publications, Milano, Italy, 1982, p. 12.

14. P. Stolley, et al., "Drug Prescribing and Use in an American Community," *Ann Int Med*, 76:537, 1972.

15. Evidence for the damage to our immune systems from this medical assault can be found in the unusual rate of increase of immune system related diseases as well as in the appearance of many new strains of drug-resistant bacteria. Thus, although penicillin originally was virtually always successful in treating gonorrhea, there are now strains of gonorrheal bacteria that are resistant to penicillin throughout the world and 90 percent of staphylococci infections no longer respond to it. (H. Smith, *Antibiotics in Clinical Practice*, Pitman Medical, London, 1977; Marc Lappe, *When Antibiotics Fail*, North Atlantic Books, Berkeley, 1986, p. xii).

16. For an in-depth critique of how western medicine's reliance upon rationalist doctrine, accompanied by an antagonistic attitude toward disease, has impeded the development of a lay-based empirical tradition in which nature (not the doctor) is seen as the true healer, see Harris L. Coulter, *Divided Legacy: Vol 1: The Patterns Emerge: Hippocrates to Paracelsus; Vol. II: Progress and Regress: I.B. van Helmont to Claude Bernard; Vol. III: Science and Ethics in American Medicine, 1800-1914*, Wehawken Book Co., Washington, DC, 1973-77.

17. William Woods, *A Casebook on Witchcraft*, G.P. Putnam & Sons, New York, 1974, p. 26.

18. Walker, op.cit., p. 1076.

19. Andrew Weil, *Health and Healing*, Houghton Mifflin Co., Boston, 1988, p. 97.

20. Richard Grossman, *The Other Medicines*, Doubleday and Co., New York, 1985, pp. 86-87.

21. See J. McKinlay and S. McKinlay, "The questionable contribution of medical measures to the decline of mortality in the United States in the twentieth century," *Milbank Memorial Fund Quarterly*, 1977, pp. 405-28. For research on England and Wales, see T. McKeown, *The Role of Medicine: Dream, Mirage, or Nemesis?* Oxford Press, Oxford, 1976.

22. Ibid.

23. John H. Knowles, M.D., "The Responsibility of the Individual," in *Doing Better and Feeling Worse: Health in the United States*, John H. Knowles, M.D., ed., Norton and Co., New York, 1977, p. 63.

24. U.S. International Trade Commission, Synthetic Organic Chemicals: United States Production and Sales, 1985, U.S. Government Printing Office, Washington, DC, 1986; The Number of Chemicals in Use from "The Quest for Chemical Safety," International Register of Potentially Toxic Chemicals Bulletin, May 1985; Number added annually from Michael Shodell, "Risky Business," *Science*, 1985, October 1985.

25. According to a report in "Diet and Stress in Vascular Disease," *Journal of the American Medical Association*, "A vegetarian diet can prevent 97 percent of our coronary occlusions." (Vol. 176, No. 9, June 3, 1961, p.806). For more on the health hazards of meat-eating (as well as its other adverse effects), see John Robbins, *Diet for a New America*, Stillpoint Publishing, Walpole, New Hampshire, 1987; and Barbara Parham, *What's Wrong with Eating Meat*, Ananda Marga Publication, Denver, CO, 1979.

26. William A. R. Thomson, M.D., *Herbs That Heal*, Charles Scribner's Sons, New York, 1976, pp. 23-26.

27. Hans Reusch, *Slaughter of the Innocent*, Civitas Publications, New York, 1983, pp. 8-10.

28. Ibid., p. 361.

29. Mike Muller, *The Health of Nations: An Investigation of the Pharmaceutical Industry's Exploitation of the Third World for Profit*, Faber and Faber, London, 1982.

30. Ben Charles Harris, *The Compleat Herbal*, Larchmont Books, New York, 1972, p. 23.

31. Ibid., p. 10.

32. Richard Wrangham, "Ape Medicine?" *Anthroquest*, No. 33, Winter 1985.

33. Griggs, p. 6.

34. According to ancient Chinese doctrine, sages did not treat those who were sick; they instructed those who were well, and they were paid for such advice. If the patient became sick, it was considered partly the doctor's fault and payments ceased. (Huang Ti, Nei Ching Su Wen, *The Yellow Emperor's Classic of Internal Medicine*, trans. Veith, I., Williams and Wilkins, Baltimore, 1949.)

Other Sources

Armstrong, B., and R. Doll. "Environmental Factors and Cancer Incidence and Mortality in Different Countries with Special Reference to Dietary Practices." *International Journal of Cancer* 15 (1975).

Doll, R. "Prevention of Cancer: Pointers from Epidemiology." Nuffield Hospital Trust, London, 1967.

Epstein, "Environmental Determinants of Cancer." *International Journal of Cancer* 15 (1975).

Fulder, Stephen. *The Tao of Medicine: Oriental Remedies and the Pharmacology of Harmony*. Destiny Books, Rochester, VT.

Higginson, J. "Present Trends in Cancer Epidemiology." Proceedings of the Canadian Cancer Conference 8, 1969.

Higginson, J. "The Role of Geographical Pathology in Environmental Carcinogenesis." *Environmental Cancer*. Baltimore: Williams and Wilkins, 1972.

Melmon, L. "Preventable Drug Reactions—Causes and Cures." *New England Journal of Mecidine* 284:1361, 1971.

PART THREE
SHE IS ALIVE IN YOU:
ECOFEMINIST
SPIRITUALITY

Earth-based spiritualities celebrate the cycle of life: birth, growth, decay, death, and regeneration as it appears in the seasonal round of the year, in the moon's phases, in human, plant and animal life, always with the goal of establishing balance among all the different communities that comprise the living body of the earth.
—Starhawk, "Feminist, Earth-Based Spirituality and Ecofeminism,"

The shift from the western theological tradition of the hierarchical chain of being to an earth-based spirituality begins the healing of the split between spirit and matter. For ecofeminist spirituality, like the traditions of Native Americans and other tribal peoples, sees the spiritual as alive in us, where spirit and matter, mind and body, are all part of the same living organism. No one aspect is any better than another; each has its own ability to grow, develop, and—in its unique way—it can enhance the whole. There is no deferring until the after-life, nor is there any supreme authority figure. Goddesses, Gods, Creators are part of each person, plant, and animal. Immanence takes the place of transcendence.

Deena Metzger writes about the importance of bringing back the Goddess with the God, and about reinvoking the sacred grove. The strength required to defend the sacred forests of northern India, Radha Bhatt feels, comes from the spiritual value of nonviolence. The oneness of spirit and body is clarified by Charlene Spretnak as she shows how spirituality is an intrinsic dimension of human consciousness and not separate from the body. Rosemary Ruether stresses the urgency for an ecological-feminist theology of nature. Neopaganism, suggests Margot Adler, is part of the modern world's search for such cultural roots. Finding oneself in nature is the subject of Dale Colleen Hamilton's short story; and, quite differently, Dolores LaChapelle traces an alternative view of human sexuality and its relationship to the natural world. Finally, Starhawk, from a witch's perspective, connects earth-based spirituality and ecofeminism with ways to transform ourselves and the world around us.

A Story of Beginnings
Starhawk

Out of the point, the swelling
Out of the swelling, the egg
Out of the egg, the fire
Out of the fire, the stars
Out of the rain of stars
   the congealing, molten world

The fire remains, see it burn in the center of the circle
Watch the flames, filled with points of light that
   spark and dance
Watch the fire, as in and out of your lungs flows breath
   the most ancient river
The air you breathe passed through the lungs of dinosaurs
   and chittering, big-eyed lemurs, ancestors
Feel yourself rocking
   cradled in the night sky womb arching around you
   alive with a billion billion dancing points of light
Breathe
Watch the flame
Listen to the voice of the story, the first story
   whispered in the secret heart of your encoded
   memories
Hear the story woman

She says
   The labor is hard, the night is long
   We are midwives, and men who tend the birth
     and bond with the child
   We are birthing, and being born
   We are trying to perform an act of magic—
   To pull a living child out of a near-corpse
     of the mother we are simultaneously poisoning,
     who is ourselves

She is alive in you as you in her
Warm your human hands at the watchfire
See the stains on the cloak
Feel the wounds too deep for healing

There are times, sisters and brothers
  when we are afraid that we will die
  and take the whole great humming dance of life
  with us
Something must change, we know that
But are we strong enough?
And will we be given time?

This is the story we like to
tell ourselves
  in the night
  when the fire seems nothing but dying embers winking
  out
  and the labor is too hard and goes on too long
  when we can't believe that we can make it
We like to tell ourselves
  that we remember the First Mother

She is alive in you as you in her
A power keener than the weapon's edge, a healing deeper
  than the wound
Feel her in your belly, at the bottom of breath
Her power is life; it is stronger

She is being who is spinning, fire covered with a
  sweet crust shell
Feel her pulse, remember in your nerves winks
  the spark of the first fire
You are alive in her as she in you
You are her
Your misty breath great clouds of gasses set in motion
  by your spinning dance
  swirl and cool and rain
  for thousands and thousands of years
  while you build up, tear down, and rearrange
  the ridges and valleys of your skin
  carve and smooth your wrinkles
And the water
  softens every sharp edge into soil
  fills the basins of your oceans
In your veins flows ocean water
Remember the lightning, sparks striking into being
  something new

Life, teeming, greedy life
That grows, cell by swelling cell, divides, devours, unites
   and changes, filling your ocean belly, flinging a green
   cloak over the land, learning to swim, crawl, run,
   stalk, fly, caress, and stand erect, made of
   earth air water fire
   and what goes beyond these and unites these
   the mystery
She is alive in us: we are alive in her as in each other
   as all that is alive is alive in us
   and all is alive

When we are afraid, when it hurts too much
We like to tell ourselves
   stories of power
   how we lost it
   how we can reclaim it
We tell ourselves
   the cries we hear may be those of labor
   the pain we feel may yet be that of birth

12
Invoking the Grove
Deena Metzger

The Trees Ask Me Home*

Soon
I'll sleep each night
with the breath of leaves
in the bed, the cough of eucalyptus,
the restless stirring of fig and lime.
There is so much life here,
rooster as alarm, hawk as sentinel,
coyote as guard; there is so much life
and ferment, death is close by.

When the human species deserted him,
tomatoes were what my father planted,
they were his true love.
With their imperative, he spent
weekends in the sun.
So I learned to talk to trees.
I see the song coming, a wing out
of the nest of bitterness,
light and dark. And further on,
those footsteps in the mulch
and that path through the new grove,
must be mine.

It seems
the story of my life
is the story of trees I've loved
some were standing, some fell down.

*See note following page.

Which Of These Forms Have You Taken?*

This year I have been growing
down into the tree
against my will
making nothing happen.
Across the woods
through the bare branch haze
of bars against the light
someone is coming with an axe.

I have known this all my life.

A few weeks ago I dreamed I was to be the poet to go to the moon.
When I got there, even though I knew I had an obligation to NASA,
I recognized that I also had other obligations to other constituencies.
I wanted to bring back words about what it was to be on the moon.
The only words that came to me as I walked about were: "I am on the
body of The Mother. I am finally on the body of The Mother." I
wanted to know, "What is it, this moon?" I wanted to see and know
the great light and I wanted to see and know the great darkness. But,
as far as I walked from the space shuttle, I could not find the moon,
because I found myself in an endless parking lot filled with VW cars
as far as the horizon. The next day I dreamed that I was in an
extraordinary grove. The air was dark and pure from the breath of
trees. There was a swift river running along one side of the grove, also
dark and pure. A small footbridge crossed the river connecting the
grove with the Los Angeles suburbs of Thousand Oaks and Sherman
Oaks. So there was the real grove on one side and the false grove on
the other. Then down through the river came a glut of VW cars.

Although this was a dream image, we know that the rivers are really
glutted, are really dying. The Rhine is already dead. And the last
groves on the planet are being cut down. When they go in Central
America and South America, in Brazil, we will not be able to breathe.

Eve, Asherah, Demeter, Diana, dryads, fairy folk, the Wee People
and many other goddesses, were worshipped in the Grove. The Greeks,
Hebrews, Celts, Druids, others established Sacred Groves. Asherah—

---

*These poems are from a talk presented to the Ecofeminist Conference at the University
of Southern California, March 1987.

the Great Mother of the Grove—is the Hebrew Goddess who was worshipped alongside El during the time of the Patriarchs and after. In Judaism she remains as the Shechinah and in Christianity she remains as Mary. She was depicted as a trunk of a tree, her arms raised to heaven. There were small Asherahs made of stone or clay, but great wooden ones, several stories high, were set in front of each temple. She remained outside the house of worship until the destruction of the Second Temple by the Romans in 70 C.E. One worshipped, therefore, outside the temple and inside the temple. Outside the temple does not mean that it is not a part of the temple. It simply means the other side. At the time of the destruction of the Temple, the Asherahs were also destroyed and they never appeared again.

The temple, particularly in the mideast, looks like the body of a woman. It is usually round-domed, shaped like a belly or breasts. The Asherah looks like a phallus. So when you worship in the temple of the sky god, you are in the body of the Mother. And when you worship the earth mother, you are standing in the body of the Father. The body of the Mother and the body of the Father have to be respected and honored.

The important question of our time, as we are trying to bring back the Goddess—that is, as we are trying to open ourselves again to the reality of the feminine principle in the universe—is: What happened when the masculine turned against the feminine? What happened to cause such a dramatic and traumatic shift in human culture? Why were, or why did, men feel compelled to turn against the feminine? It had to be an enormous grief that occurred to cause men to turn away from such loving. Aside from women rightly wondering, "What happened to us? How were we injured?" it is essential to ask, as well, "What happened to the men? What caused people in society to entirely give up the kind of caring and nurturing that comes from the Mother?"

It has been suggested, by Patricia Monaghan in *The Book of Goddesses and Heroines,* that only the great pain of disconnection from the cycle of creation could have caused such desperation in men. Cut out of—and ever afterward disdaining—the process of birth and child-rearing, disconnected from their essential relationship to the future, men become monstrous and crazed. That omission creates a madness and a despair which is perfectly comprehensible. We can easily understand the astonishing territoriality and possession which might overcome someone who did not know that he had something to do with creation, was ignorant of, or programatically isolated from, his participation in the act of bringing living things into the world.

Similarly, when women are cut out of creating the world, that is, are cut out of creativity, they also become crazed and devouring. Each expresses the same illness, albeit in different forms. Therefore, as we bring the Great Mother closer, we must be certain that we have learned how to be partners in the process of creation. Without each other, we become deranged, and the planet is destroyed.

Ecology refers to the complex relationship between organisms and their environment. In recent years the study of ecology has revealed that a working system depends upon wholeness and completeness, that a harmonious balance exists only when all the parts are included. This implies the coexistence of the inside and the outside, the dark and the light, and the masculine and feminine. These days, even as we use the term, we forget what it means, shying away from the implications in our lives, selecting out only that which serves us in the moment. We are not even ecological in our thinking about ecology. Ecological thinking and practice demands the highest consciousness and requires that each of us change the essential patterns of our life which are based more upon exclusivity, distinction, elimination, separation than upon inclusiveness, unification, and relationship.

It is appropriate that we are inviting back the Goddess at exactly the same time that men, in this culture at least, are returning to nurturing, to becoming fathers once again. (And if this is only a phenomenon of the United States we can hope that as the world suffers from the globalization of other US trends—MacDonalds, Kentucky Fried Chicken, for example—it will be affected by this one as well.) We must be careful to encourage men in this direction, and not cut them out. Just as we see and have seen men concentrating worldly power only in their own hands, we see some women trying to garner all the power associated with creation, birthing, and raising children. This tendency is subtle in the nuclear or one-parent family and extreme in the emerging mythos of parthenogenesis. The latter is, I believe, not only misguided and dangerous but ultimately as threatening to the planet as nuclear weapons.

Once men begin to experience the joy—and the difficulty—of child rearing—the delight and the diapers—once they really know and live in terms of nurturing, it will be possible also for women to nurture and structure the world. Then, together, we can bring something forth.

The tree is an essential symbol for this kind of unification—without neutralization—of distinct principles. The tree sends its roots down into the center of the earth and sends its branches up into the sky. Going down into the center of the earth means descending into the infinity of the unconscious which is as deep, far, and profound as the heavens, the ends of the galaxies. When we think of ecology we cannot only think of the planet, we have to think of the entire cosmos because we have—most probably unfortunately—developed to the point where we can affect and therefore are responsible for, the universe.

It came to me once that if we simply try to do away with nuclear weapons without changing consciousness, we will still die in a nuclear conflagration. It will come from the outside, from somewhere else in the galaxy. Our limited or distorted consciousness will not be allowed to extend itself beyond earth to populate the cosmos. So we are at a crucial time; we have to act perfectly, that is very slowly and very carefully and with a great deal of love.

The tree teaches us that the spiritual world and the material world are the same. The tree is always potentially burning. The yule log, the burning bush, the candelabra are symbolic of the transformation of the living tree into the fire of spirit. So the tree speaks to us about reconciliation, about bringing the opposites together. The tree and the grove are not only important in themselves but in what they point toward, what they stretch up toward, what they descend to, what they symbolize. When we cut down the literal tree, when we cut down the literal grove, when we cut down the forests which provide most of the essential oxygen in order to feed cattle for MacDonald's hamburgers, we cut down everything, all of culture and all of spirit.

When the sacred groves of Demeter were cut down She cursed us: "The more you eat, the more you'll want." This is the curse of imperialism, capitalism, expansionism. The curse of greed. This is the curse of our time.

How do we remove this curse? How do we restore the groves? How do we put Asherah back *outside* the temple? How do we extend the temple once more, extend the sacred to include the outside, that is, nature?

We have to restore balance and the equality of things, to recreate the ecosystem wherein everything, even the disdained, the devalued, the exploitable and endangered has to be respectfully included in the essential balance.

Those of us who are turning to the East, to Buddhism or other meditative or ecstatic practices, are working toward giving up the individual ego. It is difficult. We find this task difficult even when it is for the gods. But what we have to ask of ourselves is even more difficult. It is not only important to give up our individual egos but to begin to develop and learn the practices which can lead us to give up the cultural ego. We must learn to do this individually but, more importantly, we must learn to do this as cultures. Then, afterward, there is a more difficult task—we must give up the gender ego, again, as individuals but, also, as a body: as men and as women. And, finally, we must give up the species ego. This is the most difficult of all. This, also, we must do individually and together. Only the species, acting in concert, can give up the species ego. Still, we need to consider the idea of restoring wolves, trees, rivers, and stones to equal standing with us, affirming their equal right to life, territory, food, water, air, and to their own distinct ways of being. The word that is used to embody this understanding of the absolute equality of all things is *compassion,* but we haven't gone far enough in our understanding of this concept, its implications, and how it is to be lived. We can't begin to imagine how difficult this is to do—it is not only a task of the mind or will—and how necessary!

The path to this achievement is psychological, political and spiritual. This path makes the highest demand and requires the greatest discipline. In order to do this we must apply to our lives what we already know from religious and spiritual practices in order to create our own religion appropriate to this time and this task. Restoring a world which has virtually been annihilated is as difficult and important as creating a world. Here we are at the other end of Genesis beginning to understand that we have to proceed in the other direction, to return to Paradise, to restoring the Grove.

What Is Religion?

It is a body of teachings, a lineage, and a practice. A body of teachings is a way of understanding the universe. That is, it is physics and it is metaphysics. When physics and metaphysics become one, two different languages describing the same phenomenon, then we begin to have a viable system. When the two are one then you know you are with the universe in a profound way. When the theories of quantum physics accord with the ancient teachings of the mystics, then you know that you have reached some depth of understanding, that you are seeing what *is* rather than creating a merely usable structure. Can we say that mysticism is the experience while science is the cognition of reality?

A lineage is a progression of beings through whom these teachings have been transmitted, a progression of beings who receive, modify, amplify, and pass them on. Sometimes, as the teachings pass through, the essential divinity of the universe which these teachings describe also passes into the very nature of the being or into the world. That is, through lineage we are exposed to the ideas, teachings, and practices but sometimes we also encounter the thing-in-itself, that is, reality, that is, the divine. When the veil between ourselves and reality is parted, we may be able to see the nature of reality, or we may have the extraordinary fortune to experience essential nature—the divine. That is, we get a little "juice" from our encounter with the beings, the practices, or the teachings.

Practices, if pursued on a daily basis, also have the possibility of uniting the daily and spiritual world. This does not happen all the time, but sometimes we are the recipients of "grace," the dissolution of the veil. Then we experience the spirit within us and know that there is no difference between the spirit and ourselves.

Practices also teach us how to live in the world. That is, they guide us in applying the spiritual practices to our daily life, so that we do not separate what belongs to Caesar and what belongs to God, nor what is personal and what is political. In this state, we are both in the world while our activities are following directly from our spiritual knowledge, are a reflection of the reality of the universe. This is what it means to create heaven on earth or to return to paradise or to restore the grove or to save the planet. This is also called ethics.

Many of us here feel as if we've lost the teachings, that we come from a broken lineage, and we don't know the practices. And we have very little time in which to invent, recover, and receive anything again.

Recently, four meditations came to me which seem appropriate to our lost spiritual heritage and the tasks we have to accomplish. I believe that they may be useful to us, particularly if we do them ritually in a sequence. They may be efficacious in dissolving some of the egos which separate us from the universe and in bringing in the spirit which we need so badly.

Trespasso

This meditation allows us to know that there are other beings in the world and, after we feel the reality of another being, to dissolve the boundaries between us. All it requires is that we sit facing another being and look directly into their eyes for a period of time. During this process, awareness is important to confront and dissolve whatever arises in our minds of superiority, hierarchy, boundaries, distinction, separation, etc. Ideally, this meditation should be pursued for twenty to forty minutes. It is a rare and profound experience to know with certainty of the existence of another human being. When this meditation is done alone with a mirror, one experiences one's objective—not subjective—reality.

Tree

With your eyes closed, imagine yourself as a tree. Allow the human in yourself to dissolve. Feel your roots going down to the core of the earth, the strength of the trunk here on earth and the branches reaching to the sky. Allow yourself to be a tree and let that be sufficient.

Maintaining the Light

Once, when I was flying in a plane in late afternoon the sky was infused with a strange platinum light. Suddenly very dark clouds came across the sky and began to cover the sun until there was just a glimmer of sun left. A voice from within—or outside of me—from somewhere—said, "Keep imagining the light. No matter what, keep imagining the light. This is a practice. If you do this regularly, no matter what happens, no matter what darkness comes, you will be prepared to remember and reimagine the light. You will know it is possible, no matter what darkness comes, to hold on to the light."

With eyes closed, imagine the sun or the moon being covered by dark clouds. In your mind, keep your eye on the light behind the clouds. No matter what, keep your eye on the light.

Jung said you only need a very small flame to dispel the darkness.

Cradling the World

Proceed, as in a Zen meditation, sitting quietly and following your breath. However, instead of clearing your mind, allow images of everything or anything you love to pass across the screen of your mind and through the cradle of your heart. Allow people, faces, living and dead, known and unknown, places, plants, animals, stones, memories, dreams, activities, ideas, whatever you love, to pass through without attaching to them. As they enter your heart, imagine that you are protecting them. Allow yourself to be the protector. Do this for as long as you wish, and for the last minute of the meditation, allow yourself to hold the earth itself in this protective cradle.

This is a useful meditation to do alone on a daily basis or following zazen, meditation, or any form of prayer.

In 1980, I co-led, with Steven Kent, a group in Greece in the reenactment of the Eleusinian Mysteries, the rites of Demeter. It was the first time, as far as I know, that they were being practiced in 1500 years. In the meditation, I heard a voice which said, "When you are in Greece, you will see a hill covered with olive trees and behind it the sea, and then you will know." Although I didn't take this very seriously, preferring to assume this was fantasy, I looked for this hill as we traveled. I didn't find it. By the last days, when we were going inland to Delphi, I'd given up. But just as we were climbing to the top of the last hill on which Delphi sits, I saw a hill covered with olive trees and the Sea of Corinth brilliant in the light behind it. I hadn't known it was there.

And so I knew. What did I know? That the divinity of the universe is real. That the spiritual and material are one. That life is sacred. That the gods exist. That the Grove is the sign and the bridge. And sometimes, like at this moment, I remember that I knew.

What does it mean to bring back the Goddess?
It means that She exists.
Our task is to bring back the Goddess with the God, to re-invoke the Grove, to reforest the earth, to be aware of the spiritual reality of the universe, so that we can save the planet.

Breaking Ground

Toward the south, through the center
of a still brown patch of weeds,
a living green line,
like marble dividing stone,
cuts the hill, a caesarian section
from navel to pubic bone.
Scar on the belly of my mother
where I tore her open.
Across the canyon, a rock face
has been split into labia
and there are hundreds of buttocks and hips,
breasts cut with a water knife
from the body rock.

Here is the winter knot
before it's cut into spring.
In my belly,
the stone of light
split open,
something green emerged
and exploded into a thousand arms.

The grass has come again,
insidious spring over the disguised rock,
the mustard returns and the lupine bruise
in the raw, scabrous wind,
now acacia, bees, moths, ants, birds
ground out of uterine stone.

This is the order:
green, earth, stone, sulphur, bedrock, fire.

　　　Peace and trembling
　　　throughout the body of the Mother.

13
Toward an Ecofeminist Spirituality
Charlene Spretnak

My own patterns of awakening in the evolution of women's spirituality parallel those of many other feminists. I began life firmly entrenched in the Judeo-Christian tradition, experienced a disappointing emptiness in that orientation, and finally began making personal discoveries of the spiritual dimensions of life. Those discoveries acquired a frame of reference when I learned of the ancient prepatriarchal myths and religions that had honored female access to spiritual realities and personal power. As I began to meet other women who were making similar discoveries and who were quick to see the political implications, I knew we would never be lost again.

In truth, there is nothing "mystical" or "other worldly" about spirituality. The life of the spirit, or soul, refers merely to functions of the mind. Hence spirituality is an intrinsic dimension of human consciousness and is not separate from the body. For example, the Greek concept of *pneuma* meant breath or spirit or soul, and *spirit* comes from the Latin root for "to breathe." From one perspective, we realize that we need food, shelter, and clothing; from another that some sort of relationship among people, animals, and the Earth is necessary; from another that we must determine our identity as creatures not only of our immediate habitat but of the world and the universe; from another that the subtle, suprarational reaches of mind can reveal the true nature of being: All is One, all forms of existence are comprised of one continuous dance of matter/energy arising and falling away, arising and falling away. Only the illusions of separation divide us. The experience of union with the One has been called cosmic consciousness, God consiousness, knowing the One Mind, etc.

Theodore Roszak has observed that many western/patriarchal critics simply cannot bring themselves to endorse a system of spirituality or psychology that has no sense of sin at its center: "Fallenness, fear and trembling—so they have learned from St. Paul and St. Augustine,

Calvin and Kierkegaard, Freud and Sartre, *et al.*—are the credentials
of serious knowledge. Without the whiplash of guilt, there is no way
to enforce self-denial; and without delf-denial, there is no basis for
moral conduct."* As we know, however, there is indeed another basis:
Moral conduct can follow from one's moral identity. If we believe, and
experientially *know* through various practices such as meditation and
holistic ritual, that neither our sisters and brothers nor the rest of
nature is "the other," we will not violate their being, nor our own.
Ethics of mutual respect would not allow coercion or domination, such
as forcing someone to give birth or to kill.

The only holistic approach that involves an anthropomorphized
concept of deity is Goddess spirituality. However, just as the matrifocal
cultures were communal, harmonious, and peaceful (Minoan Crete,
for example, enjoyed a thousand years without war, and the settlements
of Old Europe were unfortified for millennia before the invasions),
thereby differing very substantially from patriarchal cultures, so the
meaning of the Goddess differs substantially from that of God. No
one is interested in revering a "Yahweh with a skirt," a distant,
judgmental, manipulative figure of power who holds us all in a state
of terror. The revival of the Goddess has resonated with so many people
because She symbolizes *the way things really are*: All forms of being are
One, continually renewed in cyclic rhythms of birth, maturation,
death. That is the meaning of Her triple aspect—the waxing, full,
and waning moon; the maiden, mother, and wise crone. The Goddess
honors *union and process,* the cosmic dance, the eternally vibrating flux
of matter/energy: She expresses the dynamic, rather than static model
of the universe. She is *immanent* in our lives and our world. She contains
both female and male, in Her womb, as a male deity cannot; all beings
are *part of Her,* not distant creations. She also symbolizes the power of
the female body/mind. There is no "party line" of Goddess worship;
rather, each person's process of perceiving and living Her truth is a
movement in the larger dance—hence the phrase "The Goddess Is All."

Women's spirituality is not synonymous with Goddess spirituality;
some practitioners of the former are uncomfortable with any
anthropomorphizing of the One. In many cases, their spirituality is
comprised of the truths of naturalism and the holistic proclivities of
women. The theme of women's elemental power is a common one,
and by that I do not mean "merely" our power to form people from
our very flesh and blood and then to nourish them from our breasts,
or the fact that we run on cosmic time, i.e., share the cycles of the
moon. I mean that there are many moments in a woman's life wherein

*Excerpted from articles by Charlene Spretnak (1977-1980) that were included in *The
Politics of Women's Spirituality* (Anchor/Doubleday, 1982).

she gains experiential knowledge, in a powerful body/mind union, of the holistic truths of spirituality. First of all, neuropsychologists have demonstrated that females are predisposed from a very early age to perceive *connectedness* in life; for example, females are more empathetic, and they remain more aware of subtle, contextual "data" in interpersonal contacts throughout adulthood. Second, the purpose of many spiritual practices such as meditation, ritual, music, and dance is to move one's consciousness beyond the mundane perception of illusion—that all beings are separate, mechanistic entities—to the consciousness of oneness. This "altered" mindstate occurs to varying degrees when women experience "reclaimed" menstruation; orgasm (the sense of having no boundaries in the postorgasmic state is often described by women as a peaceful, expansive mindstate; by men as fearsome, vulnerable, or even terrifying); and pregnancy, natural childbirth, and motherhood (as Nancy Passmore, editor of *The Lunar Calendar,* has observed, "Certainly the distinction between me and not me becomes a little blurry, to say the least, when one has been inhabited as a mother"). The experiences inherent in women's sexuality are expressions of the essential, holistic nature of life on Earth; they are "body parables" of the profound oneness and interconnectedness of all matter/energy, which physicists have discovered in recent decades at the subatomic level. Every woman who has practiced meditation and is aware of the holistic composition of the universe—whether through Goddess spirituality, Eastern religion, or modern physics— recognizes that her postorgasmic mindstate is something quite different from what males have described as *le petit mort* (the little death); rather, the boundary-less, free-floating, non-discriminating sense of oneness that females experience could more accurately be called *le petit satori* (the little glimpse of enlightenment). In a culture that honored, rather than denigrated such "body truth," the holistic realities would be guiding principles of ethics and structure.

Men, too, experience moments of heightened awareness when everything seems different, more vividly alive. They have often written that such instances occur during the hunting of a large animal, the landing/killing of a large fish, the moments just before and during combat. Not feeling intrinsically involved in the processes of birthing and nurture, nor strongly predisposed toward empathetic communion, men may have turned their attention, for many eras, toward the other aspect of the cycle, death. Certainly much of men's art and literature has shown an obsession with this theme, and the male-orchestrated global arms race is suicide on a grand scale. But many men, too, have life-affirming "awakenings," often related to naturalism, and, like women, report spiritual experiences in near-death situations wherein one feels sublimely peaceful and is drawn toward union with a compelling light or union with one's family members who died previously.

That there are similarities and very real differences between the sexes is not news. What is new is our refusal to accept patriarchal perceptions and interpretations of those differences. To achieve a sane society that reflects, spiritually and culturally, holistic truths, we must encourage awareness, or "mindfulness," of such truths. Admittedly, women seem to have an elemental advantage, but men may consider that old feminist saw: Biology is not destiny. All minds contain all possibilities. The sexes are not opposites or dualistic polarities; the differences are matters of degree, whether negligible or immense. Inner growth, not war, is our natural state, and much could be done to foster it. For example, during the past decade men have been encouraged to be with their wives/lovers during labor and delivery, and they report feeling a much stronger bond with those children in whose birthing they had participated than with the older siblings from whose births the fathers had been banned by patriarchal custom. A holistic orientation would also include teaching children the connectedness among all beings through raising them with non-sexist principles.

.   .   .

Politics built on the lie of natural male supremacy is death-oriented and corrupt with exploitation of "the other." The damage wrought by patriarchy cannot be halted by patchwork reforms of that system, nor will technological "fixes" save the Earth and us. Only the acceptance of *a postpatriarchal, holistic attitude toward life on Earth* will bring about truly comprehensive change. Feminist spirituality is a means of both evolving that attitude and activating the processes which will lead to that change.

The great silence has been broken at last. Women are coming together to cultivate the powers that can result from exploring matrifocal heritage, personal and collective mythology, natural healing, meditation, dreamwork, celebrating the cycles of nature (i.e., our surroundings and our own bodies), and ritual. As we all bear scars from having been raised under patriarchy, the ability to heal ourselves and each other psychically and physically is essential to the growth of women's culture. Ritual can generate and transform tremendous fields of force. That energy is always there for us to tap and manifest. Rituals created within a framework of women's spirituality differ in form and content from the empty, hierarchically imposed, patriarchal observances with which most of us grew up. They involve healing, strengthening, creative energy that expands with spontaneity from a meaningful core of values.

We are not interested in masculinist, linear approaches that would first attack the defects in the status quo and only later would consider the creation of a new society. Our models of change, our meetings, and our public actions all express *on our own terms* an encompassing political struggle. We are building a revolution of the psyche as well as the society. The postpatriarchal options that we are evolving have roots in the peaceful, egalitarian, body-honoring, Earth-revering, gynocentric cultures. To *remember* our potentials and to begin to live these possibilities with our sisters and brothers as we initiate change is our political process. Always, we work to expand our circles.

Cultivating the female mind, acknowledging the female source of wisdom and harmony—these practices must extend beyond our own bodies and our own circles. Of all the patriarchal outrages—racism; harassment of homosexuals; increasing violence against women; forced prostitution; pornography; non-personhood for women in legal, educational, and medical areas; economic oppression—it is nuclear power and weaponry that promise irreversible effects. But our activism is not a matter of "either this issue or that;" all of the above stem directly from our society's acceptance of patriarchal values. As we work in each area, we will voice the *connections* among the issues.

How to save us all from annihilation, how to birth a just world of inner and outer peace and harmony? . . . One essential element of our strategy should be achieving broad public awareness that the human race *does* have a heritage of long eras of peace among societies that lived by holistic values. There are so many books on the history of wars, why none of the history of peace in the prepatriarchal cultures? Well-meaning antinuclear and peace activists often say, "We are trying for something new in the history of man [sic]: peace." This is not so. Peaceful and progressive societies thrived for millennia where gynocentric values prevailed, for example, in Minoan Crete and Old Europe. In short, we have lived sanely before, we can do it again.

A second element must be our self-regeneration. To avoid being overwhelmed by the dimensions of our struggle, we should carefully maintain our most essential political resource: us. Addressing what we would call "burn-out," Elizabeth Cady Stanton, an indefatigable hera of the first wave of feminism, warned her colleagues, "To develop our real selves, we need time alone for thought and meditation. To be always giving out and never pumping in, the well runs dry too soon." Feminist process, then, involves living the new possibilites *now,* as we struggle.

Can we adopt yet another political slogan? Here is one that will contribute to our long-range success in whatever personal or public areas we may address: *Watch Your Mind.* Trust your body knowledge. Feed your natural tendencies toward multilayered perceptions, empathy, compassion, unity, and harmony. Feel your wholeness. Feel our oneness. Feel the elemental source of our power. Discard the patriarchal patterns of alienation, fear, enmity, aggression, and destruction. It is not necessary to force them away; by merely focusing awareness on the negative, masculinist thoughts as they begin to arise and then opting not to feed them any more psychic energy, their power becomes diminished and they fade. The wisdom of our body/mind can wash over those artificial habits of thought as waves rising from our center.

We have choices. We have will. We have insight and awareness that can be acknowledged and developed—or denied. We can move far beyond the patriarchal boundaries. The authentic female mind is our salvation.

14

The Give and the Take*

Dale Colleen Hamilton

Emma divided her attention between the Devil's Club and the television. She was sitting on the couch in Rose's living room, a knife in her hand, peeling the outer and inner bark from several branches of Devil's Club. But her attention was mostly on the television. An entire sequence of the national news had been devoted to Meares Island and Emma was holding on to every word, booing and cheering at the appropriate places.

Rose was in the kitchen, watching a pot of clam chowder that was about to boil and, at the same time, filling jars with the Devil's Club bark Emma was stripping. The chowder boiled and she turned it down. There were still three empty jars on the table, waiting to be filled with bark. She took the enamel wash basin from its place on the wall and entered the living room, intending to fill the basin with more bark.

But the bowl in Emma's lap was almost empty. She held the knife limply and the pile of Devil's Club, waiting to be stripped, lay untouched at her feet. Emma's mouth was slightly open and her lips appeared blue in the cold light thrown by the black and white television screen. On the wall was a carved wooden mask. It stared at the back of Emma's head and Emma stared at the TV.

Rose stood in the doorway for a moment, then returned to the kitchen, the empty basin in her hand. She turned when she heard Emma call out to her. "Rose, come and see this, quick! We're on the news!"

Rose watched from the doorway as the face of an interviewer was replaced with her own, then Emma's. The camera followed them through the bush, as Rose pointed out medicinal and edible plants. The camera zoomed in on a stand of wild columbine.

Rose thought back to the day the TV crew had come to Opitsat. What they *didn't* show on the TV was where the interviewer and the cameraman, as they were packing up to leave, had stepped all over

*This article is an excerpt from *Bonegames*, a novel in progress.

that same patch of columbine, trampling it with their feet and heavy equipment.

The columbine on the television screen faded and was replaced with shots of clear-cut mountain sides and ruined streams. The voice from the TV was Rose's and it filled her living room.

"Those logging companies come in here and they tear down a whole forest and waste wood and spray chemicals. And when the rain comes, the soil and those chemicals wash down into the streams. We're not gonna let them do that here. This island is like our garden and you can't have somebody clear-cutting your garden."

Emma cheered and applauded from the couch. Rose took a step back from the TV, scrutinizing her image on the screen. Then the newscast was over and her head was replaced by a box of sanitary pads. As the commercial began, the volume swelled, although neither of them touched the dial. A very young, very thin and very white woman told them about absorbancy, convenience and disposability, never once mentioning the word blood.

Rose disappeared into the kitchen and returned a moment later, dragging a kitchen chair. She placed it directly in front of the TV, her back to the screen. The light from the television played on Rose's shoulders and blue rays leaked from around her head. Rose faced Emma squarely, and said nothing.

"Rose, you wanna talk to me? We can turn the TV off if it bothers you."

Rose waved her hand, as if to dismiss the television, and spoke. "I want you to do something for me before you go."

"What do you mean, before I go?"

"I know you'd rather be spending your time at the protest camp."

"Rose, I . . . "

"I know it's true."

"I guess I would like to be there. But I don't want you to think I've lost interest in studying with you."

"You don't find much time for it lately."

"I know, I'm sorry. I guess I've gotten caught up in the protest."

"Just make sure you know why you're doin' it. Just as long as you're not doin' it cuz you like seein' it on the TV and in the newspapers."

"I just keep thinking; what good is it to be studying the plants on Meares if they all get wiped out?"

"I know. I think you should go. I'd go if I was your age."

"C'mon, don't give me that. I've seen you crawling over logs and lifting sacks. You could come and join the blockade too."

Rose ignored her suggestion, lowering her voice to a whisper.

"I want you to do something for me before you go."

Emma wondered what mundane task Rose had in mind. While she waited for Rose to continue, she picked up the knife again and started peeling Devil's Club bark into the bowl. The old woman pulled her chair closer to the couch and took the knife from Emma's hand; as if signaling that she wanted her undivided attention.

"What is it that you want me to do, Rose?"

Rose's voice went a tone lower. "First you have to fast for four days; eat nothing, drink only water."

"Why?"

"To prepare for the ceremony. I want you to do a ceremony."

Emma barely heard Rose's announcement. A pain, originating in her hand, shot up her arm and spread. One of the Devil's Club thorns had lodged in her thumb. The thorn of the Devil's Club is many times larger than the wild rose or hawthorn and much more painful to extract. As Rose pulled, tears appeared in Emma's eyes and she drew in a breath as though breathing in fire.

Neither of them spoke as Rose attended to the bleeding gap left by the thorn. Only when Emma's thumb was cleaned with plantain tea and covered in comfrey salve did they resume their conversation. Emma began, wondering if she'd heard the old woman correctly. "Did you say you want me to do a ceremony? What kind of ceremony?"

"I'd do it with you, but I'm getting too old to sleep outside."

"Sleep outside? What kind of ceremony is this, Rose?"

"You'll have to spend the night alone, outside."

Emma sat up on the edge of the couch, holding her thumb in her lap. "Why?"

"You know about sicknesses in the body, but there's spirit sicknesses too. Sleeping outside alone will help you."

Emma leaned back into the lumpy couch, finding no relief from the throbbing pain in her thumb. Just at that moment, she felt very old and tired. "What do I have to do, exactly?"

Emma shaded her eyes against the glare from the TV. Rose's skin glowed blue. "Spend the night inside a tree."

"*Inside* a tree?"

"It's a hollow tree. I'll draw you a map so you can find it."

"Where is it?"

"About half way between here and C'is a Qis."

"That's a long way from the village." Emma had stated the obvious, so Rose didn't even acknowledge her words.

"What am I suppose to *do* inside this tree?"

"Spend the night. Just spend the night."

"Alone?"

"Alone."

Rose was already drawing a map on the back of a long cash register receipt from the grocery store. Emma's mind wandered. She had a sudden desire to be as far away as possible from Meares Island, in a large grocery store in a large city, filling up a cart with all her favorite food, regardless of cost or calories.

She wished she was back in her clinic in Tofino, prescribing antibiotics and setting broken bones. When she studied with Rose, she got a glimpse of a very different kind of medicine; but it was never more than a glimpse. She didn't have to wear a white medical jacket to be branded as a white doctor; one white face amongst the dark. "Couldn't I just sleep outside in the yard, or something?"

Rose ignored her question. "Inside the tree, you build yourself a bed of cedar; dead cedar for your mattress and live cedar for your pillow."

"No sleeping bag or foamie?"

"You take nothing with you, except this columbine root to chew on and a medicine bag and a blanket."

"Why don't you get one of your daughters or nieces to do it?"

"They've already done it. It's your time."

"The last time I tried camping outside alone, I ended up sleeping in my car with the doors locked."

"What are you afraid of?"

"I don't know; wild animals, hostile men, the dark, not knowing what's out there . . . "

"And not knowing what's inside there?" Rose tapped her on the chest as she spoke. "Afraid of thoughts you can't hide from?"

Emma turned back toward the TV, feigning interest in the weather report before she spoke again. "What do I do inside this tree?"

"Wait."

"Wait for what?"

"And pray."

"Pray for what?"

Rose tapped Emma on the chest again, as if that answered her questions. Rose pulled something from the pocket of her cardigan sweater and pressed it into Emma's palm, holding her hand shut over it.

"Here's something else you can take with you." Rose didn't allow Emma to open her hand, still holding it in a tight fist. "It's a ceremonial fire stick. You can keep it."

Emma matched Rose's solemn tone. "Thank you, Rose."

Rose released Emma's hand and allowed her to look at the object. In her hand, Emma found a cheap disposable Bic lighter. Rose threw back her head and laughed.

In the background, the TV threw an image of a young white woman drinking deeply from a cup of coffee. As she lowered the cup, a look of carefully calculated satisfaction spread over her face.

.   .   .

Emma pulled the map from inside her raincoat, sheltering it from the rain with her hand. The cash register receipt was getting soggy and the pencil marks Rose had made were beginning to fade.

Rose's map directed Emma to enter the trail at the mudflats and hike in from there. The trail made an abrupt turn and began to climb. Emma approached the steep incline with an unexpected burst of energy. She had expected to feel weak and faint, having not eaten for four days. But the hunger pangs had passed after the second day and she now felt as though she could go without food indefinitely.

Up until the fourth day, images of food had rolled through Emma's head. She dreamed of food she had never tasted. . . . baby calves' livers, artichoke hearts and blood pudding. But the fourth day had been calmer inside and filled with bursts of energy which saw her awake before the alarm clock, and now served to propel her over the huge fallen logs which criss-crossed the trail.

She gorged herself on images of the rainforest. On Meares Island, trails are permanently temporary. Without someone else in the lead, she found herself pushing aside branches and undergrowth which constantly threatened to reclaim the trail.

By the time Emma reached the crest, she was breathing heavily. The combined smell of cedar, balsam, fir and spruce, all activated by the rain, made her nostrils flare and then relax, soothing her throat and lungs.

Emma had expected to see big trees, but she was unprepared for what lay ahead of her. As she rounded a sharp bend in the trail, she came up against a wall of solid cedar. She looked up, and up, and up. The top of the tree was obscured by fog, giving a Jack-and-the-beanstalk impression. Before her was a tree of mythical height and size.

Blinking against the rain, Emma moved closer. She wrapped her arms around the tree, with the intention of measuring the circumference by the number of arms lengths. But once the first measurement had been made, she found herself unable and unwilling to move. She buried her nose up against the bark and inhaled. The tree seemed to be growing even as she held it in her arms.

Emma knew all the statistics. Men armed with measuring tapes had declared that some of the largest cedars in Canada are to be found on Meares Island. Those men with measuring tapes record the circumference and the diameter and count the number of tree rings to determine the age. Logging companies see trees as "X" number of marketable board feet of timber equalling "Y" amount of profit. Photographers photograph them, artists draw them, carvers carve from them and writers write about them. At that moment, Emma didn't want to use this tree in any way, nor did she feel the need to reproduce it as statistics or art.

Emma finally let go of the tree, dropping her arms and stepping backward. As she stepped, her foot came to rest on a deadfall log. Without thinking, Emma put all her weight on to that foot, and as she did, the soggy rotting wood gave way and she found herself sprawled on the forest floor.

She moved her arms and legs tentatively at first, but felt no pain. The earth beneath her was soft from centuries of fallen spruce needles and cedar branches and decaying wood. Emma was in no hurry to get up and closed her eyes against the rain. She moved her legs and arms again, creating a faint angel. She had often made angels in the snow, but this angel, in this rainforest—this angel was not white.

She continued to move her arms and legs, the angel image around her growing deeper. Then came a sound, like wingless flight. Emma's arms and legs froze, extended fully, spread-eagle on the ground. The sound continued. She stood up quickly and, in her haste, scattered the angel image carved into the forest floor.

The sound grabbed at Emma's guts. She hurried along the trail now, looking neither left nor right, her eyes lowered. She pulled her rain hat down over her ears and, with the rain beating on it, she could almost shut out the other sound.

.   .   .

Rose's map was good and Emma found the hollow cedar easily. It was not as large as some of the others, but it was entirely hollow at the base and open on one side, forming an entrance way and a sheltered interior just barely large enough for one person.

Emma crouched at the entrance to the tree, inspecting the interior before she entered. The sound had followed her and, as she stuck her head inside the tree, it seemed to amplify in both volume and tone; like placing an ear next to a seashell.

The walls inside the tree were soft and crumbling to the touch. Emma stuck her head in further and turned her face upward, still remaining outside the tree. It was impossible to tell how far the hollow extended up the trunk, or exactly what might be up there in the darkness.

The smell was pure cedar and struck Emma as very familiar. The interior of the tree reminded her of an old cedar hope chest at her grandparents' farm. It was the familiarity of the smell that encouraged Emma to venture inside the tree.

She sat in the center of the hollow, letting her eyes adjust to the darkness. The sound continued. Emma was growing accustomed to it now and took off her rain hat, letting the sound wash over her. Being inside the tree was like being simultaneously indoors and outdoors. Emma found it somewhat comforting to be inside the shelter of the tree, where it became less obvious that she was alone in the rainforest with night approaching.

Rose had warned her that night comes early in the rainforest, so Emma prepared for the ceremony, following Rose's instructions. She crawled backward through the opening. Outside the tree she felt exposed; oversensitive to light and to sound and to all that surrounded her.

She began by looking for cedar boughs with which to make her bed, repeating Rose's instructions to herself as she searched: "Dead cedar as your bed and live cedar as your pillow."

Emma searched through the undergrowth and found a large branch of cedar, apparently broken off by the wind. Cut off from its source, the branch had turned brown and dry. It was brittle to the touch and Emma found it relatively easy to break off several smaller pieces. She gathered the branches into her arms and piled them inside the tree.

Finding live cedar was not as easy. It seemed that all the branches were well out of her reach and Emma wondered if she'd be able to follow Rose's instructions exactly and, if she didn't, what difference it would really make. Emma searched on both sides of the trail but could find no live cedar anywhere near the ground.

As she retraced her steps, having given up the search, a branch of very green very live cedar came into view. It was well off the trail and Emma had to push her way through a patch of sahlal in order to reach it, the leaves brushing clean pathways on her muddy raincoat.

Emma was just about to strip a green bough from the fallen branch when she remembered something Rose had told her. She'd taught Emma a prayer of sorts and had extracted a promise from Emma to use it when gathering cedar for her night in the tree. "Mother Cedar, may I take some of your dress to make a bed for myself?"

Although there was no one for miles, Emma looked around before speaking out loud. The thought of talking to a tree made her feel ridiculous. But as she spoke, her voice grew stronger. Hers was the only human voice in the forest and, in its singularity, rose above all judgment and ridicule.

Rose had failed to mention whether she should wait for Mother Cedar to reply. Talking to a tree was stretching it, but waiting for an answer caused something to snap. "Doctor" Emma arose and rebelled.

Rationality had returned. Emma looked around as if she had just come out of a dream and immediately began to plot a sensible course of action. She would abandon the idea of a ceremony, go back to the boat, and hopefully make her way home before dark; whereupon she would cook herself a huge seafood meal and get into her own warm bed.

But she made no move to leave. Rationality only whispered through the forest and was lost, like a passing wind. If this was part of Rose's medicine, then Emma would swallow it and await the benefits. She silenced Doctor Emma for the time being. There were times when the good doctor was useful, but this was not one of those times.

She asked the question again: "Mother Cedar, may I take some of your dress to make a bed for myself?" There was no response; no loud claps of thunder or voices from above. Emma took the silence as her answer and proceeded to take the boughs she needed; and then, for no apparent reason, she pulled a hair from her head and laid it over the original branch; leaving something of herself in exchange for what she had taken. Rose had not taught her this; as far as she knew, no one had taught her this.

The slight pain of pulling the strand of hair from her head and the symbolic act of offering it to the tree seemed to clarify something for Emma, although it wasn't at all clear what had been clarified. All she knew was that this act had slowed her down and made her really consider exactly how much she was receiving and exactly how much she was giving.

Emma tried to imagine a logger praying at the foot of a cedar tree, chainsaw revving, asking Mother Cedar: "May I run my saw through your entire body and drag you to a mill and then a factory to be made into paper wrappings for fast food and advertising flyers and disposible diapers for babies' bums? Amen."

·   ·   ·

The cedar boughs were now in place and Emma laid out the blanket. Rolled inside the blanket was the pouch Rose had prepared. As Emma emptied the pouch of its contents, examining each item in turn, she tried to piece together the instructions Rose had given her.

Inside the pouch was an abalone shell, an eagle feather and a bundle of four dried herbs—sage, cedar and sweetgrass; and the fourth herb was called "holkmeen," or that was as close as Emma could come to pronouncing it. Rose didn't know the English name and they couldn't seem to find it in any of the books. Hemlock John had given Rose the sweetgrass, which grows mostly in the east, and taught her how to use it in ceremonies. In the bottom of the pouch was the ceremonial fire stick, in all its disposable plastic splendor.

Emma activated the lighter and lit up the cedar walls around her, giving the interior an auburn glow. The flame seemed to emphasize the gathering darkness outside the tree. In the rainforest, even the late afternoon light had a quality of dusk about it. Emma moved the lighter toward the abalone shell, trying to recall Rose's words.

"Put the herbs into the abalone shell, one at a time. Each one means something different, so use them all and do it slow. Then light the herbs on fire and use the feather to move the smoke around yourself. Take the smoke to you, as if you're taking a bath in it."

The abalone walls of the shell danced blues and greens and tiny fingers of silver in the firelight. As Emma touched the fire stick to the herbs, they burst into flame, but only for a moment. As the flame flickered out, having spent its fuel, a sweet smoke was emitted.

With her head bent over the shell, the smoke encircling her, Emma's fingers found the eagle feather and used it to waft the smoke around the interior of the tree. Then she took the smoke toward herself, embracing it, washing her face, her arms, her entire body. It entered her nose and her mouth and got caught up in her hair and her clothes.

Rose had talked about the four elements and, at the time, it had sounded very abstract, especially coming from a practical woman such as Rose. But now Emma understood what Rose had meant. The smoke obscured her vision inside the tree; she could barely see the shell in front of her. But everything else seemed to be getting clearer. Every object, every tiny move, every thought became a symbol.

The Shell . . . Water.
The Feather . . . Air.
The Flame . . . Fire.
The Herbs . . . Earth.
. . . and the Tree, binding together the elements.

.   .   .

The columbine root. Emma pulled it from her pocket and placed it in her mouth. She gave it a few tentative chews and swallowed. It tasted like a domesticated vegetable gone wild; there was nothing bland about it. She held the root under her tongue, letting it dissolve slowly. Then, as instructed, she closed her eyes and did nothing, just sat and waited; which, for Emma, was more of an endurance test than a reprieve. Ordinarily, Emma was too impatient for any sort of meditation. Normally, her mind would be racing, thinking about all the things she could be doing if she wasn't sitting there doing nothing.

But in the tree, just sitting seemed to come easier. There were no distractions, except for the humming sound, which Emma now found comforting. She began to feel she could remain still indefinitely.

When Emma opened her eyes, it was dark, inside and outside. She closed them again and retreated into the sound. Still, Emma remained still.

.   .   .

Two hands came down hard on her legs, just above her knees. Human hands. She felt the hands rise up from her legs. Then they came down again, harder this time. The hands rose and fell, rose and fell, slapping her legs until they tingled. Then a rhythm emerged. The hands were her own. She was drumming.

A sound came from her throat; a high note then a low note, both notes far beyond her usual range. It was more of a chant than a song, with no words and as repetitive as her drumming. The humming faded away into the background as Emma's song grew stronger.

.   .   .

Emma's head jerked up. It must be almost dawn, she thought, but she could see no sign of light. She groped for the Bic lighter, but it seemed to be gone. Panic started in her stomach and climbed up her throat. Emma let her chin fall to her chest and she resumed her song, shutting out everything else.

.   .   .

Dream images rushed in behind Emma's eyelids. She was up against a solid wall of sound. Then the wall gave way, a door opening, and inside, a dark room and a ceremony, a bonegame. The players are gambling with bones, the bones of their ancestors; hidden and retrieved, hidden and retrieved.

Emma reaches out for a bone, but before she can take hold, the dream transports her to another landscape. It is a grove of trees, a dream wind exposing the underside of branches. The branches twist and curl upon themselves until they become carved wooden masks. There is a sense of danger, but it is faceless. The danger lies in a mindset, an attitude.

Faceless people emerge from beyond the trees and don the masks, spreading out to form a circle, a human chain, around the grove of trees.

The carved masks are animal in design and primitive in construction; birds and animals of the rainforest; in dream colors that could never occur to the waking eye. Then Emma is no longer an observer; she is drawn into the dream and reaches up toward a tree, plucking a mask from a branch about to snap under the weight. The mask she chooses is of a bird, a Hummingbird; and a familiar humming fills the mask.

Inside the mask, she is surrounded in cedar. It is smooth and slightly damp on her face, newly carved, aromatic. Inside the mask, she knows that eye contact is essential; all other features, save the eyes, are masked. Only the eyes can relay the message. She can see the masks of others standing with her; so vivid in color and detail that Emma knows she has had some hand in their creation.

Outside the mask, the rain and wind are rising. Emma knows, without seeing, that the painted features on her Hummingbird mask are being washed away. She looks down the chain of people, meeting all of their eyes, watching the painted features fade and drip and wash away in the rain until it is impossible to identify the animal or bird represented by the masks. Only the original wood remains.

Simultaneously, speaking only through their eyes, the people in the chain remove their masks. And underneath the masks, their faces are scored with deep lines of paint, like petroglyphs carved in rock. Some are painted red, some black, some yellow, some white. They raise their faces, without warning and without signal, to the rain. The paint is washed away, revealing their naked features. There is no need for adornment here.

.   .   .

It was raining hard and several drops made their way through a hole in the hollow trunk, dropping on Emma's face. She straightened her back and sat bolt upright, as though some cold sharp object was being run up and down her back. She relaxed her spine as she realized where she was; surrounded in cedar; only the most determined morning light managing to sift its way through the rainforest and into the tree.

Emma felt something inside her mouth and thought at first that a tooth had come loose during the night. She ran her finger inside her mouth. She shivered. The soft fleshy spot beneath her tongue must surely be the only warm place on her entire body. From beneath her tongue, she pulled a small brown object, worn smooth as a river rock. It was the remainder of the columbine root.

The root had served its purpose. Emma held it in one hand and dug a small hole with the other; pushing aside the bed of cedar boughs, her fingernails clawing the earth beneath it. As she dug, her fingernails met with resistence. Emma assumed it was a rock and dug around it with her fingers. As she lifted it from the earth, she realized it was not a rock at all, but a bone; what kind she couldn't tell. She scraped the dirt from its slightly porous surface and held it up to the light. It fit perfectly into the palm of her hand and she held it there.

Then she crawled out of the tree, like a bear ending a long hibernation, and turned her face upward. The rain ran down her face, and the dream images from the night before washed over her.

Emma buried the tiny piece of columbine root, along with the bone, placing a strand of her hair in the hole before covering it with earth. It was a small ritual, but it was her own.

15
Toward an Ecological-Feminist Theology of Nature
Rosemary Radford Ruether

An ecological-feminist theology of nature must rethink the whole western theological tradition of the hierarchical chain of being and chain of command. This theology must question the hierarchy of human over nonhuman nature as a relationship of ontological and moral value. It must challenge the right of the human to treat the nonhuman as private property and material wealth to be exploited. It must unmask the structures of social domination, male over female, owner over worker, that mediate this domination of nonhuman nature. Finally, it must question the model of hierarchy that starts with nonmaterial spirit (God) as the source of the chain of being and continues down to nonspiritual "matter" as the bottom of the chain of being and the most inferior, valueless, and dominated point in the chain of command.

The God/ess who is primal Matrix, the ground of being-new being, is neither stifling immanence nor rootless transcendence. Spirit and matter are not dichotomized but are the inside and outside of the same thing. When we proceed to the inward depths of consciousness or probe beneath the surface of visible things to the electromagnetic field that is the ground of atomic and molecular structure, the visible disappears. Matter itself dissolves into energy. Energy, organized in patterns and relationships, is the basis for what we experience as visible things. It becomes impossible any more to dichotomize material and spiritual energy. Consciousness comes to be seen as the most intense and complex form of the inwardness of material energy itself as it bursts forth at that evolutionary level where matter is organized in the most complex and intensive way—the central nervous system and cortex of the human brain.

If we follow Teilhard de Chardin's interpretation of evolution, the radial energy of matter develops along the lines of increasing complexity and centralization. At certain "boiling points" of life energy, there is a critical leap to a new stage of being, from minerals to plant life, from plant life to animate life, moving through increasing stages of intelligence until the breakthrough to self-conscious intelligence.[1]

It becomes evident that one can no longer make the dichotomy between nature and history. Nature itself is historical. The universe is a great being that is born, grows and presumably will die. Critical moments of transformation appear at stages of the universe's growth, bringing into being new possibilities. These were latent in what existed before and yet represent something new, something that could not simply be expected from the pre-existing forms of being. Nature contains transcendence and freedom, as well as necessity. The change from mineral being to plant life, from plant life to animate life, and then to self-conscious intelligence is not just quantitative, but qualitative transformation. At each stage a qualitatively new dimension of life comes into being.

So far the evolutionary view of matter and radical energy in Teilhard de Chardin and others could lead simply to a new version of the chain of being. The chain of being has been laid on its side, so to speak. But this view still preserves the same presuppositions of the superiority of the "higher" over the "lower" forms and hence the domination of the "highest" form—namely, the human—over the rest, solely for human self-interest. Indeed, Teilhard does not question the racist assumptions that white western development is the privileged line of human development that has a right to control and reshape the rest of humanity.[2] This hierarchicalism of evolutionary theory has to be modified by several considerations.

We come to recognize the continuity of human consciousness with the radial energy of matter throughout the universe. Our intelligence is a special, intense form of this radial energy, but it is not without continuity with other forms; it is the self-conscious or "thinking dimension" of the radial energy of matter. We must respond to a "thou-ness" in all beings. This is not romanticism or an anthropomorphic animism that sees "dryads in trees," although there is truth in the animist view. The spirit in plants or animals is not anthropomorphic but biomorphic to its own forms of life. We respond not just as "I to it," but as "I to thou," to the spirit, the life energy that lies in every being in its own form of existence. The "brotherhood of man" needs to be widened to embrace not only women but also the whole community of life.

The more complex forms of life represent critical breakthroughs to new stages of existence that give them qualitatively more mobility and freedom for response. But they are radically dependent on all the stages of life that go before them and that continue to underlie their own existence. The plant can happily carry out its processes of photosynthesis without human beings, but we cannot exist without the photosynthesis of plants. The more complex forms of life are not the source and foundation of the less complex forms, just the opposite. An animal depends on a whole ecological community of life processes of plants, insects, other animals, water, air, and soil that underlie its existence. Still more, human beings cannot live without the whole ecological community that supports and makes possible our existence.

The privilege of intelligence, then, is not a privilege to alienate and dominate the world without concern for the welfare of all other forms of life. On the contrary, it is the responsibility to become the caretaker and cultivator of the welfare of the whole ecological community upon which our own existence depends. By what right are we the caretakers of nature when nonhuman nature takes care of its own processes very well and, in most cases, better without us? Human self-consciousness carries with it a danger that exists in no other form of creaturely life. Nonhuman creatures, to be sure, eat and are eaten by others. There is violence and bloodshed in nature, but it takes place within its own built-in balances. If one creature rapidly and drastically increases its population, it kills off its own life-support system and so dies off until it reaches a population back in balance with its ecological community.

Humans alone perpetuate their evolutionary advances primarily through cultural-social means. We don't grow our clothes on our bodies or our tools in the nails at the ends of our hands; we create these as artifacts. So we can continually change and develop them as part of our technology. More than that, we have the ability to create dysfunctional relationships with the earth, with our ecological community, and with each other, and to preserve them socially. We alone can "sin." We alone can disrupt and distort the balances of nature and force the price for this distortion on less fortunate humans, as well as the nonhuman community. We cannot do this forever. Finally, the universe will create inversions, under the weight of human distortion and oppression, that will undermine the whole human life-support system. But we may be able to bring the earth down with us in our downfall. We may destroy much of the work of evolutionary development back to the most primary level of minerals and photosynthesis, and leave even this deeply poisoned against the production of life. We are the rogue elephant of nature.

Thus we have not so much the privilege of intelligence, viewed as something above and against nonhuman nature, but the responsibility and necessity to convert our intelligence to the earth. We need to learn how to use intelligence to mend the distortions we have created and how to convert intelligence into an instrument that can cultivate the harmonies and balances of the ecological community and bring these to a refinement. We can turn the desert wilderness or the jungle into the garden. But we need to do that not simply by bulldozing what is and ignoring all other needs but our own, but by understanding the integrity of the existing ecological community and learning to build our niche in that community in harmony with the rest. We do this out of a genuine recognition of our interdependence. We cannot violate the ecological community without ultimately destroying our own life-support system. The notion of dominating the universe from a position of autonomy is an illusion of alienated consciousness. We have only two real options: either to learn to use our intelligence to become *servants* of the survival and cultivation of nature or to lose our own life-support system in an increasingly poisoned earth.

This conversion of our intelligence to the earth will demand a new form of human intelligence. The dominant white western male rationality has been based on linear, dichotomized thought patterns that divide reality into dualism: one is good and the other bad, one superior and the other inferior, one should dominate and the other should be eliminated or suppressed. The biological base of these patterns is specialization in left-brain, rational functions in a way that suppresses the right-brain, relational sense. This one-sided brain development seems more dominant in males than in females, possibly because of later verbal development in males.[3]

This biological tendency has been exaggerated by socialization into dominant and subordinate social roles. Dominant social roles exaggerate linear, dichotomized thinking and prevent the development of culture that would correct this bias by integrating the relational side. Women and other subordinate groups, moreover, have had their rational capacities suppressed through denial of education and leadership experience and so tend to be perceived as having primarily intuitive and affective patterns of thought. Thus socialization in power and powerlessness distorts integration further and creates what appears to be dichotomized personality cultures of men and women, that is, masculinity and femininity.

What we must now realize is that the patterns of rationality of left-brain specialization are, in many ways, ecologically dysfunctional. Far from this rationality being the mental counterpart of "natural law," it screens out much of reality as "irrelevant" to science and reduces scientific knowledge to a narrow spectrum fitted to dominance and control. But the systems it sets up are ecologically dysfunctional because they fail to see the larger relational patterns within which particular "facts" stand. This rationality tends toward monolithic systems of use of nature. Linear thinking, for example, directs agriculture, or even decorative planting, toward long rows of the same plant. This magnifies the plants' vulnerability to disease. Humans then compensate with chemical sprays, which in turn send a ripple effect of poisons through the whole ecological system. Nature, by contrast, diffuses and intersperses plants, so that each balances and corrects the vulnerabilities of the other. The inability to see the forest for the trees is typical of linear thinking.

Linear thinking simplifies, dichotomizes, focuses on parts, and fails to see the larger relationality and interdependence. Ecological thinking demands a different kind of rationality, one that integrates left-brain linear thought and right-brain spatial and relational thought. One has to disrupt the linear concept of order to create a different kind of order that is truly the way nature "orders," that is, balances and harmonizes, but that appears very "disorderly" to the linear, rational mind. One observes a meadow with many kinds of plants and insects balancing each other, each with their ecological niches, and then one learns to plant for human use in a way that imitates these same principles, in a more simplified and selective fashion. Converting our minds to the earth means understanding the more diffuse and relational logic of natural harmony. We learn to fit human ecology into its relation to nonhuman ecology in a way that maximizes the welfare of the whole rather than undermining and subverting (polluting) the life system.

Converting our minds to the earth cannot happen without converting our minds to each other, since the distorted and ecologically dysfunctional relationships appear necessary, yet they actually support the profits of the few against the many. There can be no ecological ethic simply as a new relation of "man" and "nature." Any ecological ethic must always take into account the structures of social domination and exploitation that mediate domination of nature and prevent concern for the welfare of the whole community in favor of the immediate advantage of the dominant class, race, and sex. An ecological ethic must always be an ethic of ecojustice that recognizes the interconnection of social domination and domination of nature.

Nonhuman nature, in this sense, is not just a "natural fact" to which we can "return" by rejecting human culture. Nature is a product not only of natural evolution but of human historical development. It partakes of the evils and distortions of human development. There is virtually no place on the planet where one can go to find "nature untouched by human hands." Even if humans have not been there before, their influence has been carried by winds, water, and soil, birds, insects, and animals, who bear within their beings the poisoning effects of human rapine of the globe. Nature, in this sense, can be seen as "fallen," not that it is evil itself but in that it has been marred and distorted by human misdevelopment. The remaking of our relation with nature and with each other, then, is a historical project and struggle of re-creation.

Nature will never be the same as it would have been without human intervention. Although we need to remake the earth in a way that converts our minds to nature's logic of ecological harmony, this will necessarily be a new synthesis, a new creation in which human nature and nonhuman nature become friends in the creating of a livable and sustainable cosmos.

Endnotes

1. Pierre Teilhard de Chardin, *The Phenomenon of Man*, Harper & Row, New York, 1959, pp. 53-74.
2. Ibid., pp. 209-210.
3. Sally P. Springer and Georg Deutsch, *Left Brain, Right Brain*, Freeman, San Francisco, 1981, pp. 121-130.

16

The Juice and the Mystery*

Margot Adler

Women are looking at the myths of the ancient Goddesses and seeking insights from the fragments of ancient traditions. Sometimes working within established church communities, sometimes creating their own, women have created a body of lore, songs, chants, and ritual techniques—some of sparkling originality. Feminist bookstores devote shelves to studies of women's spirituality, Witchcraft and mythology. Many mainstream churches are preparing new liturgies with inclusive language. The United Church of Christ has just published a new book of worship where God is described in feminine as well as masculine terms. And within the Unitarian Universalist Association, for example, a curriculum on feminist theology, "Cakes for the Queen of Heaven," is being widely distributed.

But some of us have gone further in the exploration and re-creation of the old, pre-Christian traditions. As many as one hundred thousand people in America, both women and men, call themselves Neopagans. Neopagans are searching among the archaic images of nature, among the ruins of traditions lost, in order to find, revive, and re-create the old polytheistic nature religions. The fascination with long dead pagan traditions is part of a search for cultural roots. Since most Neopagans are white, they often look toward Europe, just as Alex Haley looked to Africa. Neopagans are searching among these traditions and creating new religions—in the same way that members of the Society of Creative Anachronism are re-creating the Middle Ages—not as they were, but as they would like them to be.

"Pagan" is a strange word for most of us. It doesn't have quite the flamboyant and inflammatory effect on most people as the dreaded "W" word—"witch"— but it has its own assortment of negative or misleading associations. In the mainstream culture—and especially in literature (e.g., the novels of Hawthorne and Huxley or the pages of

*This article formed the basis of a talk given at the Unitarian Universalist Association's General Assembly in the fall of 1987.

The New Yorker)—"pagan" has come to mean "nonreligious" and more
or less free-spirited. The word's roots are far different. "Pagan" comes
from the Latin *paganus,* which means a country-dweller (*paganus* is
derived from *pagus,* Latin for rural district). Likewise, "heathen"
originally meant someone who lived on the heaths. After Christianity
won its victory over the older polytheistic religions, often the last
people to be converted were those who lived in the unpopulated rural
areas, the Pagans and the Heathens. In fact, the word was originally
a term of insult, like hick.

But to anyone steeped in the classics, or in the lore of aboriginal
peoples, "pagan" simply means a member of a polytheistic religion,
such as the ancient Greek or Egyptian religions, or a member of one
of the indigenous folk or tribal religions found all over the world.

In my own life, at the age of twelve I found myself obsessed by the
legends of the Greek goddesses. Growing up in the 1950s Artemis
and Athena represented images of strength and wisdom. There were
few images of powerful women in the culture at large. But despite the
power of these images, it was only much later, during the first years
of the 1970s, during a search for a spiritual framework that would fit
in with notions of ecological sanity, that I found myself studying the
ancient Pagan traditions, thanks in large part to two essays written
around that time by the historians Arnold Toynbee and Lynn White.

Toynbee noted that, in popular pre-Christian Greek religion,
divinity was inherent in all natural phenomena, the godhead was
diffused, it was plural not singular. He added that with the coming
of Christianity, "the divinity was drained out of nature and was
concentrated in one unique and transcendent God . . . " Similarly,
Lynn White wrote in his now famous essay, "The Historical Roots of
Our Ecological Crisis," that "Christianity, in absolute contrast to
ancient paganism . . . not only established a dualism of man and
nature but also insisted that it is God's will that men exploit nature
for his proper ends. By destroying Pagan animism, Christianity made
it possible to exploit nature in a mood of indifference to the feeling
of natural objects."

Many Christians would strongly dispute this view. Even White, in
the end, held up St. Francis as an alternate model, and Toynbee stopped
short of advocating a return to Pagan polytheism. Still, both writers
resonate with the same kind of critique that was developed in greater
detail by Neopagans during the 1970s.

Neopagans are a very diverse group of people. They include feminist
goddess worshipers, Celtic revivalist witches, creators of Greek,
Egyptian, Norse and Druid revivals, various forms of Shamanism, and
assorted other Pagan religious experiments. They have different names
for their deities; they often disagree on politics and lifestyle issues.

There are over one hundred newsletters published by Neopagans; there are perhaps over one thousand different groups and over fifty local and national yearly gatherings. And despite a diversity that brings together aging hippies and computer nerds, vegetarians and chain smokers, the Neopagan community generally gets on pretty well. Perhaps because this anarchistic bunch does seem to share a few basic principles:

1. Neopagans tend to think of their religion as based on what one does, not on what one believes.

This is a feature of many tribal religions. Even within Judaism, it is not your belief in God that makes you a Jew; it is the customs and practices that keep you a part of the community.

Most Neopagan religions have few creeds and no prophets. They are based on seasonal celebration, the cycles of planting and harvesting, on custom and experience rather than the written word. They are based on myth and metaphor rather than literal understanding. One can relate to Neopaganism as one relates to a poem or a work of art. As one scholar, Robert Ellwood, once wrote, "Neo-Paganism is a religion of atmosphere instead of faith, a cosmos, in a word, constructed by the imagination." Since the religion is alogical or prelogical, it is harder to imagine a dispute over dogma. The current dispute between creationists and evolutionists would seem absurd, since few would assume that religious truths are literal truths.

2. Pagans don't proselytize.

A polytheistic perspective assumes that there are multiple pathways to the divine. In many of the ancient Pagan religions, the gods and goddesses were tied to a particular place. They were not universal. There were bloody wars for territory in ancient history, but relatively few religious wars. Holy wars seem to be monotheism's unfortunate gift to the world.

The Neopagan polytheistic perspective is grounded in the view that reality is multiple and diverse. Most Neopagans do not assume that their spiritual path is the appropriate one for anyone but them. It is perfectly all right if you find what you are looking for elsewhere.

The basic assumption behind the polytheistic perspective is anarchist and decentralist, and therefore a bit scary for most people. It assumes one goal of life is to be at home in a world filled with chaos and complexity. It assumes that there is not going to be some golden day when there will be one truth, one way, one government, one attitude toward life.

Just as the health of a forest or meadow is measured by the number of different insects and plants and creatures that make it their home, so diversity in the spiritual world will mark the health of the human community. The polytheistic vision doesn't preclude monotheism as an appropriate *individual* path, but it does insist that the larger vision is multiple—that the universe is too rich and large and varied to be captured so easily by a single prophet, system or holy book.

This Pagan viewpoint can sometimes serve as a critique to Goddess monotheism, as well as patriarchal monotheism. It poses a challenge to those aspects within the feminist spiritual community and within feminist Wicca that look to a transcendent female deity.

3. Divinity is immanent in nature. The world is holy.

If divinity is multiple and diverse, it is also diffused throughout the world. It is not something only "out there" and "above." Divinity is inherent in all nature. This world, the here and now, the body, the mind, sexuality, all are holy. And a spiritual path that is not stagnant ultimately leads one to the understanding of one's own divine nature and the divine nature of all life.

4. You can have the juice and the mystery without totalitarianism.

In our modern, industrialized world, ecstatic rituals, ceremonies, and initiations into the processes of life and death and rebirth have almost always been the province of small and forgotten tribal groups or dogmatic religious sects. The educated and the literate have given up ecstasy along with discarded creeds. Neopagans have brought back the rituals and ecstatic techniques—the dancing and the chanting—but within a nonauthoritarian framework. They have also erased the line between the sacred and the secular; they understand that humor and laughter is part of ecstatic practice. They understand that you don't need a lot of money, or fancy temples, or hierarchies, or even, sometimes, a permanent ministry. You can set up a sacred space in your front yard. And your friends can bring the food and the candles. Perhaps most importantly, Neopagans generally believe that, when the drum stops and the dancing and chanting ceases, you can come back to a very grounded and rational self. But a self still at one with the juice and the mystery.

17

Sacred Land, Sacred Sex

Dolores LaChapelle

This exploratory essay ventures into the vast expanse of radical inquiry into the nature of the relationship between human sexuality and the natural world. Others have begun with the individual and then gone on to question the sexual mores of our culture. This approach is too anthropocentrically narrow for my purposes. Instead, I go to the roots of the matter by considering three different approaches, each of which recognizes the reciprocal relationship of human and nonhuman: 1. primitive cultures; 2. Taoism, with its direct ties to the primitive; and 3. D. H. Lawrence, the only modern literary figure who has ventured into this terrain of human sexuality and nature.

This essay leaves the reader with more questions than answers but the first step in our search for a modern ecological consciousness is learning to ask the right questions. We have only begun to do that. Let us start with a passage from D. H. Lawrence.

> Oh, what a catastrophe, what a maiming of love when it was made a personal, merely personal feeling, taken away from the rising and the setting of the sun, and cut off from the magic connection of the solstice and equinox! This is what is the matter with us, we are bleeding at the roots, because we are cut off from the earth and sun and stars, and love is a grinning mockery, because, poor blossom, we plucked it from its stem on the tree of Life, and expected it to keep on blooming in our civilized vase on the table.

Today, more than half a century later, it is even more obvious that we are "bleeding at the roots"; yet, judging from the dozen books published last year on the fiftieth anniversary of Lawrence's death, the full implications of this "love," which he spent his lifetime exploring, are as little understood as they were in his own day. Of his contemporaries only the perceptive Scandinavian novelist, Sigrid Undset grasped the importance of Lawrence's work. In 1938 she wrote:

> So many-sided was Lawrence and so intensely did he live his life that he became a representative figure—the man of mystery who

> symbolized his civilization at the moment when it reached a crisis.
> It is among other things a crisis of population and an economic crisis.
> In the language of mythology it means that the phallus has lost its
> old significance as a religious symbol. . . . Much of what is
> happening in Europe today and yet more that will doubtless happen
> in the future are the brutal reactions of mass humanity to the problem
> which the exceptional man, the genius, D. H. Lawrence, perceived
> and faced and fought in his own way.

The following year, 1939, the "brutal reactions" which Undset so clearly anticipated began with Hitler's invasion of Poland, quickly escalating until the slaughter became worldwide; yet, once the war was over, it was "back to normal" with an unprecedented "baby boom" as fears and uncertainties about the future were covered over with an emphasis on settling down and raising a family. It was "the world all in couples, each couple in its own little house, watching its own little interests, and stewing in its own little privacy," as Lawrence so graphically stated in *Women in Love*.

In the 1960s, when the children of this middle-class "baby boom" reached maturity, they rebelled against the affluent "system" bequeathed to them, confusedly proclaiming themselves on the side of all life, and against exploitation of that life in any way. In trying to help the victims of exploitation such as the blacks and the poor, they discovered that they too were powerless against the "system"; and while experimenting with freer, uncommitted forms of sexuality, they frequently found sex meaningless. Furthermore, while working alongside their men in these crusades, the women began to realize that they were as exploited as any other minority. Out of this impasse came many aspects of the "women's movement," with its confusion over the "rights" of man *versus* woman. We are no nearer a solution to these conflicts than we were in Lawrence's time. If anything, there is more hostility, more anger and more hatred between the sexes. We are obviously asking the wrong questions, if we are getting such devastating "solutions."

Forsaken by the Mother of All Beasts

When Undset mythologically defined the crisis which our culture is facing in terms of the phallus losing its old significance as a religious symbol, she was referring to our European cultural inheritance of 2,000 years of Judeo-Christian emphasis on sex for procreation. To get to the roots of what sex is for among human beings, we have to go beyond this temporary 2,000-year anomaly, to the total span of the 300,000 years of Homo Sapiens' life on Earth. When we do this, we discover that, as in so many other aspects of human behavior, some of our basic sexual patterns we share with our ancestors, the higher primates.

The high primates made a breakthrough from the usual mammalian sexual pattern, that in which all the females come into heat at the same time of year, thereby creating intense rivalry among the males during this limited time. Usually the dominant male secures a harem of females, leaving the other males to wander alone or rove in "bachelor" bands. Such activity effectively breaks off any continuity of relationship among the entire herd or tribe.

In the higher primates all this is changed. With females coming into heat throughout the year, at any one time some females are always available, so copulation becomes an ongoing activity. This continuous sexual atmosphere leads to social relationships based on sexual status, and ritualized forms of sex become a form of communication about other matters. Among higher primates, sexual postures, such as mounting and presenting, are examples of nonreproductive sexuality. Many different kinship ties develop, as well as various relationships to consorts of the opposite sex. Freeing sexual patterns from procreation alone increases the bonding within a group.

Sexual activity continued to serve as the major bonding mechanism for human tribes of gatherer-hunters. For over 99 percent of the time that human beings have been on this Earth, they have lived in this way. Only in the last ten thousand years have they begun to live by agriculture. Ten thousand years is only four hundred human generations. In so few generations there is no possibility of major genetic change. "We and our ancestors are the same people," as the anthropologist, Carleton Coon, succinctly pointed out; therefore, the same physiological and psychological structures form the roots of our behavior patterns today.

Until quite recently, agriculture was considered to be an enormous step forward for the human race, one which vastly improved human life; but during the last fifteen years new areas of research have made this idea seem very dubious indeed. It has shown that hunting and gathering can provide higher quality and more palatable food than agriculture; furthermore, crop failures cannot wipe out the entire food supply of hunter-gatherers because their food supply is so diverse. Only ten thousand years ago a few groups began agricultural practices; yet by two thousand years ago the overwhelming majority of human beings lived by farming. What happened to cause this incredible shift to agriculture all over the Earth in only eight thousand years? Although clues have been accumulating during the past few decades, it was not until 1977 that the answer became clear, when Mark Cohen wrote *The Food Crisis in Prehistory*.

Drawing on more than eight hundred research studies, Cohen concludes that human populations grew so large that hunters caused the extinction of great numbers of large mammal species by the end of the Pleistocene, thus forcing large numbers of humans to resort to agriculture. Although still more research indicates it is not this simple, the end result is the same. Cohen points out that the major advantage that agriculture has over a gathering-hunting life is that it provides more calories per unit of land per unit of time, and thus supports denser populations. He explains that fifty species of large mammals were extinct by the mid-Pleistocene in Africa, two hundred species in North and South America by the end of the Pleistocene and in Europe the enormous herds of grazing animals were gone about the same time. Paleolithic hunters had destroyed the easiest, most tasty protein source. Mythologically, we can say that the hunters realized that the Mother of All Beasts no longer sent Her animals to them for food.

"Biosphere" and "Ecosphere" Cultures

Over a period of several thousand years, human beings developed several strategies to deal with this new situation, some of which led to "biosphere" cultures and others to "ecosystem" cultures. Agriculture—a biosphere strategy—required more work than gathering and hunting. It therefore encouraged larger families of children to provide more workers which, in turn, meant more intensive agriculture, and so on, in an ever increasing spiral of scarcity, hard work and destruction of soils. Eventually, this led to enslaving other peoples as workers.

Biosphere cultures assumed that nature was no longer the overflowing, abundant Mother. She had withdrawn her plenty; the never-ending stream of animals was gone. Nature was not to be trusted anymore; therefore, humans must take affairs into their own hands. Within a short period of time—the last 500 years of the era encompassing the 10,000-year spread of agriculture—all of the world's so-called "great ethical systems" arose, beginning with Confucius and Buddha (approximately 500 B.C.), through the Hebrew prophets and Plato and ending with Christianity, in the beginning of our present era. What these systems represent is the establishment of religious systems based on "ideas" put forth by individual persons: Buddha, Moses, Jesus, St. Paul and others.

Before exploring the second type of culture, the ecosystem cultures, it is necessary to consider the two basic, underlying ways of looking at life. One emphasizes the birth or coming into being of new things, and the other emphasizes the death or disappearance of old things. Some forms of Judeo-Christianity and Buddhism focus on the final phase, the inevitable decline, destruction, and death of all things.

Buddhism, in some of its forms, teaches the way of deliverance from the wheel of rebirth, from the impermanence and ongoing passing away of all things. This universal impermanence of things arouses an ultimate anxiety in the rational mind. Christianity, in some of its forms, focuses on the endings of things, the transience of life, preferring to concentrate on the "ideal" of life after death in a perfect state called heaven. In these "ethical" world religions, life on this Earth, or on this "plane of being," is transitory, unimportant, even illusory; therefore, the Earth itself becomes expendable, of no real value. This view permits total exploitation of nature.

The other type of worldview is exemplified by Taoism, which focuses on the initial stage of the process, the birth, the coming into being of new things, "the never-ceasing procreativeness" of life. There is no separation between human and nonhuman. The human mind came out of nature and is identical with the structure of the cosmos. Nowhere in Taoism is there a "great man" who formulated "ideas" out of his head as in the ethical religions. The legendary Lao Tzu and the historical figure Chaung Tzu are the most noted proponents of the Tao; but it is clear from their writings that nature was considered much too complex for the human mind to order. Human society could only be brought into order by fitting itself into the order of nature, because human society was only a smaller part of the whole of the *Tao*.

With the distinction between these two viewpoints on life clarified, we can now turn to "ecosystem" cultures. We find that instead of taking up agriculture, these people moved into marginal areas, high mountains, deserts, deep jungles, or isolated islands, and learned to pay attention, to watch carefully. They learned to revere all of life as it was considered their body and their life. They developed rituals which acknowledged the sacredness of the land; thus enabling them to remain aware of the sacred cycles of taking life to live, but also of giving life back, so that the whole of the land could flourish, not just humans. Because their economic basis consisted of a limited natural region such as a watershed, within which they made their whole living, it was possible for them to notice when a particular species of animal or plant became scarcer and harder to find. At such times they set up taboos limiting the kill. They began to understand that they could destroy all life in their environment if there were too many human beings there placing excess demands on it. They came to understand that sex must be part of the sacred cycle. Misused, it caused destruction, not only within the human tribal group, but among all the life around them. Used with due reverence for its power, it brought increased energy and unity with all other forms of life.

In the primitive cultures which developed out of the "ecosystem" way of life—based on "sacred land, sacred sex"—much of the wisdom of the tribe was devoted to "walking in balance with the Earth." Human population was never allowed to upset this equilibrium. Early ethnologists in North America found that child-spacing and child-rearing practices that grew out of this approach to the Earth showed remarkable similarities in tribes as far apart as the Arctic and the Southwestern desert. Infanticide, abortion, the lack of punishment of children, and the quiet, "good" children proved a continual source of amazement to these early researchers. Among tribal people, the birth of a child was not an "accident" left up to the individual parents, but instead was regulated by ritual, or contraception, or abortion, so that the particular child would fit into the overall health and stability of the entire ecosystem.

In some cultures the food/reproduction/energy cycle is so attuned that there is no need for conscious birth control. The !Kung have lived in the Kalahari desert for at least eleven thousand years. Recently, because of the drop in the water table, they have been forced to begin moving near the farming villages of the settled Bantu. Here the !Kung women are losing their equal status, children are becoming more aggressive, and the once stable population is exploding. Population stability among the nomad !Kung is mostly due to the scarcity of fat in their diet, which delays the onset of menstruation. First babies are usually born when their mother is about nineteen. They are nursed for four years. The mother rarely conceived during that time, because nursing women need one thousand extra calories per day; therefore, she does not have enough fat left for ovulation to take place.

For these "ecosystem" people it is not appropriate to speak of the human beings' relation to the universe, for their way is one of universal interrelatedness. Humans are not the focus from which the relations flow. For instance, Dorothy Lee, in her study of the Tikopia natives, found that an act of fondling or an embrace was not phrased as a "demonstration" or an "expression" of affection, that is, starting from the ego and defined in terms of the emotions of the ego, but instead as an act of sharing within a larger context.

By way of illustration there follow three detailed examples: In the Ute Bear Dance sex was used to bond the widely scattered hunting bands into the tribe as a whole; in the Eskimo game of "doused lights" sex was used as an emotional cathartic; and, in the final example, a modern Odawa Indian shows that the sharing of sex still contributes to the bonding of the tribe.

During most of the year the Ute tribe was split into small kinship groups hunting in widely separated parts of the high Rocky Mountains. Once a year—after the first thunder—the entire tribe met for the annual spring Bear Dance. Because the female bear chooses her mate, the woman chose which man she would dance with by plucking his sleeve. For three days the dance continued, filled with the spirit of the bear. From time to time a couple would leave the dance and "take their blanket up into the brush of the hillside to let out the spirit of the bear and the thunder of spring that had grown too strong in them." Many healings took place during the Bear Dance. At noon of the third day, the Dance ended and gradually, over a period of days, the big camp broke up. A woman who plucked the sleeve of a man during the Bear Dance might visit the bushes with him for an hour, or for the entire night, or might stay with him for the entire year's hunting, until the next Bear Dance, or even for "many snows." Here ritualized, sacred sex served the function of putting the individuals together again as a tribe, and back in connection with their land through their totem animal, the bear.

Peter Freuchen tells of an Eskimo game—"doused lights"—where many people gathered together in an igloo. Lights were all extinguished and there was total darkness. No one was allowed to say anything and all changed places continuously. At a certain signal each man grabbed the nearest woman. After a while, the lights were lit again and now innumerable jokes could be made over the theme: "I knew all the time who you were because . . . " This game served a very practical purpose, if bad weather kept the tribe confined for a long time. The possibility of serious emotional trouble is ever-present, because the bleakness and loneliness of the Arctic can mean little food, or an uncertain fate. When the lamp is lit again after this ritualized sexual game is over, the whole group is joking and in high spirits.

Wilfred Pelletier is a modern Odawa Indian who left his island reserve in Canada. He became a success in the white man's world, but he found it wanting and returned to his reserve. He says that his own introduction to sex was provided by a relative. "I still look on that as one of the greatest and happiest experiences of my life. From that time on, it seems to me that I screwed all the time, without letup. Not just my relatives, who were not always available, but anywhere I could find it, and it always seemed to be there . . . On the reservation people were honest about their feelings and their needs, and as all the resources of that community were available to those who needed them, sex was not excluded. Sex was a recognized need, so nobody went without it. It was as simple as that."

In these examples, sexual activity served as a bonding mechanism for the tribe. The Tukano tribe provides us with an example of an even more expansive sexuality. They derive their entire ecologically sophisticated cosmology largely from the model of sexual physiology. The Tukano live in the rainforest of the northwest Amazon Basin, with its difficult climate and easily depleted natural resources. In their worldview the Sun Father, a masculine power, fertilizes the feminine element, the Earth. Creation is continuous because the energy of the sun, which to the Tukano is seminal light and heat, causes the plants to grow and humans and animals to reproduce. This procreative energy of the sun flows in limited quantity continuously between all parts of the universe. Humans can remove only what is needed for their life and only under particular ritual conditions. Whatever energy is borrowed must be put back into the circuit as soon as possible. They practice birth control and understand about microclimates and phenomena such as parasitism and symbiosis. The Tukano do not see nature as something apart from humans, so there is no way that human beings can confront or oppose it, or even try to harmonize with it. The individual human, however, can unbalance the cosmic system by personal malfunctioning within the overall system, but can never stand apart from it.

Sex and the Pattern of Existence

In the past, a linear cause and effect model generally has been used to explain how cultures function. This model, with its dualistic presuppositions, has been inherent in western civilization since the time of the Greeks. Only since the famous Macy Conference (1947-1953), which "invented cybernetics," has the West been moving toward the "systems model" of thinking. In the East, however, the "systems" way of thinking dates from the Taoists of very ancient times.

Taoism does not consider that the order in nature comes from rules laid down by a celestial lawgiver, as in our western "laws of nature" concept; but from the spontaneous cooperation of all the beings in the universe brought about by following the *li,* the pattern of their own natures. The earliest meaning of the word *li* came from the pattern in which fields were laid out for cultivation in order to follow the lay of the land. *Li* also stood for the basic patterns of propriety expressed in ritual. Laying out fields was a ritual undertaking. Hence, the Earth itself was the ordering principle for a particular place, and ritual helped to divine its pattern. In ancient times, the word *li* was also used to describe the pattern in things such as the markings in jade or the fibres in muscles. *Li* was eventually used to stand for the principle of organization in the universe. It is the order to which parts of the whole have to conform by virtue of their very existence as parts within that whole. If they do not behave in a particular way (according to their *li*) they lose their relational position in the whole and become something other than themselves. This is one of the underlying reasons for the elaborate seasonal rituals practiced throughout Chinese history. Since human beings were considered an integral part of nature, to follow their own *li* required that they conform to the ongoing seasonal pattern, the *li* of nature.

Because of the very early development of writing in China, Taoism not only provides us with written material coming directly out of the oral, original primitive concept of human with nature—uncorrupted by any later "ethical religious" systems—but also gives us the advantages of centuries of further development and elaboration of these concepts within one of the most "civilized" cultures in the world. According to Taoism, the energy of the universe operates through the interaction of yin and yang (female and male). Taoism developed some of the most sophisticated methods of any culture for dealing with sexual energy, within and between humans and nature. Its sexual techniques were used to increase the energy, not only between man and woman, but within the human group as a whole, and between the humans and their land. From these relationships came the exquisite sex/nature poetry of China.

The most important ritual was called "The True Art of Equalizing the Chi's" or "Uniting the Chi's" (*Chi* means flow of energy) of male and female, dating back to at least the second century A.D. The ritual of "Uniting the Chi's" occurred on either the nights of the new moon, or full moon after fasting. It began with a ritual dance, "Coiling of the Dragon and Playing of the Tiger," which ended either in a public group ritual intercourse, or in a succession of unions involving all those present in chambers along the sides of the temple courtyard. A fragment of the highly poetic book of liturgy for this ritual called the *Huang Shu* survived. During the Ming dynasty most of these Taoist sexual ritual books were destroyed. Fortunately, some were preserved because they had been translated by the Japanese in about the tenth century.

In both the Chinese sexual rituals, and in primitive tribal rituals, sex itself was made numinous. In the Chinese rituals it is not clear what deities were worshiped, but they seem to have been star gods, the gods of the five elements, and the spirits residing in and controlling the various parts of the human body.

To understand why the Taoists devoted so much attention to sexual techniques, it is necessary to understand the importance of the structure of the pelvic region with its central bony mass, the sacrum. Because western culture puts so much emphasis on the rational mind, (specifically, the rational, left hemisphere of the neocortex), the Taoist insistence on the importance of the lower mind, located four fingers below the navel (*tantien* in Chinese and *hara* in Japanese), seemed utter nonsense until quite recently. In the 1920s when D. H. Lawrence emphasized the "solar plexus" he was ridiculed; but, in the last two decades, with the growing popularity of such disciplines as Tai Chi, Aikido and other martial arts, as well as body therapies such as Rolfing, the pelvic area is coming to be recognized as our "sacred middle," the area within us where the flow of energy (*Chi*) takes place between us and the cosmos. The functions of sex, prenatal life, birth, assimilation of food, as well as deep emotions, all emanate or take place in this area. "Sacred middle" refers to the area of sacrum, the bony plate which gets its name from the same Latin root as the word sacred. The lower five vertebrae, which in the adult become fused into a single, curved, shield-shaped plate, make up the sacrum. Since the muscles of the entire pelvic girdle are attached here, this area is central to being human. The enlarged human brain developed only after we achieved true upright posture; and furthermore, all the muscles involved in walking, standing, and sitting converge here.

Much of the corrective work accomplished through Rolfing has to do with breaking down the overrigidity of the abdominal muscles so prevalent in our culture. It often completely eliminates many states of underlying anxiety. This connection between what we generally conceive of as a "mental" condition, and the actual facts of its cure through manipulation of muscles within the pelvic region, defies the conventional western connections; yet the Chinese have always considered the *tantien* the seat of strong emotions. When trained by Tai Chi it can also sense the emotions of other people, as well as registering currents within the Earth. Modern experiments with dowsers suggest that the pelvic area is the particular physical location within the dowser's body which indicates water beneath the Earth.

The most ancient of the martial arts, Tai Chi, was developed in the Taoist Shaolin monastery in the mountains of China. Each of its 108 forms deals specifically with the muscles discussed above. It is these same muscles, which Tai Chi liberates, that are crucial for the practice of Taoist sexual techniques. For the man these muscles are essential for the Taoist technique of orgasm without ejaculation. For the woman, during the moment of vaginal orgasm, the fascial and coccygeal muscles of themselves, with no immediate conscious effort, can prevent the entry of semen and thus provide an automatic method of birth control, when needed.

Sex for Procreation, or Harmony with Nature?

Ritualized sex in both primitive societies and in Taoism came from entirely different roots than sexual activities in modern western culture—where the emphasis has been on procreation. In the latter culture, male ejaculation is of great importance, as it is tied in with fertility and the male ego. In ritualized sex, however, the main concern is "dual cultivation," bonding within the group, and harmony with nature. None of these functions need ejaculation to succeed, hence male ejaculation, but not male orgasm, becomes unimportant. This completely eliminates some of the most important male emotional problems, due to such things which western culture labels as "premature ejaculation" and "impotence," two categories actually created by an overemphasis on male ejaculation. Freed from the preoccupation with ejaculation, the *jade peak,* as the Chinese call the male organ, naturally acts as it was designed by nature to act, unless there is physical disability. In ritualized sex, which is not confined to the genital area, the entire body and the brain receive repetitive stimuli over a considerable period of time. This leads to a condition called "central nervous system tuning," which has a clear physiological basis.

The organs of the body are homeostatically interconnected by the nervous system and the brain. The autonomic nervous system (ANS) consists of both the parasympathetic (PNS) and the sympathetic (SNS) nervous systems. The entire SNS can be excited by stimulation of only a few nerves, thus readying the muscle structure and stopping or reducing activity in organs, such as the digestive system, not immediately needed for escape or fighting. The ergotropic (energy expending) response occurs when the SNS is stimulated, resulting in increased muscle tone, excitation of the cerebral cortex and desynchronized cortical rhythms. The parasympathetic nervous system (PNS) responds only to more generalized stimulation and results in pleasurable states such as sleep, digestion, relaxation and, among animals, grooming activities.

Generally speaking, if one of these systems, either PNS or SNS, is stimulated, the other system is inhibited. Tuning occurs, however, when there is such strong, prolonged activation of one system that it becomes supersaturated and spills over into the other system and it, in turn, becomes activated. If stimulated long enough, the next stage of tuning is reached, where the simultaneous, strong discharge of both autonomic systems creates a state of stimulation of the median forebrain bundle, generating not only pleasurable sensations, but, in especially profound cases, a sense of union or oneness with all those present. This stage of tuning permits right hemisphere dominance, often enabling solution of problems deemed insoluble by the rational hemisphere. Furthermore, the strong rhythm of repetitive action, as done in sexual rituals, produces positive limbic (animal brain) discharge, resulting in increased social cohesion. This contributes to the success of such rituals as bonding mechanisms.

All these benefits which follow on "tuning" apply even more powerfully in ritualized sex; such "tuning," however, cannot come about through the usual quick orgasm of western style sex, programmed as it has been mainly for procreation. Such an orgasm resolves only immediate sexual tensions. Ritualized sex requires considerable time to allow for full "tuning" of all the interconnected systems of the body. Jolan Chang quotes Li T'ung Hsuan of the seventh century in his commentary on the "thousand loving thrusts" of the "jade peak":

> Deep and shallow, slow and swift, direct and slanting thrusts, are by
> no means all uniform. . . . A slow thrust should resemble the jerking
> motion of a carp toying with the hook; a swift thrust that of the flight
> of the birds against the wind.

From his own experience, this modern Chinese, Jolan Chang, adds in a footnote that the "thousand thrusts" can easily be done in half an hour at a very slow rhythm.

Taoist sexual rituals sensitize the entire body; whereas, in western culture we have forced most of the passion of living into the narrowness of genital sexuality. But any time there is a total response, in any situation, the whole being is there and, because the **whole** being is sexual, sexuality is always there in any total response. It **can** occur in any relationship, with an animal, with a flower, with the world itself. Some of the criticism of D. H. Lawrence came from his total response to nature. Ford Madox Ford, his stuffy Edwardian type editor, reported that, while walking and talking of literary matters one day, Lawrence went "temporarily insane." He knelt down and tenderly touched the petals of a common flower and went into an "almost super-sex-passionate delight." Ford admitted that this was "too disturbing" for him.

While written accounts of Taoist sexual practices date back to over a thousand years ago, when it comes to primitive ritualized sex, we have no written material. Such cultures were not literate, and in the case of North American Indians, by the time they became literate many of their cultures were largely destroyed. Of course, anthropologists have written on these matters, but they have usually dealt only with surface manifestations. Fortunately, because of a most unusual combination of personal talents and circumstances in his life, the linguist, Jaime de Angulo has contributed some insight into the Indians' own understanding of the place of sex in their world.

The combination of his shamanic knowledge and his academic knowledge of psychiatry and medicine, along with his incredible linguistic ability, gave Jaime access to areas of Indian thought denied to other white people. The poet, Robert Duncan, reports that Jaime got the idea from the Indians that

> you could cross over not just between the living and the dead, as in
> Shamanism, but also from one sex to another. He found the Indian under-
> standing reasonable enough. We get confused about something like
> homosexuality. But sex and gender are not the same thing. . . . At one
> point when I confused sex and gender, Jaime said, "You're Western in
> your thinking, you think that male and female are genders. For Indians
> there can be five genders in a language, five genders in a tribe."

In English we have only three genders: male, female and neuter. According to a number of sources, there can be as many as eleven to fifteen genders in some tribes. The most commonly known example of crossing from one sex to another is the "contraire" in certain Plains Indian tribes. Influenced by "thunder," this man could marry a warrior and was considered a sacred personage.

According to the dictionary, "engendering" means "to produce, give existence to living beings." Looked at from Jaime's point of view, it is obvious that humanity alone cannot engender children. Instead, it is the entire living environment which produces the child and keeps it alive: the air, soil, plants, and animals of its immediate environment. We are the children of our particular place on Earth. This is why the land is sacred, sex is sacred, and eating is sacred; because they are all parts of the same energy flow as the Tukano and the Taoists conceived it. The Indians repeatedly acknowledge "all our relatives" in their sacred sweat lodge ceremonies. The hot rocks, the water which is thrown on the rocks, the sage—all are part of the same family. Other cultures have never lost this understanding of being part of the whole, the Tao. Western culture did forget. But now we have been forced by ecological disasters on every side to begin to recognize the inter-relatedness of all. As Lawrence observed:

> The last 3,000 years of mankind have been an excursion into ideals, bodilessness, and tragedy and now the excursion is over. . . . It is a question, practically, of relationship. We *must* get back into relation, vivid and nourishing relation to the cosmos. . . . The way is through daily ritual, and reawakening. We *must* once more practice the ritual of dawn and noon and sunset, the ritual of kindling fire and pouring water, the ritual of first breath, and the last. . . . We must return to the way of "knowing in terms of togetherness". . . . the togetherness of the body, the sex, the emotions, the passions, with the Earth and sun and stars.

18
Lakshmi Ashram:
A Gandhian Perspective
in the Himalayan Foothills*
Radha Bhatt

I come from one of the villages in the far interior of the middle Himalayas, an area remote from so-called modern development. Yet I doubt if these villages are really "backward," if judged by human values. The area is rich in humanity, although there are problems that need social change to bring solutions. My organization, Lakshmi Ashram, is helping the people of this area to bring about such change, along the lines of Gandhian ideals.

I would like to present some of my experience of work in this field, gained over the past thirty-two years. To my mind the most important factor in bringing about change in society is fearless thinking among the people, and Gandhi's contribution to the world was his generation of this power of fearlessness, particularly in the hearts of the downtrodden and poor. Thereafter they were able to stand up and say, "We won't tolerate this injustice." This fearlessness is a basic factor in bringing about long-lasting social change.

The exploited and weak people and classes are so because they have lost the courage to stand up against injustice and exploitation. After a while, a sense of fatalism becomes fixed in the minds of these people, and they lose any confidence they once had in themselves. When this happens, people cannot even understand or recognize the nature of the injustice or exploitation to which they are subjected.

It is very difficult to generate the capacity of fearlessness in exploited people, but Gandhi was able to do so. He was able to regenerate their ability to analyze justice and injustice, and to fight for justice; to understand equality and inequality, and to resist inequality. The

*Reprinted by permission from *Speaking of Faith*, Diana L. Eck and Devaki Jain, eds., New Society Publishers: Philadelphia, PA, 1987.

fearlessness of the common people was a great strength which he discovered and brought out into the struggle for political liberation in India. And Gandhi gave it a right sense of direction in the revolution of social values. It was of great significance that this revolution, political and social, was carried out by the farmers, the women, and the other downtrodden people of India.

I was not lucky enough to experience firsthand the movements of women and men led by Gandhi, but I saw the fearless power of which he spoke among the farming women of Kumaon in 1967. At that time, Lakshmi Ashram was campaigning alongside the village people against the liquor shops. The women of the Garud area had stood firmly against the government liquor shop in their village, and every day hundreds of women were picketing in front of it because they wholeheartedly believed it was a dangerous threat to their families and their economic well-being. Over a period of six months, the campaign was taken up by some hundred villages, but still the district authorities continued simply to wait and watch. It was finally decided that a few women should go and talk with the district magistrate. Four women were selected who were absolutely committed to liquor prohibition. These illiterate women needed someone with them to make all the arrangements for their 60-kilometer journey by bus to the district headquarters. I was deputed to accompany them, for I doubted if they had the courage to speak face to face with the district magistrate. They could not even speak in Hindi, only in their local Kumaoni language.

Yet the next day in front of the district magistrate they spoke so fearlessly and perfectly that I was astonished. They started arguing with him, and the talk began to get quite heated.

"If I don't agree, how can you stop the liquor shop?" shouted the district magistrate.

"We can set fire to the shop," the women spoke firmly and calmly.

"That is an offense. Do that and you will find yourselves in handcuffs," he said.

"Then come with ten thousand handcuffs. We are not just one or two. Thousands of us are picketing the liquor shop. We have no fear of jail or even death, for our lives are completely destroyed by this drinking. We can face every danger."

The district magistrate looked into the eyes of these illiterate village women and found them ablaze with determination.

No, not with handcuffs, I will come myself to see these fearless women like yourselves, he thought to himself.

The district magistrate was so overwhelmed by the atmosphere that he ordered the shop to be closed down, and said, "This is the miracle of Gandhi, whose spirit is working in these women."

In the eight districts of the middle Himalayas where I have been working these last thirty-two years, the people are exploited in many ways. They have had no equal chances of development. In such an exploited and underdeveloped society the women find themselves in an even worse position, for they are considered secondary persons within their own society. Even today they do not get even 5 percent of the available opportunities for development, education and freedom. So they have come to accept this as their fixed due with a spirit of fatalism.

These women, however, are not weak in any way. Working hard in the fields and forests, by the rivers, and in the mountains, they have become very perseverant and tolerant. They are wise and practical, bearing the responsibilities of their families without the help of their men. But social injustice had killed their self-confidence to such an extent that they could not contemplate any thought of change or self-discovery in their lives. They used to say, "We are just like cows in the *goth*," the *goth* being the cowshed on the ground floor of their homes. And thus were they considered by society.

To gain their active participation and give them the confidence to act together fearlessly for social change is not very easy, yet if it can be achieved it is very effective. This was the experience we in the ashram had gained, but still I had my doubts as to whether the village women themselves would be able to lead such revolutions. The women of Khirakot village changed my apprehension by their action. They shed new light on my whole way of thinking.

Khirakot is a village in the Someshwar valley with a population of one hundred fifty families. It lies just above the Kosi River on the lower slopes of the hillside. Above the village is their own village forest, while higher up lies the government reserve forest. Most of the men of this village are away in employment. Out of some five hundred men only twenty-five or thirty remain in the village. Therefore, the responsibilities of daily life within the family are borne by the women.

The pine trees of the village forest of Khirakot were lopped to such an extent that only the lower stems were left on the land. These branches were lopped off and used for fuel, but this in turn caused a complete depletion of the pine needles that are used as bedding in their cattle sheds.

One morning the women coming down from the distant government reserve forest with heavy headloads of dry pine needles felt it was just too much for them to walk so far every day. It meant leaving their children and cattle alone at home for hours at a time, and finally reaching home so tired that the rest of the day's work was impossible to finish.

They discussed the matter among themselves, and decided that they should protect their village forest against the lopping off of branches for fuel by their own and neighboring village women. If the pine trees grew bigger, then needles would be available close to their homes. And if the forest were managed properly, then fuel wood would also be obtainable from these trees without destroying the whole tree. They spread their ideas among the other women of the village, and they all became convinced, not by holding any formal meeting, but by talking at the water places or along the village paths where they met one another.

Thus, after four years of continuous efforts by the collective leadership of these women, a fine pine forest can be seen above Khirakot village. The forest has already begun to provide dry pine needles for their cowsheds. This leadership is not tired, but rather increasingly enthusiastic about ideas. In January 1983 they involved the menfolk in their endeavors. Every family of the village agreed to pay a rupee a month as salary to a forest guard, a young man from their village. The women's group collected the money and helped the young man guard the forest.

This is a rare example of collective enterprise in the present day atmosphere of the welfare state that is India, where people have lost their initiative for such collective action and have instead grown accustomed to asking for grants from the state, even for a very small work project.

The method that can succeed in such leadership is completely nonviolent, with no aggression, no hatred, no competition. Nonviolence is one of the main principles of Hindu philosophy. Gandhi, who tried to act in a nonviolent manner both as an individual and collectively, had his family roots in the Hindu Vaishnava tradition. There, in his daily family life, he gained a deep inner consciousness of truth and nonviolence. Truth was his aim, and nonviolence was the means to attain it. Truth was his God, and nonviolence was his religion. Once, when someone asked him to which religion he belonged, he replied, "Previously I used to say I believed in God, but now I say I believe in Truth. I was saying that God was Truth, but now I am saying that Truth is God. There are people who disagree with the existence of God, but there is none who differs as to the existence of truth. Even an atheist believes in truth."

This sense of nonviolence also permeates the consciousness of the women among whom I have been working all these years. Yes, this awareness is more alive, stronger and clearer in the women than among the men. The following example will make this clear.

This incident goes back to 1957 when India was moved by the revolutionary action of Bhoodan, the land-gift movement. Our organization, Lakshmi Ashram, was spreading this idea in the far-flung villages and valleys of Kumaon. I went from village to village and door to door, along with other girls of my ashram. We walked along the high and narrow paths, our rucksacks on our backs, conveying the message that the big landowners should be able to spare and donate a part of their land to the landless people of their village. In the Himalayan region, however, there are few true landlords, and the majority are small farmers with holdings roughly similar in size. Even so, one can find a poor landless man or widow in every village.

That day we had walked a distance of some thirty kilometers, and had conducted four small meetings in villages along the way. It was getting dark, evening was closing in, and we had finished the last meeting of that day. We had found accommodation for the night in the house of a typical farmer of that village. While he was preparing food in his kitchen for us, we were sitting under the low roof of his house around an open fire in the middle of the room, which was full of smoke. He had been joined by some men and children from the neighboring houses.

Then a figure appeared out of the thick cloud of smoke and sat herself down beside me. Her clothes were torn. She said calmly, "I want to donate one *nali* (1/20 of an acre) of my land as Bhoodan."

"But how much land have you got in all?"

"I have some, by the grace of God," she said.

"She has only three *nalis* of unirrigated land," said one of the village men.

She kept quiet.

"Why do you want to donate something when you have such a little piece of land?"

She spoke after a short pause. "I have two sons. If God had offered me three, wouldn't I have distributed the same land among them?"

We were all impressed, and words were not necessary.

"Do you have any landless person in your village to whom you want to give it?" I asked again.

"Yes, one widow who has a son."

"Is she somehow related to you?"

"No, she is a Harijan. But she is a human being, and she also has a child. Just like me. Please don't try to stop me. This is my religion. I am illiterate, but still I know that our religion preaches that we should share our meal. Lord Krishna has said, 'The one who cooks for himself is a sinner, therefore eat, only after distributing among others.'" (*Bhagavad Gita*, 2.13)

These hill women have such a sense of relision, not in their minds alone, but in their hearts, and in their souls. It is this that gives them the strength for nonviolent action, be it in development work, revolutionary social change, or in opposing injustice and exploitation.

Gandhi has declared many times that nonviolence is the tool of the brave, and that there is no place in nonviolence for cowardliness. This kind of brave action was taken by these hill women when they fought against the timber contractors in Chamoli district, hugged the trees, and flung their bodies before the axes. Their action gave birth to the famous nonviolent ecological movement known in India and throughout the world as "Chipko." Similar action was taken by the women of Khirakot when they fought against the businessman and the government who had started a soapstone quarry on their village land, which had spoiled their village forest, their cultivated land, their drinking water, and the footpaths to their fields. They were bold enough to struggle for two and a half years against these two big powers in India. They were so powerful that they could motivate the men of their own families and villages for this cause. They were able to proclaim strongly, "This is our forest, our land, and our paths, and the businessman is exploiting us. We will not tolerate it."

The women of the villages in Kumaon have succeeded because their actions were nonviolent, for nonviolence is the only tool for such people. And where are the roots of this nonviolence? I believe they are deep in the culture and religion of our people.

19

Feminist, Earth-based Spirituality and Ecofeminism

Starhawk

Ecofeminism is a movement with an implicit and sometimes explicit spiritual base. Yet to use the term "spirituality" is itself almost misleading, for the earth-based spirituality that influences ecofeminism has nothing to do with systems of thought which divide "spirit" from matter.

The spiritual traditions of Native Americans, Africans, Asians and other tribal peoples, and the pre-Christian traditions which survived in Europe, have in common a worldview in which the sacred is seen as immanent in the living world. Whether we talk about Goddess, God, or Great Spirit, we are it as it is nature as we are nature, and *here* is where it's at. To say that ecofeminism is a spiritual movement, in an earth-rooted sense, means that it encompasses a dimension that profoundly challenges our ordinary sense of value, that counters the root stories of our culture and attempts to shift them.

Earth-based spirituality influences ecofeminism by informing its values. This does not mean that every ecofeminist must worship the goddess, perform rituals, or adopt any particular belief system. We are not attempting to promote or enforce a spiritual practice: in my own tradition, we do not proselytize and we believe firmly that our way is not the one, right, true and only one for everyone. Many people live very fulfilled and satisfying lives without doing anything that we would typically call spiritual, and that's fine.

What we are doing, however, is attempting to shift the values of our culture. We could describe that shift as one away from battle as our underlying cultural paradigm and toward the cycle of birth, growth, death, and regeneration, to move away from a view of the world as made up of warring opposites toward a view that sees processes unfolding and continuously changing.

Riane Eisler, in *The Chalice and the Blade,* describes this underlying difference as that between the dominator and partnership models of society.[1] The metaphors of the mainstream traditions, the stories we see on TV every night, the underlying structures of our major institutions are based on battle and domination. War is the organizing principle of society: its hierarchical structures determine the management of corporations, schools, prisons, hospitals, universities, churches and, of course, governments. War sets a pattern for unequal power relations, between men and women, light people and dark, rich and poor, human beings and nature. War teaches us to need an enemy to conquer and overcome and to see those who are different as lesser, dangerous, inhuman.

When birth becomes our underlying metaphor, however, the world shifts. The cosmos becomes a living body in which we all participate, continually merging and emerging in rhythmic cycles. Birth is a process that takes its own time and is subject to its own laws. Although it is common, it still remains a mystery: inherently surprising, never wholly knowable or controllable, a process moved by forces so intense that they take us out of superficiality and throw us into the depths of the life-stream.

In cultures where the cycle of life is the underlying metaphor, religious objects reflect its imagery, showing us women—Goddesses— ripe in pregnancy or giving birth. The vulva and its abstracted form, the triangle, along with breasts, circles, eyes, and spirals, are signs of the sacred.[2] These images are often interpreted as those of mere "fertility cults," as if their purpose was only to ensure more and more fertility, but such explanations miss the point. The birth images also refer to stories, now lost, mythologies, rich systems of symbolism, and ideologies about the processes of creation and generation.

Earth-based spiritualities celebrate the cycle of life: birth, growth, decay, death, and regeneration as it appears in the seasonal round of the year, in the moon's phases, in human, plant and animal life, always with the goal of establishing balance among all the different communities that comprise the living body of earth.

Of course, I cannot speak for all earth-based traditions or for any except my own—and even there I speak *out of* a tradition, not *for* it. We have no dogma, no authorized texts or beliefs and no authoritative body to authorize anything; nor do we want one, for earth-based spirituality prizes individual inspiration and autonomy. The tradition I am a part of stems from the pre-Christian Goddess-worshipping religions of Europe, and we are called Witches, a word that stems from an Anglo-Saxon root meaning "to bend or shape." Witches were shamans—benders and shapers of reality—but shaman is a word so overused and commercialized today that I don't claim it for present-day Witches. A shaman is a healer who is trained within a traditional society and uses her or his skills in the service of that community.

Today's Witches are mostly urban people living in the mobile, fragmented, technological modern world. Although some Witches grew up in family traditions that survived the times of persecution, most of us have come to the Craft in adulthood. Rather than using our skills, such as they are, to preserve a traditional community, we are faced with the task of reshaping western culture.

The attempts by the Catholic and Protestant churches in the sixteenth and seventeenth centuries to discredit the Old Religion, to identify Witchcraft with Satanism and devil worship, or the casting of evil spells, their persecution of Witches and murder of millions of women and men, were part of the vast cultural brainwashing in that era that attempted to undermine the last vestiges of an organic worldview and establish a vision of the world as a mechanistic hierarchy.[3] The word "Witch" still carries negative associations for some people, but I use it because it expresses the reality of the reversals our culture needs to undergo to regain balance and sanity.

Witchcraft survived secretly through the times of persecution and began a small revival in the 1950s, which expanded in the countercultural atmosphere of the 1960s. The seventies saw it begin a major growth spurt as feminists began searching for alternatives to the patriarchal mainstream religions. Feminist spirituality encompasses many traditions and movements, and many women are involved with re-emerging Goddess traditions that do not identify themselves as Witches. Feminists are also involved in challenging patriarchal structures and language within Judaism, Christianity, Buddhism, Hinduism, etc.[4]

The political wing of the feminist movement was at first against spirituality of all sorts, identifying the mystical with the patriarchal religions which historically had served to control the poor and the oppressed. They feared that a focus on the spiritual would prevent people from taking action. And perhaps also some feared a shift in perception that goes deeper than conventional political wisdom.

Nevertheless, throughout the seventies and eighties, more and more women, and also men, began exploring feminist approaches to spirituality, coming to identify with a vision of the world as a living being, learning to celebrate that vision in ritual, act out of that vision to preserve the life of the earth, and build community around it.

Earth-based spirituality provides both an imperative toward action in the world and a source of strength and renewal of the energies that often burn out in political action.[5] By the eighties, feminist spirituality provided some of the major energy left in the feminist movement, as well as a strong influence in the profeminist men's movement, in the direct action wing of the peace and anti-intervention movements, and in some of the more radical wings of the ecology and wilderness preservation movements. Instead of replacing political action, earth-based spirituality provides a repository of energy that can resurge in new cycles of political momentum. Ecofeminism, arising in the late seventies and eighties, inherits this history.

Earth-based spirituality is based on three core concepts. The first is that of immanence: that Goddess is embodied in the living world, in the human, animal, plant, and mineral communities and their interrelationships. Among scientists, this concept has been formulated as the Gaia hypothesis (although using the name of an ancient Greek Goddess reflects our continuing western cultural bias: Lovelock could have named his theory after any of hundreds of living earth goddesses still worshipped in tribal cultures around the world). Luisah Teish, author of *Jambalaya,* writes of the West African teaching that "We are all cells in the body of God."[6]

Immanence challenges our sense of values. When the sacred is immanent, each being has a value that is inherent, that cannot be diminished, rated, or ranked, that does not have to be earned or granted.

Immanence also shifts our definition of power. Power is not only power-over—the ability to manipulate, control and punish—but also power-from-within, the inherent ability each of us has to become what we are meant to be—as a seed has within it the inherent power to root, grow, flower, and fruit. Power-from-within is not limited and there is no scarcity of it in the universe. My power does not preclude your having power, rather my skills and knowledge may augment your own.

According to Teish, the Yoruba teaching is that we each have an original contract with creation, an individual "ache" or personal power. The rituals of Witchcraft also help us discover and develop our personal power, the unique gift we each have to bring to the world. But that power can only be fully realized when we respect the ache, the power-from-within, the inherent right to be, of all.

Personal power increases when we take on responsibility, and develops through our personal integrity, living our beliefs, acting on our ideas, striving for balance. We cannot gain power-from-within by trying to get something for nothing. Gifts carry with them a responsibility to return something. We give back energy we draw out of the cosmos—ultimately, we give back ourselves. If we learn from spiritual practices of a community—for example, from the Native American sweat lodge or the African bimbe—we only gain real power if we return energy and commitment to the real life, present-day struggles of those communities. Power-from-within must be grounded, that is, connected to the earth, to the actual material conditions of life, for the material world is the territory of the spirit in earth-based traditions.

Immanence is also a concept that works against the passivity sometimes attributed to spiritual philosophies. For when this world is seen as the living body of the Goddess, there is no escape, nowhere else to go, no one to save us. This earth body itself is the terrain of our spiritual growth and development, which come through our contact with the fullness of life inherent in the earth—with the reality of what's going on here. When what's going on is the poisoning and destruction of the earth, our own personal development requires that we grapple with that and do something to stop it, to turn the tide and heal the planet.

Inherent value extends to everyone. The full implications of this idea may make some of us uncomfortable. Those of us who live in North America, are white, and have class privilege, in particular, are used to living in a culture which values our lives much more highly than those of people in other countries, of people with darker skin, or of people with fewer economic advantages.

Earth-based spirituality values diversity. We learn from ecology that the more diverse a system, the more capacity it has for survival. But we have grown up in a world in which difference is associated with danger. To be different means to be lesser or greater, valued or valueless, conqueror or conquered.

The second base concept of earth-centered spirituality is that of interconnection. All parts of the living body of the earth are linked. All things are interconnected, including the human and natural worlds. Earth-based spirituality is based on our love for nature, our identification with the seasons, cycles, animals and plant communities.

This deep connectedness with all things translates into compassion, our ability to feel with and identify with others—human beings, natural cycles and processes, animals, and plants. Our definition of self expands, and we know that our own interests are linked to black people in South Africa as well as to forest-dwellers in the Amazon, and that their interests in turn are not separate from those of the eagle, the whale, and the grizzly bear.

Earth-based spirituality does not see human beings as separate from nature, nor does it imagine the human order and the natural order as opposites at war. The present social order, of course, serves interests inherently at odds with those of natural systems, but to change that order we must change the essential fallacy of thinking that we are somehow removed from nature. To ally ourselves with nature *against* human beings, as some environmentalists do, does nothing to challenge the essential split in our thinking. In the worldview of the earth religion, we *are* nature, and our human capacities of loyalty and love, rage and humor, lust, intuition, intellect, and compassion are as much a part of nature as the lizards and the redwood forests.

Interconnectedness also furnishes the basis for our political understanding. When we see the world as inherently interconnected, we also understand that political issues are not separable.

This understanding means that feminists, Pagans, and other individuals who have identified with the perspective of interconnection support many of the opinions expressed by environmentalists. For example, the headline of a recent article in the *Earth First! Journal* asks: "Is AIDS the Answer to an Environmentalist's Prayer?" Its author, Daniel Connor, proposes that "the AIDS virus may be Gaia's tailor-made answer to human overpopulation."[7] Similar views about famine have been expressed by Dave Foreman, one of Earth First!'s founders, who has opposed sending aid to famine victims in Africa.[8]

From the point of view of earth-based spirituality, such solutions are unacceptable because they deny compassion, and unethical because they violate the personal integrity we are called to by our understanding of the immanent presence of the sacred. The concept of integrity is colloquially expressed by the saying, "putting your money where your mouth is." In other words, we cannot propose, or accept, solutions that we are unwilling to practice ourselves. If we ourselves are eating, we cannot condone others starving. We cannot ask others to make sacrifices for the earth that we are unwilling to make ourselves, or take risks we are unwilling to share.

Another problem with such solutions to the population problem (aside from the echoes they evoke of other "final solutions") is that the people who are dying of environmental breakdowns, in the form of famines and disease, are those who have all along been written off by the dominant culture as having little or no value. We cannot shift the values of our culture by accepting, even unconsciously, its ranking of some human beings below others. We cannot restore inherent value to trees, wilderness, and earth unless we also restore it to every human being on the planet.

When environmentalists applaud the demise of Africans and homosexuals, they ally themselves with the same interests that are killing people of color, gay people, women, and other vulnerable groups. Those same interests are destroying the earth's ecosystems and raping the wilderness.

Narrow viewpoints and lack of awareness are dangerous to any movement, because they are essentially false, based on false understandings and misinformation. For example, to see famine as a process of nature is to remain ignorant of the historical reasons for drought and poor land use connected with colonialism and exploitation. Famine in Africa is human-caused, not natural, the result of political decisions to focus crop production on exports rather than subsistence, of misguided intervention by western experts teaching agricultural methods that disturbed ecological balances, of decisions by world economic institutions that encouraged underdeveloped countries to incur huge foreign debts which they must attempt to service, on all the economic and political structures which remove from people power to make decisions about their own lives. "Powerlessness lies at the very root of hunger," states Frances Moore Lappe in *World Hunger: Twelve Myths,* a book every ecologist should read.[9]

What both feminism and Paganism bring to ecology is that knowledge that every movement, to be effective in the defense of the earth, must see its interconnections with other movements and issues, for its own survival. Unless we understand the interrelationships of human systems of oppression, and the oppression of the earth, we cannot develop a strategy and program of political action that makes sense. It is in the interests of those who rule to prevent us from seeing these connections—because such knowledge is power. Famine in Africa is a critique of our policies, of the same agricultural practices that are turning the Midwest into a desert, of the values of profit over inherent value, gain over use, that are at the root of the exploitation of wilderness. We cannot save the wilderness without challenging those values. For as long as those values remain as the shapers of culture, the forces which produced famine in Africa will continue to produce it elsewhere, and the result will not be a peaceful or long-term drop in population, leaving the wilderness to the animals, but increased pressure to exploit marginal lands in ways that destroy their capacities to recover, as we see happening in the Amazon rainforests.

We might look at AIDS as we do the diseases and parasites that kill trees weakened by acid rain—as a symptom of a declining and increasingly toxic environment. (Leaving aside theories of more active and deliberate perpetuation.[10]) Again, the message of AIDS is one we cannot afford to ignore or misread. Our conscious or unconscious willingness to write off those we identify as "other"—our racism, homophobia, whatever—makes us stupid, keeps us focused on challenging the wrong structures and divided from those who might be our allies. Ignorance does not make for a winning strategy, nor is callousness a good foundation for a movement to heal the earth.

Compassion, our ability to feel with another, to value other lives as we value our own, to see ourselves as answerable and accountable to those who are different from us, has survival value. For, through compassion, we can open up a multifaceted view of the world that allows us to begin to understand problems in their true complexity.

Compassion allows us to identify powerlessness and the structures that perpetuate it as the root cause of famine, of overpopulation, of the callous destruction of the natural environment. From that understanding, we could develop strategies that challenge powerlessness in many arenas. We could develop alliances with those whose interests and issues parallel ours, strategies consonant with a Pagan sense of integrity.

The contribution of feminism to ecology is its critique of power relations. Feminists point out to ecologists that overpopulation is bound up with social structures that deny women power over their own bodies and options for their lives other than that of breeder. "The higher the level of female education, (and, therefore, of women's income and occupational status) the lower the birth rate. . . . A study done in Thailand in 1970 showed that women had about half as many children if they had received even five years of education than if they had received none. . . . all the women indicated that they would rather have had fewer [children] than they had had."[11] " . . . Rapid population growth results largely from the powerlessness of the poor," state Frances Moore Lappe and Joseph Collins in *World Hunger: Twelve Myths.* Their excellent discussion demonstrates that "population growth will only slow when far-reaching economic and political changes convince the majority of people that social arrangements *beyond the family*—jobs, health-care, old age security, and education (especially for women)—offer both security and opportunity.[12]

Mass death has never been an effective, long-term method of population reduction, any more than crash diets really help in losing weight. If it were, then surely World War II would have seen the end of the problem. The only sure way of reducing population is to increase the security of life, while opening opportunities for women for work, education, and public power. When women have the power to freely choose when, to whom, and how to bear children, when they can count on their children surviving to adulthood, when they do not need to fear poverty and loneliness in old age unless supported by their own progeny, populations decline. Feminists rightly question why environmentalists often fail to comment on this aspect of the population question.

Overpopulation is also connected to war. Governments restrict women's control over reproduction and enforce childbearing to ensure national strength on the battlefield. Any movement truly concerned with overpopulation would therefore necessarily become an antimilitarist movement as well.

An ecofeminist movement would address African famine in a multifaceted way: first, by supporting whatever effective immediate relief can be offered, because to deny food to the hungry is indecent. It destroys in us the capacities for compassion that are our only hope for the earth's survival. Nevertheless, we can be aware that such measures are, at best, temporary stopgaps, and begin pressuring for the political and economic changes that can support long-term recovery.

We could pressure for development aid that encourages ecological sensitivity, and appropriate technology that fits the climate, the soil, and the culture, that is oriented toward women who do much of the actual farming in Africa, that puts control of land and resources in the hands of the people who live on the land. And we can be aware that such measures would have economic reverberations that affect us, and be willing to make changes in our own lives.

A movement informed by the values of earth religion would address all issues in such multifaceted ways, and construct a political agenda that reflects our understanding of interconnections. What follows is my personal formulation, a sketch meant to stimulate thinking, not a final platform. Its order does not necessarily represent priorities of importance: a list is necessarily linear, but the issues are all interconnected.

Liberty and Justice for All

When we all have inherent worth, the institutions we create must recognize and defend that worth for everyone: women, men, children, and the aged; the dark-skinned and the light; the healthy and the ill; the strong and the disabled; those who live in industrialized societies and those who live in the Third World, in traditional Native cultures, and in the lands we have considered our enemies; lesbians, gay men, heterosexuals and bisexuals and omnisexuals as well as those who practice any religion and those who don't. And when we say "for all," we include the animals and plants and the environment itself as part of our community. And this value is not an abstraction, but becomes manifest in the opportunities we make available and the economic structures we create that can feed the hungry, shelter the homeless, provide health care and education to all as a right, and place the sacred value of each being above the right to exploit the earth and profit off other's labor. To do this, we need to construct a new economics, with sustainability as its base.

A Sustainable Livelihood for Everyone

Acknowledge that everyone has an equal right to the gifts of the earth and the accumulated labor of the past. Everyone has a right to a sustainable livelihood. Transform the economic system accordingly. Support land reform in Third World countries and reduce economic pressures that force production for export; support development projects and programs that focus on the needs of women and children, and that favor those who produce food for subsistence. Support small farms in this country and the restructuring of Third World debts to take pressure off land to produce exports. Create appropriate technology to provide subsistence and meaningful work abundantly rewarded. Provide jobs and education for women and men who have been denied them. Support small businesses and collective enterprises. Devote research money to new technologies that use renewable resources.

A Sustainable Environment for Everyone

End nuclear weapons, nuclear power, the dumping of toxins, the cutting down of the Amazon rainforest, the logging of old-growth forests everywhere, the further development of wilderness and the sacred lands of Native peoples. End military intervention and colonial adventurism that destroy and maim human beings, degrade the environment, and waste resources. Control industrial and agricultural processes that pollute the environment, cause acid rain, and destroy air and water quality. Change to agricultural processes that build and preserve soil, and to technologies appropriate to the human and natural environment. Preserve wildlife and wilderness.

Support a Multiplicity of Spiritual Directions

How? Basically, by not interfering with the practices of groups or individuals as long as they don't interfere with the rights of others; by countering stereotypes and educating people about earth-based spiritualities; by protecting the land, the wilderness, and the ancient sacred places of all traditions; by not allowing privileges to some traditions that are denied others; and, basically, by keeping church and state separate. Earth-based spirituality should never be inflicted on anyone. If and when we can truly practice our traditions openly, without fear or prejudice, those who are drawn to our ways will find us easily. Those who aren't will find a way that fits them.

I do not envision these changes happening easily or gracefully. How do we envision changes happening? People cling to power, wealth, and privilege, and cannot necessarily see that they might benefit, in the long run, by sharing more equally. But our belief in the immanent value of all, and our understanding that the means we use themselves determine the ends we will create, place inherent restrictions on the means of persuasion we can use.

The shift we need to make is both a shift in consciousness and a major restructuring of all the institutions of society. We need to engage in active, nonviolent resistance to the destruction being mounted all around us. At the same time, we need to develop and make real our alternative visions; start the businesses, live in the households, grow the gardens that embody our ideals. In so doing, we can experiment with our ideals on a small scale and find out if they actually work in practice.

In all of this, we need support and community. The rituals of earth religions are tools we can use to bond together, as are common work and common struggle. The communities we create must themselves be structured in ways that embody our ideals.[13]

Feminist spirituality, earth-based spirituality, is not just an intellectual exercise, it's a practice. For those of us called to this way, our rituals let us enact our visions, create islands of free space in which we can each be affirmed, valued for our inherent being. In ritual we can feel our interconnections with all levels of being, and mobilize our emotional energy and passion toward transformation and empowerment. We can bring a new sense of play, music, rhythm, and communal feeling to political work. And when we get wild and silly together, we learn not to take ourselves too seriously.

Transformation is inherently creative, and each of us is part of the creative being who is the universe herself. Although the structures of war and domination are strongly entrenched, they must inevitably change, as all things change. We can become agents of that transformation, and bring a new world to birth.

Endnotes

1. Riane Eisler, *The Chalice and the Blade*, Harper & Row, San Francisco, 1987, xvii.
2. A thorough survey of the symbolism of early European Goddess cultures is found in Marija Gimbutas, *The Goddesses and Gods of Old Europe*, University of California Press, Berkeley, 1982.
3. Further information about the Witch persecutions can be found in Starhawk, *Dreaming the Dark: Magic, Sex, and Politics*, Beacon Press, Boston, 1982, 183-219. Another important work on this period is Carolyn Merchant, *The Death of Nature: Women, Ecology and the Scientific Revolution*, Harper & Row, San Francisco, 1980. See also: David Kubrin, "Newton's Inside Out: Magic, Class Struggle and the Rise of Mechanism in the West," in Harry Woolf, ed., *The Analytic Spirit*, Cornell University Press, Ithaca, NY, 1981.
4. The literature on feminist spirituality is too vast to be referenced here, but some works reflecting the variety of approaches are: Carol Christ and Judith Plaskow, *Womanspirit Rising*, Harper & Row, San Francisco, 1979; Charlene Spretnak, ed., *The Politics of Women's Spirituality*, Anchor, Garden City, NY, 1982; Starhawk, *The Spiral Dance: Rebirth of the Ancient Religion of the Goddess*, Harper & Row, San Francisco, 1979; Merlin Stone, *Ancient Mirrors of Womanhood*, Beacon Press, Boston, 1979; and Luisah Teish, *Jambalaya*, Harper & Row, San Francisco, 1985.
5. For further exploration of the building of spiritual/political community, see: Starhawk, *Truth or Dare: Encounters with Power, Authority and Mystery*, Harper & Row, San Francisco, 1987.
6. Personal communication in a course entitled "The Wisdom of Native Spiritualities," taught at the Institute for Culture and Creation Spirituality, Oakland, CA, fall 1987.
7. Daniel Connor, "Is AIDS the Answer to an Environmentalist's Prayer?" *Earth First!* Yule Edition, December 27, 1987, Vol. VIII, No. II, p. 16.
8. Although I disagree with some of the opinions expressed in its journal, I also consider *Earth First!* to be the most exciting and effective environmental group around,

because of its commitment to direct action, decentralized organizing, and uncompromising defense of wilderness. It deserves support as well as loving criticism from feminists and Pagans.

9. Frances Moore Lappe and Joseph Collins, *World Hunger: Twelve Myths*, Grove Press, New York, 1986, p. 4.

10. For a full discussion of several alternative theories regarding the origins of the AIDS virus, including the germ warfare theory, see *Covert Action Information Bulletin*, No. 28, summer 1987.

11. Lisa Leghorn and Katharine Parker, *Woman's Worth: Sexual Economics and the World of Women*, Routledge & Kegan Paul, Boston, 1981, p. 96.

12. Lappe and Collins, op.cit., p. 26

13. I'm running out of space in this article, but a much fuller discussion of resistance, renewal and the structuring of community can be found in my latest book, *Truth or Dare: Encounters with Power, Authority and Mystery*, Harper & Row, San Francisco, 1987.

PART FOUR
THE CIRCLE IS GATHERING:
ECOFEMINIST COMMUNITY

> What community may be is humanity's next evolutionary step, giving
> more and more people the opportunity to live in ways consistent with
> our deepest needs. If we can understand those needs, and practice
> what it takes to meet them, we can find the strength to grow, and
> perhaps also to bring about the kind of changes that must be made
> if the planet is to survive. —Helen Forsey, "Community—Meeting
> Our Deepest Needs"

Reclaiming our natural right to care for each other and the place in
which we live is the fundamental building block of ecofeminist
community. If we are to get beyond alienated, self-interested society,
our daily life has to reflect the values we espouse. For just as it is true
to say that what we do to the web we do to ourselves, so it is also the
case that what we do to each other, we do to the world around us.
Therefore, the less we participate in and depend upon the institutions
and governments which oppress people and place, and instead rely on
our own communities, the more we live with integrity and self-
determination. As well, our communities, too, must be creating a
truly new social fabric based on valuing differences and the
interdependence of all of life, not simply repeating the same oppressive
social patterns of the old order.

This final section reflects the immediate need to incorporate the
understandings of ecological feminism into our lives, thus transforming
our individual selves and our communities, and grounding us in an
understanding of all our relations. Dorothy Dinnerstein urges us to
see that our present uses of gender, which feminism challenges, keep

both sexes infantile and that they must change to allow human beings to assume collective responsibility for the well-being of all of life. The work of Joanna Macy provides some of the theory and practice that will take us beyond our separate and fragile selves. Helen Forsey takes us on a personal journey toward community life showing how, for her, it has developed quite naturally out of ecofeminist ideals. As feminists, the process of how we make decisions becomes as important as the decisions themselves. In an interview with Caroline Estes, consensus and community are linked as features of sustainable human organization. Margo Adair and Sharon Howell look at patterns of power in personal relationships as a reflection of patterns of domination that permeate our society. They suggest ways to break out of these kinds of interactions, enabling the building of life-affirming communities. And lastly, I provide glimpses of a rural community's life, telling stories of one group's struggle to come together, working with new-found power from-within, valuing cultural differences with Indian friends, and learning the meaning of kindred love.

Lost Arrows
and the Feather People
Ursula K. LeGuin

                          Small claws of an acorn woodpecker
                          In the roofpeak over my head:
                          squawks and purring, "wackawacka,"
                          exploratory taps
                          on the housewall.

If it, if they're right, is war,
life in a battle, every kitchen
Iwo Jima, and the bed Thermopylae,
then we have to be warriors—winners
or else won, prizes, Sabines slung
like quarters of mutton behind the he-roes.
We have to be armed.
Every kid a Colt, a .22,
machineguns for the grownups,
bombs for the real biggies,
the bossmen, los generales.
All chiefs. No injuns.

                          The mourning dove
                          calls in the digger pines
                          across the creek
                          across the rainy air.

Why do I keep thinking
you can, if you just know how,
and it takes luck too, what doesn't—choose.
Instead of being drafted or enlisting
and bearing arms in defense of god and cunt
and los generales, choose to be
not a hero. To be
something else. What else?
A deserter?

                          Sun has gleamed out.
                          A silent wind
                          stirs wet branches.
                          From the big oak's new limegreen
                          leaves, soft-lobed,
                          drops bright water.

A hippie? A victim?
Somebody there isn't any use for.
A civilian?

"Wackawackawackawacka!"
in the oakworlds, the leafnations,
the dwelling places of the people
with red-feathered heads,
always joking and talking.

A squaw, maybe.
Yes. But one who doesn't yippiyi
when the braves ride back
waving scalps, who doesn't watch
the wardance, doesn't give a shit.

Lice, squabbles, acorns.
Always joking and talking.

Why do I keep thinking
about courage, about honor,
things I know nothing about?
But if honor, if they're wrong, is what
is lost in battle?

The black-capped chickadee
speaks a few times
clearly,
as if teaching a language.

O Arjuna,
if we used our hunger,
used our anger, otherwise?
Rilke the poet said, "a *falling* happiness,"
and turned the world over for me.
Turning the world over in my hands
in tai chi turning
from right to left, from up to down,
I keep wondering about an honor
that might, with luck, if you knew how,
be like the new leaves of oak trees,
tender; about a valor
that would not withstand, but run away,
downhill, as easy as creek water.
If soul knew not to let itself be lost
as falling rain is lost,
what would be lost?

The hawk is back,
to cry her hungry two notes
over the wild pastures
where the deermice
walk in their dwelling places.
The hawk is back
and angry.
She stoops to kill,
falls
like an arrow of bright rain.

As rain is lost
and runs away
into the world.

Well, it is so,
probably, almost certainly;
but I wish I could hear it
not only from woodpecker and chickadee,
see it not only in the barred wind-feather,
know it not only in the deermouse kiva,

but also in the words
and in the ways
and dwelling places
of my own people.

20

Survival on Earth:
The Meaning of Feminism

Dorothy Dinnerstein

Webster's[1] defines feminism as "a. the theory that women should have political, economic and social rights equal to those of men; b. the movement to win such rights for women." But in a human realm whose dictionaries define as a "theory"—i.e. a debatable idea—the notion that women should have such rights, feminism must define itself in terms far broader than this: other core changes, in such a realm, are inseparable from change in our uses of gender. Women whose energies are focused on achieving equality within the status quo—within a short-term future, that is, in which present social reality continues otherwise essentially unaltered—are hoping for what cannot happen.

Indeed, "status quo" is itself a weird misnomer for our present collective condition. The reality we inhabit—the reality within which I write this and you read it: our driven predatory depersonalized human realm, fragile and frantic, blind with passion to prevail, fanatically greedy, rigidly and mortally coercive—is surely anything but stable. We are moving fast—nose-diving—toward ecological catastrophe and/ or nuclear Armegeddon. If we cannot pull out of this nose-dive the short term future can evaporate at any moment. And to pull out of it—to avert the death of living earthly reality—means mustering a huge, a miraculous, spurt of human growth and change: fast change; change within persons and within intimate groups, and change in the nature of the larger societal units (cultural, economic, political and regional) on whose level the developments we call historic take place.

What happens in those larger societal units happens in three-way interaction with developments within persons and within intimate groups. It would be folly, I think, to suppose that we can mastermind the outcome, or even identify all the crucial features, of this process. An adequate overview of the changes that might make it possible for earthly life to go on now is not within our mental reach; our pooled intelligence—even with the prosthetic extensions which it has so cleverly devised for itself, and of which it is so stupidly proud—falls far short of that task.[2] Such an overview might well tell us that there is no chance—none at all—for this planet's organic fuzz to outlive the twentieth century. What I am discussing here, then, are some *necessary* conditions for a living earthly future. What the *sufficient* conditions are is another question, and maybe we're lucky not to know the answer to it. *Without hope—open-eyed hope, which by definition embodies uncertainty and counsels action, not blind hope which is passive and shuns available fact—we are already dead.* And an equal-rights-for-women stance that remains oriented to an otherwise unchanged social reality *is* blind hope: hope resigned, on some silent level of feeling, to the truth of what it denies: the imminence of world-murder. It is a business-as-usual strategy; a self-deceptive device for whiling away time; a blind to-do; a solemn fuss about concerns that make no sense if we have no future, as the end of earthly life draws closer (an end that is bound to come sometime, but why now? and why at human hands?). Surely one should, at every moment, choose: fiddle frankly while Rome burns (because music is intrinsic to the moment; like love, it fulfills itself by being made; sing "I am! I am!" while bearing witness to your world's annihilation) or try to put the fire out. Business-as-usual, which carries intrinsic reference to a future, is blank denial, the most primitive of those defense mechanisms that Freud challenged us to outgrow.

Feminism is a living movement, I am saying, a movement honest with itself, only insofar as it embodies active radical try-to-put-the-fire-out hope; active long-shot optimism, based on the widest knowledge we have—tentative, partial knowledge—and on love for the widest reality that human feeling at its mammalian core can authentically embrace—earth life; optimism that has faced the possibility of failure, and felt through (come to terms with, and put in its proper place) the silent hatred of Mother Earth which breathes side by side with our love for her, and which, like the hate we feel for our human mothers, poisons our attachment to life.

Central to a humanly whole feminist vision is awareness that our traditional uses of gender form part of an endemic mental and societal disorder; part of the everyday psychopathology, the normal taken-for-granted mishugas, that is killing our world. Not only do our old sexual arrangements maim and exploit women, and stunt and deform men, the human way of life that they support moves, by now, toward the final matricide—the rageful, greedy murder of the planet that spawned us—and seems bent on reaching out into space for new planets to kill. In doing what we do with gender we humans not only constrict and distort ourselves; we also rape and desecrate earthly nature, and threaten to lay waste, as fast as we can get to it, to whatever may be alive in outer space. I say "we humans," not "those men," because while it is of course mainly men, not women, whose military and economic games threaten to decreate what our grandparents called Creation, they play these games with tacit female consent. Maybe we could not stop them if we tried. But so far we have not found ways to try—not on the scale which could make such effort realistic rather than purely symbolic/expressive.

As girls, we were trained, shaped, schooled to become the responsibly nurturant members of the human family, alert to the needs of vulnerable, dependent beings.[3] Now grown up, rejecting that old male-female division of responsibility, but equipped still with the traditional skills we were taught; demanding that men and boys must learn them too, but aware that time is short and such learning inexorably slow; knowing that the public realm, which men still rule, is in mortal trouble, and the earth itself a vulnerable being, a vitally endangered creature, needy, damaged already, and dependent on human protection from further human assault—now, at this moment, we crazy feminists may well be the most sanely conscious little part of our ailing lifeweb. From the perspective of this consciousness, what feminism most urgently means is something very much broader than the right to equal pay for equal work, or to orgasm (though such rights are of course essential parts of it). It means *withdrawing from old forms of male-female collaboration, not only because they restrict female access to some major sources of power, status, and pleasure,[4] but now, most centrally, because they express and support the insanity that is killing the world.* And it means *mobilizing wisdoms and skills with which our female history has equipped us, and focusing them upon the chance that this worldmurder can be interrupted—stopped; reversed—and human life re-ordered: re-worked into forms harmonious with those we now threaten to smash:* forms as shapely as trees and stately as gorillas; as elegant as giraffes and exuberant as coral reefs; as gaily wise as elephants and whales; as loving and free as lions and housecats; as green as grass, and brave as flowers.

The core meaning of feminism, I am saying, lies, at this point, in its relation to earthly life's survival. Equal rights goals matter, first of all, because they have to do with psychic growth, fast growth, growth away from the infantilisms, male and female, which support and are supported by our old uses of gender, and toward human responsibility; responsibility for our own self-creation; for our complex and internally contradictory bodily and psychic traits; for the place we have carved out for ourselves in the earthly lifeweb; and for the life and death power over nature that has come to lie in our ingenious, unwise hands. Feminism is a crucial human project—a project worthier of adult passion than war or the manufacture of plastic bottles—only insofar as it moves us toward outgrowing the mental birth defect, the normal psychopathology, that makes us so deadly a danger, now, to the living realm that spawned us; the birth defect that makes us—clever, inventive, affectionate, tool-using ape-cousins who seem to have "dreamed ourselves into existence"[5]; sociable, playful mammals who laugh, weep, talk, talk, and talk—an ecological cancer, and a nuclear time bomb, in the body of the earth.

At the heart of this birth defect, at the core of human malaise, is scared refusal to believe that we *are*, in fact, collectively self-made beings, responsible for our own existence; culture-dependent, two-legged primates whose crucial biological assets—our brains and our hands—are usable only insofar as we acquire, through learning, the prosthetic equipment which, over eons, we ourselves (our human and proto-human ancestors, that is) seem collectively to have fashioned; perishable equipment, easily lost forever; equipment upon which we so heavily rely that without it the creatures we seem slowly to have become as we brought it slowly into being would be too disabled to reconstruct it; tools, skills, language and the concepts it carries, and pooled knowledge of earthly fact; detachable equipment, progressively elaborated, refined, and extended, the beginnings of which seem apt to have taken shape in tandem—in back and forth interdependence—with the evolution of our complex central nervous systems, our upright bodies, and our subtle, versatile hands.[6]

This human fear of facing human self-creation—this core refusal of our collective responsibility; responsibility for what we are, for the realm we have made, and for the earthly lifeweb that has nurtured our existence; all of which we now seem about to wipe out—stands face to face, at this point, with what the psychically androgenous Mumford, at eighty,[7] begged us to mobilize: "mammalian tenderness and human love." It is a confrontation implicit in every part of world-conscious human life and central, I think, in feminism, which is (among other things) a bid for female sharing of public power. *But the question for women is what kind of public power we want to share: the kind that is killing the world or the kind that is focused on keeping the world alive?*

These contrasting modes of power—life-hostile power, bent on damaging what it cannot kill or control (polluting, maiming, reducing it; desecrating or degrading it; boxing it in) and nurturant power, which cherishes the freedom and integrity and health of what it loves—seem to have coexisted, till this century, in fragile balance.[8] World War I, followed in my lifetime by Hitler, Hiroshima, and the steadily growing weight of world-killing machinery since Hiroshima—the stockpiled thunderbolts of a crazed and dimwitted Jove; enough of them by now to denude the earth of life how many times over?—herald a fateful tipping of that fragile balance.

Can this tipping conceivably still be righted, reversed? The runaway societal-technological trends that underlie it are of course fueled in large part by malignant human impulses, impulses to realize the old enraged eye-closing thumb-sucking infantile-omnipotent dream of making the world go away, of shutting it out or wiping it out, since it refuses to obey the baby's wishes.[9] Still, what fuels a trend need not wholly steer history. Clearly, devices for wholesale death are metastasizing, and international political machinery moving us—heavily, steadily—toward extinction. But human impulses toward the protection of life, impulses more volatile than political machinery, more flexible and agile, may at the same time be gathering momentum; we may yet mobilize Eros, put Thanatos in its proper psychic place[10] and turn the deathly tide.

Feminism has bearing on this gathering of momentum—feminism is a vital part, that is, of current history—only insofar as feminism spells out, and embodies in its practice, the links between change in our uses of gender and reversal of our descent into nuclear and/or ecological hell. Maybe—who knows?—we can still manage this reversal. But doing so means starting to outgrow normal human psychopathology: starting, in other words, to surmount ordinary moral cowardice and mental sloth. It means repudiating violence, active and passive, and renouncing coercive exploitative lifeways—using our rage, like our shit, not for ammunition as our monkey cousins do, but humanly: to fertilize green growth. It means mobilizing the core interest and empathy which (alongside anger, fear and cannibalistic cravings) we feel toward each other; our impulse to understand and comfort and forgive each other; our built-in attraction to the humanly created human realm (the realm to whose presence our large brains, upright posture and clever hands refer, just as our eyes refer to light and our ears to sound); and our protective filial concern for earthly nature.

Such mobilization would take all the strengths we could muster. It would draw on the traditional talents which women and men, respectively, now embody: talents whose exercise in our present extremity might hasten their merging (and thereby deepening) inside each human skin. It would call forth the energy we need—all of us, in all the earth's nations—to start changing our old uses of gender, uses that now support the infantile violence and greed, the infantile fusion of irresponsibility and felt omnipotence, that are killing our world. And it would foster those new strengths, those new forms of resourcefulness, which would start to take shape as we worked out new modes of community and primary-group life.[11]

Men, for example—far more, on balance, than women—have traditionally felt responsible for the public realm. They have embodied skills for speaking out in this realm: skills for foreseeing, and summarizing, historic event; for articulating moral and philosophical principles; for organizing broad collective action. With some impressive and instructive exceptions, it is men, throughout recorded political and religious history, who have been the main leaders and rulers, the main prophets and priests.

Indeed it is mainly men—a few highly gifted men: in our own time, men like Freud, Mumford, Norman Brown—who have been in a position to articulate in the public realm the counter-considerations that women in private life—many women, ordinary women—have all along embodied; the counter-considerations which, taken seriously, limit human enthusiasm for human (mainly male human) exploit: the doubts that women, within safe boundaries, have all along powerlessly ventilated in a running critique, a subordinates' critique, sealed off from the flow of formal historic event to which it refers. This societal safety valve, this "court jester" mechanism,[12] has channelled off potentially subversive female energy, and at the same time vicariously ventilated truant male misgivings, letting the male-steered stream of public events move undeflected—and with substantial tacit female consent,[13] we must remember—toward what by now looks like all-but-inevitable nuclear and/or ecological hell. Can this sealed-off subordinate critique become part of that stream of overt public event in time to redirect its flow? Maybe it can; but for this to happen, the critique itself must be extended. What a few male critics of male exploit have all along been saying in public, and innumerable female court jesters in private—that history-making is shot through with crazy, life-hostile urges—omits mention of a basic concomitant of those lethal urges: if we want to renounce them, we must change what we do with gender. Since such change means abolition of male privilege (privilege to which wise and kind men, as well as mean and foolish ones, are deeply addicted), men are understandably slow to grasp its bearing, now, on earthly life's fate.

Indeed we female jesters ourselves, once we start to grasp this bearing, must either put up or shut up. Self-respect tells us to choose: throw away our clown hats, dive deep, and surface as feminist survival activists, or praise our lords and pass the final ammunition. What becomes clear is that the misgivings women have all along been ventilating—the critique we have ambivalently mumbled, in private, about the realm where "with streaming banners noble deeds are done"—must now be articulated in a more responsible, actively insurgent public context; a context embodying change in our old uses of gender. Central to such change, wherever women and men live together, is movement toward male sharing of the life-maintaining, nurturant work that women have all along done: intimate, personal work that will be in important ways transformed—as will world-making public work as well—when that public realm's demands are fused with the demands of fragile, growing young life.

Such change will necessarily take time. But its beginning, if that beginning is strong, announces a deep turn toward life. It is a commitment to the future which alters the present, like pledging allegiance or planting trees. [14]

We are feminists, then, for many reasons; but feminism matters now, most centrally, because the old uses of gender that it challenges have kept human beings, no matter how busily and well they work at their everyday tasks, humanly feckless. They have helped both sexes stay infantile, helped us deny collective responsibilities which we can escape at this point only by dying off (or by moving off into space, some folks must dimly feel; but see footnote 15.) [15]

The possibility that we may after all pull through this emergency— that there may after all continue to be a warm brainy human race, rooted in a sweet earthly lifeweb—depends on the rate at which we can break through the collective developmental stalemate, the collective refusal of responsibility, of which our old uses of gender are a core expression: refusal of responsibility for our own self-creation, and refusal of responsibility to keep the lovely living earth—now mortally imperilled by our foolish cleverness, our callow nastiness, our silly self-conceit, our brute compulsion to prevail—alive.

What survival now demands, in sum, is fast steps—fast giant steps— toward growing up. And a necessary condition for such growth is change in our uses of gender. This is a kind of change which most men, bound and blinded by cast privilege, tend to resist; although— and also *because*—it promises to deepen their humanity, to free them from warping constraints, they by and large fear it. So the task of initiating these fast giant steps—the task of mobilizing human life-love and starting to outgrow the species-specific mental birth defect of which our uses of gender are part and our assault on the ecosphere an expression; the task of focusing human energy on protection of the lifeweb for whose fate we humans have by now, willy-nilly, made ourselves responsible—is a task, at this point, which rests largely in female hands. What happens next may well depend on us.

Endnotes

1. Ref. Webster
2. Ref. Worldwatch and Global 2000: these useful surveys suggest both the dimensions of our survival problems and the impossibility of knowing whether or not coordinated human effort could still, at this point, bring them under control.
3. Ref. Chodorow, Gilligan, Ruddick
4. —and constrict male existence, of course, in ways at least equally maiming: so maiming that the victim is typically unaware of the constriction.
5. Ref. Mumford Reflections
6. Ref. Washburn's *Tools and Human Evolution*. Also *Man Makes Himself*. Archeologic findings since *Tools and Human Evolution* are ambiguous, but I think this still remains the most plausible hypothesis, unless we fall back on creationism as an explanatory principle.)
7. op.cit.
8. Mumford described this unsteady balance in "Culture of Cities" and "The Myth of the Machine." Freud analyzes its psychic roots in *Civilization and Its Discontents*. Brown continued that analysis in *Life Against Death*. Women writers of widely varying perspectives and sensibilities, Colette, Woolf, and de Beauvoir, for example, throughout their work, compare its expression in female and male experience.
9. Some people—these days probably most—shut the world out. Partly or wholly, they even now deny the real probability of earthly life's destruction, and in that way—on some dark split-off mental level maybe willingly—increase that possibility: being alive and human can get to feel like more trouble thàn it's worth. Others, maddened by assault on their need to prevail, seem wholly and overtly willing to wipe the world out. Vengeance for reality's refusal to confirm infantile omnipotence can be either active or passive, that is: it can be either assaultive or withdrawing. In this respect the quiet apathy of the apolitical masses and the reckless bellicosity of an active Reaganite have much in common.
10. i.e., a more tolerable place. What this place should be for humans (as compared with other intelligent beings who seem in some way aware of death: apes, whales and elephants, for instance, who have memory, foresight and imagination but not, apparently, culture or history—not the sense, that is, of a cumulatively evolving social reality) is a question for which our old religious answers have never been wholly adequate. If they had, we would not have been moving, all along, toward our present mortal crisis. It is a question whose meaning we need time to come to better terms with—more time than we now seem likely to have. Yet even a small step toward such a coming-to-terms, a sense of movement in that direction, might at this moment be crucial. (Ref. Brown: "using the death instinct"—whatever that is—"to die with.")
11. It feels crazy to be writing this. How—by what benign wildfire contagion—could it happen? Yet how could we live if we agreed there was no chance it could happen? Maybe nonactivists' secret hope is that something the crazy activists do will turn the unthinkable tide, with whose approach all of us (in our varying, but mostly numb and silent ways) are obsessed. And surely what activists have to hope—what saner hope is possible?—is that this "something" will be the massive worldwide burst of constructive energy that the aging Freud challenged us to muster. Quote from *Civilization and Its Discontents*.
12. Ref. *Mermaid and the Minotaur*, chapter 19.
13. It is vital, clearly, that this tacit female consent be withdrawn: that our old complicitous grumble (maternal, but cowed; unimpressed, but self-deprecating; worried, but sheepishly proud of our big boys; amused by their silly bravado, but protective of their tender egos; afraid *for* them, but afraid *of* them; angry and contemptuous, but deferent; doubtful, but dazzled) become active, unqualified resistance. Those bully boys are killing us, and our children, and the earth's sweet

plants and beasts—and we, human and standing by, share by default their guilt. Standing by, we are co-responsible for their lying and their stealing, their predation and pollution, their ravaging assault on everything that lives: co-responsible, by default, for the murder of earthly reality.

14. As I and others have pointed out (e.g. Ruddick, Gilligan, Chodorow), this and some of its concomitants are among the centrally necessary conditions for the kind of human societal change that might allow our grandchildren to grow old, our coral reefs to flourish, and elephants to multiply in large green spaces.

15. Enthusiasm for space travel is rooted, I think, in hostility to earthly life. And how I wish that folks possessed by this enthusiasm could just buzz off and leave this boring green ball to us who want no other home! If—if—space journeys were launched from a thriving sturdy earthlife lifeweb—from a mother-planet unthreatened by human short-sightedness life-hatred and greed—I would ask only that astronautical enthusiasts go away, enjoy their hobby, and leave the rest of us in peace: that self-important cosmic comings and goings be governed by some simple rules of courtesy and justice: that they be paid for by folks who want them to happen and can afford the wild expense, not by hungry children and lonely impoverished old women and displaced demoralized Native Americans and desperate migrant farm workers; and that they manage not to be the noisy nuisance they now are to planetary homebodies like me. As things are, astronautical ardor smells vile to me. It stinks of matricide: of sweet baby boys gone ugly.

21
Awakening to the Ecological Self

Joanna Macy

I believe that we are summoned now to awaken from a spell. The spell we must shake off is a case of mistaken identity, a millennia-long amnesia as to who we really are. We have imagined that we are separate and competitive beings, limited to the grasp of our conscious egos, hence essentially fragile, endlessly needy. This delusion has brought us some high adventures, but also much suffering, and it will destroy us and our world if we don't wake up in time.

For our own sakes and the sake of all beings, we are called to rediscover our true nature, coextensive with all life on this planet. We are called to break out of the prison we've made for ourselves, turn the key of that isolation cell, and walk out into the world as into our own heart, coming home to the full reach of our being, home to our power, home to our ecological self.

The Roar of Awakening

This is happening. An ecological selfhood is emerging. I feel it in myself; I see it in my sisters and my brothers as, out of deep concern over what is happening to our world, they begin to speak and act on its behalf.

The larger, ecological sense of self and self-interest is especially, and dramatically, evident in the many actions where people put their lives on the line for another species. I see it in my sisters of the Chipko or "tree-hugging" movement in Northern India as they risk injury and death to protect the remaining woodlands, blocking the axes and chainsaws with their bodies. I see it in the Greenpeace sailors as they put their frail, bobbing rubber boats in the way of the giant factory ships, so that the whales can escape to the depths of the sea. In such campaigns, conventional, customary notions of self and self-interest are being shed like an old skin or confining shell.

One day, under the vine-strung jungle trees of eastern Australia, I was walking with my friend John Seed, director of the Rainforest Information Center. I asked him how he managed to overcome despair and sustain the struggle against the mammoth lumber interests. He said, "I try to remember that it's not me, John Seed, trying to protect the rainforest. Rather I am part of the rainforest protecting myself, I am that part of the rainforest recently emerged into human thinking."

This ecological sense of selfhood combines the mystical and the pragmatic. Transcending separateness and fragmentation, in a shift that Seed calls a "spiritual change," it generates an experience of profound interconnectedness with all life. This has in the past been largely relegated to the domain of mystics and poets. Now it is, at the same time, a motivation to action. The shift in identity serves as ground for effective engagement with the forces and pathologies that imperil us.

In our confusion as to our true nature, we are like the tiger cub in the ancient Indian fable. His mother having died in childbirth, the orphaned cub was adopted by a herd of wild goats, who suckled and raised it as one of their own. He learned to bleat and graze, although it was hard to nibble grass with pointed teeth and the vegetarian diet kept him thin and meek. One night a fierce old female tiger attacked the herd, which fled in all directions—except for the cub who just stood there, gazing at this apparition and devoid of fear. Then he bleated and bit off some grass. "Why are you making that silly sound?" roared the old tiger, "What are you chewing? What are you doing here among those goats?" And when she was answered by a few pathetic "baaa's," she seized the cub by the scruff of the neck and carried him first to a pond, to see his own reflection on the surface of the water, and then to her cave. There she forced between his teeth a piece of raw meat, the appropriate food for a tiger. The cub gagged and tried to spit it out, but catching a taste of the blood, began to chew and swallow, feeling an unfamiliar gratification. A strange, glowing strength went through his body. He arose and gave a mighty yawn, as if awakening from a long sleep. Stretching his legs, spreading his paws, lashing his tail, he released from his throat the tremendous and triumphant roar of tiger.

For most of us, I hasten to add, the awakening recognition of our forgotten identity involves the cessation, rather than the onset, of meat-eating, but it brings the same kind of release. It brings release from a false and confining notion of self. In our case, unlike the tiger cub, the false self-concept has become an extremely dangerous one; it is fundamental, I believe, to the crises that threaten our planet.

The crises of our planet-time, whether viewed in military or ecological or social terms, result from a dysfunctional and pathogenic concept of self. It is a mistake about our place in the order of things. It is the delusion that the self is so separate and fragile that we must delineate and defend its boundaries, that it is so small and needy that we must endlessly acquire and endlessly consume, that it is so aloof that we can—as individuals, corporations, nation-states or as a species—be immune to what we do to other beings.

As Deena Metzger writes,

> A fundamental question of our time is whether we can conquer the personal ego so that we can conquer the cultural, religious and species egos as well. I do not know if Judaism or Christianity can encompass the idea that neither the sun nor the human is the center of the universe. In this century we must be broken as violently as we were broken by the vision of Copernicus and Bruno, echoed, fearfully, by Galileo.

Metzger is right. Yet I want to add that my own sense of what is required and what is beginning to happen is not so much a "being broken" as a being released, a humbling but also gratifying shift to a more expansive, accommodating and joyous identity.

A variety of factors converge in our time to promote such a shift in the sense of self and self-interest. Among the most significant are 1) the psychological and spiritual pressures exerted by current dangers of mass annihilation, 2) the emergence from science of the systems view of the world, and 3) a renaissance of nondualistic forms of spirituality. These three developments also contribute strongly to the ecofeminist movement itself.

The courses I teach and the workshops I lead focus attention on these three factors—planetary peril, systems thinking and nondualistic religions, specifically Buddhist teachings and practice—and use them as vehicles in facilitating the shift to the ecological self. Let's look at them in turn to see how.

Personal Response to Planetary Crisis

The shift toward a wider, ecological sense of self is in large part a function of the dangers that threaten to overwhelm us. Given accelerating environmental destruction and massive deployment of nuclear weapons, people today are aware that they live in a world that can end. For example, public opinion polls indicate that over half the population expects nuclear weapons to be used, and two-thirds believe that once they are used, the resultant nuclear war cannot be limited, won, or survived. The loss of certainty that there will be a future is, I believe, the pivotal psychological reality of our time.

Over the past ten years my colleagues and I have worked with scores of thousands of people in North America, Europe, Asia and Australia, helping them confront and explore what they know and feel about what is happening to their world. The purpose of this work, known as "Despair and Empowerment Work," is to overcome the numbing and powerlessness that result from suppression of painful responses to massively painful realities.

As their grief and fear of the world is allowed to be expressed without apology or argument, and validated as a wholesome, life-preserving response, people break through their avoidance mechanisms, break through their sense of futility and isolation. And generally what they break *into* is a larger sense of identity. It is as if the pressure of their acknowledged awareness of the suffering of our world stretches, or collapses, the culturally defined boundaries of the self.

It becomes clear, for example, that the grief and fear experienced for our world and our common future is categorically different from similar sentiments relating to one's personal welfare. This pain cannot be equated with dread of one's own individual demise. Its source lies less in concerns for personal survival than in apprehensions of collective suffering—of what looms for human life and other species and unborn generations to come. Its nature is akin to the original meaning of compassion: "suffering with." It is the distress we feel on behalf of the larger whole of which we are a part.

I have learned through my work that there is immeasurable pain in our society—a pain carried at some level by each and every individual— over what is happening to our world and our future. Given our culture's fear of pain and the high value it sets on optimism, feelings of despair are repressed. Hidden like a secret sore, they breed a sense of isolation. But when one's pain for the world is redefined as compassion, it serves as a trigger or gateway to a more encompassing sense of identity. It is seen as part of the connective tissue that binds us to all beings. The self is experienced as inseparable from the web of life in which we are as intricately interconnected as cells in a larger body.

Such a view of the human condition is not new, nor is the felt imperative to extend self-interest to embrace the whole in any way novel to our history as a species. It has been enjoined by many a teacher and saint. What is notable in our present situation, and in the Despair and Empowerment Work we have done, is that the extension of identity can come directly, not through exhortations to nobility or altruism, but through the owning of pain. That is why the shift in sense of self is credible to those experiencing it. As poet Theodore Roethke said, "I believe my pain."

Despair and Empowerment Work draws on both general systems theory and Buddhist teachings and practice. Both of these inform our methods and offer explanatory principles in the move beyond the ego-based identifications. Let's now turn to see how they serve the shift to the ecological self.

Cybernetics of the Self

The findings of twentieth-century science undermine the notion of a separate self, distinct from the world it observes and acts upon. As Einstein showed, the self's perceptions are shaped by its changing position in relation to other phenomena. And these phenomena are affected not only by location but, as Heisenberg demonstrated, by the very act of observation. Now contemporary systems science and systems cybernetics go yet farther in challenging old assumptions about a distinct, separate, continuous self, showing that there is no logical or scientific basis for construing one part of the experienced world as "me" and the rest as "other."

As open, self-organizing systems, our very breathing, acting, and thinking arise in integration with our shared world through the currents of matter, energy, and information that flow through us. In the web of relationships that sustain these activities, there are no clear lines demarcating a separate, continuous self. Organism and environment are linked in a continuous chain of events. As systems theorists aver, there is no categorical "I" set over against a categorical "you" or "it."

The abstraction of a separate "I" is what Gregory Bateson calls the "epistemological fallacy of Occidental civilization." He asserts that the larger system of which we are a part defies any definitive localization of the self. That which decides and does can no longer be neatly identified with the isolated subjectivity of the individual or located within the confines of his skin.

> The total self-corrective unit which processes information or, as I say, "thinks" and "acts" and "decides," is a *system* whose boundaries do not at all coincide with the boundaries either of the body or of what is popularly called the "self" or "consciousness."
> The self as ordinarily understood is only a small part of a much larger trial-and-error system which does the thinking, acting and deciding. This system includes all the informational pathways which are relevant at any given moment to any given decision. The "self" is a false reification of an improperly delimited part of this much larger field of interlocking processes.

The false reification of the self is basic to the ecological crisis in which we now find ourselves. We have imagined that the "unit of survival," as Bateson puts it, is the separate individual or the separate species. In reality, as throughout the history of evolution, it is the individual *plus* environment, the species *plus* environment, for they are essentially symbiotic.

> When you narrow down your epistemology and act on the premise "What interests me is me, or my organization, or my species," you

> chop off consideration of other loops of the loop structure. You decide
> you want to get rid of the by-products of human life and that Lake
> Erie will be a good place to put them. You forget that the eco-mental
> system called Lake Erie is a part of *your* wider eco-mental system—and
> that if Lake Erie is driven insane, its insanity is incorporated in the
> larger system of *your* thought and experience.

Although we consist of and are sustained by the currents of
information, matter, energy that flow through us, we are accustomed
to identifying ourselves with only that small arc of the flow-through
that is lit, like the narrow beam of a flashlight, by our individual
perceptions. But we don't *have* to so limit our self-perceptions. It is
as logical, Bateson contends, to conceive of mind as the entire "pattern
that connects." It is as plausible to align our identity with that larger
pattern and conceive of ourselves as interexistent with all beings, as
to break off one segment of the process and build our borders there.

Systems theory helps us see that the larger identification of which
we speak does not involve an eclipse of the distinctiveness of one's
individual experience. The "pattern that connects" is not an ocean of
Brahman where separate drops merge and our diversities dissolve.
Natural and cognitive systems self-organize and interact to create larger
wholes precisely through their heterogeneity. By the same token,
through the dance of deviation-amplifying feedback loops, the
respective particularities of the interactive systems can increase.
Integration and differentiation go hand in hand. Uniformity is entropic,
the kiss of death.

The systems view of the world, unfortunately, has not characterized
or informed the uses our society has made of systems science. The
advances permitted by its perceptions of pattern and models of circuitry
have been mainly employed to further values and goals inherited from
a mechanistic, reductionistic interpretation of reality. Systems thinker
Milady Cardamone hypothesizes that it is the feminine-like qualities
of the systems approach that has kept our society from fully grasping
this holistic style of perceiving the universe.

Molecular biologist and Nobel prize winner Barbara McClintock
reveals, however, how practical and revolutionary the results can be
when science is done from the perspective of the ecological self. Her
discovery of the interactive nature of the cell, as opposed to the
previously accepted master control theory, came out of her ability to
see the cell and feel herself as part of the system. "I actually felt as if
I were down there and these (internal parts of the chromosomes) were
my friends."

The Boundless Heart of the Bodhisattva

In the current resurgence of nondualistic spiritualities, Buddhism is distinctive in the clarity and sophistication it offers in understanding the dynamics of the self. In much the same way as general systems theory does, its ontology and epistemology undermine any categorical distinctions definitive of a self-existent identity. And it goes further than systems cybernetics both in revealing the pathogenic character of any reifications of the self and in offering methods for transcending them.

Dependent co-arising, or *pratitya samutpada*—the core teaching of the Buddha on the nature of causality— presents a phenomenal reality so dynamic and interrelated that categorical subject-object distinctions dissolve. This is driven home in the doctrine of *anatman* or no-self, where one's sense of identity is understood as an ephemeral product of perceptual transactions, and where the experiencer is inseparable from his or her experience. The notion of an abiding individual self—whether saintly or sinful, whether to be protected, promoted or punished—is seen as the foundational delusion of human life. It is the motive force behind our attachments and aversions, and these in turn exacerbate it. As portrayed symbolically in the center of the Buddhist Wheel of Life, where pig, cock, and snake pursue each other endlessly, these three— greed, hatred, and the delusion of ego—sustain and aggravate each other in a continuous vicious circle, or deviation-amplifying feedback loop.

We are not doomed to a perpetual rat race; the vicious circle can be broken, its energies liberated to more satisfying uses of the threefold interplay of wisdom, meditative practice, and moral action. Wisdom (*prajna*) arises, reflected and generated by the teachings about self and reality. Practice (*dhyana*) liberates through precise attention to the elements and flow of one's existential experience—an experience which reveals no separate experiencer, no permanent self. And moral behavior (*sila*)—according to precepts of nonviolence, truthfulness, generosity—helps free one from the dictates of greed and aversion and other reactions which reinforce the delusion of separate selfhood.

Far from the nihilism and escapism often attributed to it, Buddhist practice can bring the world into sharper focus and liberate one into lively, effective action. What emerges, when free from the prison cell of the separate, competitive ego, is a vision of radical and sustaining interdependence. In Hua Yen Buddhism it is imaged as the Jeweled Net of Indra—a cosmic canopy where each of us, each jewel at each node of the net, reflects all the others and reflects the others reflecting back. As in the holographic view in contemporary science, each part *contains* the whole.

Each one of us who perceives that, or is capable of perceiving it, is a *bodhisattva*, an "awakening being." We are all *bodhisattvas*, capable of waking up, capable of recognizing and acting upon our profound interexistence with all beings. Our true nature is already evident in our pain for the world, which is a function of the *mahakaruna,* great compassion. And it flowers through the *bodhisattva's* "boundless heart" in active identification with all beings.

Christina Feldman, like many other women Buddhist teachers today, points out that this *Bodhisattva* heart is absolutely central to spiritual practice. It is more transformative of ego and more generative of connection than the desire to be perfect or pure or aloof from suffering. It is already within us, like a larger self awaiting discovery. "We find ourselves forsaking the pursuit of personal perfection and also the denial of imperfection. To become someone different, to pursue a model of personal perfection is no longer the goal. . . . Learning to listen inwardly, we learn to listen to our world and to each other. We hear the pain of the alienated, the sick, the lonely, the angry, and we rejoice in the happiness, the fulfillment, the peace of others. We are touched deeply by the pain of our planet, equally touched by the perfection of a bud unfolding. . . . We learn to respect the heart for its power to connect us on a fundamental level with each other, with nature and with all life."

The experience of interconnection with all life can sustain our social change work far better than righteous partisanship; that is the teaching of Vietnamese Zen monk Thich Nhat Hanh. During the 1960s in Vietnam he founded Youth for Social Service, whose members rescued and aided homeless, hungry, and wounded villagers on both sides of the war. From their ranks he created a nonmonastic order called Tiep Hien, now gradually spreading in the West under the name Interbeing.

His poem "Please Call Me by My True Names" is a remarkable and, I believe, prophetic expression of the ecological self. To quote a few lines:

> Do not say that I'll depart tomorrow
> because even today I still arrive.
>
> Look at me: I arrive in every second
> to be a bud on a spring branch,
> to be a tiny bird . . . in my new nest,
> to be a caterpillar in the heart of a flower,
> to be a jewel hiding itself in a stone.
>
> The rhythm of my heart is the birth and death
> of all that are alive . . .

I am the frog swimming happily
in the clear water of a pond,
and I am also the grass snake who,
approaching in silence, feeds itself on the frog . . .

I am the 12 year-old girl, refugee on a small boat,
who throws herself into the ocean
after being raped by a sea pirate.
I am also the pirate,
my heart not yet capable of seeing and loving . . .

Please call me by my true names
so that I can hear all my cries and my laughs at once,
so that I can see that my joy and my pain are one . . .

Please call me by my true names
so that I can wake up . . .

Beyond Altruism

What Bateson called "the pattern that connects" and the Buddhist's image as the Jeweled Net of Indra can be construed in lay, secular terms as our deep ecology. "Deep ecology" is a term coined by Norwegian philosopher Arne Naess to connote a basic shift in ways of seeing and valuing. It represents an apprehension of reality which he contrasts with "shallow environmentalism," the band-aid approach applying technological fixes for short-term human goals.

The perspective of deep ecology helps us to recognize our embeddedness in nature, overcoming our alienation from the rest of creation and regaining an attitude of reverence for all life forms. It can change the way that the self is experienced through a spontaneous process of ever-widening identification. It launches one on a process of self-realization, where the self to be realized extends farther and farther beyond the separate ego and includes more and more of the phenomenal world. In this process notions like "altruism" and "moral duty" are left behind.

"Altruism implies that ego sacrifices its interests in favor of the other, the *alter*," says Naess. "The motivation is primarily that of duty. . . . It is unfortunately very limited what people are capable to love from mere duty or more generally from moral exhortation. Unhappily the extensive moralizing from environmentalists has given the public the false impression that we primarily ask them to sacrifice to show more responsibility, more concern, better morals. . . . The requisite care flows naturally if the self is widened and deepened so that protection of nature is felt and perceived as protection of ourselves."

Please note: virtue is not required for the emergence of the ecological self! This shift in identification is essential to our survival at this point in our history precisely *because* it can serve in lieu of "ethics" and "morality." Moralizing is ineffective; sermons seldom hinder us from pursuing our self-interest as we construe it. Hence the need to be a little more enlightened about what our self-interest is. It would not occur to me, for example, to exhort you to refrain from sawing off your leg. That would not occur to me or to you, because your leg is part of you. Well, so are the trees in the Amazon Basin; they are our external lungs. We are just beginning to wake up to that, gradually discovering that the world *is* our body.

Economist Hazel Henderson sees our survival dependent on a shift in consciousness from "phenotype" to "genotype." The former, she says, springs from fear of the death of the ego, and consequent conflict between the perceived individual will and the requirements of society or biosphere. "We may be emerging from the 'age of the phenotype', of separated ego awareness, which has now become amplified into untenable forms of dualism. . . . The emerging view is rebalancing toward concern for the genotype, protection of species and gene pools and for the mutagenic dangers of nuclear radiation, chemical wastes and the new intergenerational risks being transferred to our progeny, about which economics says little."

Grace and Power

The ecological self, like any notion of selfhood, is a metaphoric construct, and a dynamic one. It involves choice. Choices can be made to identify at different moments with different dimensions or aspects of our systemically interconnected existence, be they hunted whales or homeless humans or the planet itself. In so doing, this extended self brings into play wider resources—resources, say, of courage or endurance—much like a nerve cell opening to the charge of fellow neurons in the neural net. For example, in his work on behalf of the rainforest, John Seed felt empowered *by* the rainforest.

There is the experience then of being acted "through" and sustained by something greater than oneself. It is close to the religious concept of grace but, as distinct from the traditional western understanding of grace, it does not require belief in God or supernatural agency. One simply finds oneself empowered to act on behalf of other beings—or on behalf of the larger whole—and the empowerment itself seems to come "through" that or those for whose sake one acts.

This phenomenon, when approached from the perspective of systems theory, is understandable in terms of synergy. It springs from the self-organizing nature of life. It stems from the fact that living systems evolve in complexity and intelligence through their interactions. These interactions, which can be mental or physical, and which can operate at a distance through transmission of information, require openness and sensitivity on the part of the system in order to process the flow-through of energy and information. The interactions bring into play new responses and new possibilities. This interdependent release of fresh potential is called synergy. And it is like grace, because it brings an increase of power beyond one's own capacity as a separate entity.

As we awaken, then, to our larger, ecological self, we find new powers. We find possibilities of vast efficacy, undreamed of in our squirrel cage of separate ego. Because these potentialities are interactive in nature, they are the preserve and property of no one, and manifest only to the extent that we recognize and act upon our interexistence, our deep ecology. Then will we be able to survive together, then will our days be long. I close with a Laguna Pueblo prayer:

> I add my breath to your breath
> that our days may be long on the earth
> that the days of our people may be long
> that we shall be one person
> that we may finish our roads together.

22
Wings of the Eagle

A Conversation with Marie Wilson
Spokesperson for the Gitksan-Wet'suwet'en Tribal Council

Marie Wilson: When I read about ecofeminism I find that the attitudes toward women and the feelings inside myself are different. It's difficult to explain, but it's as if women are separate. Though I agree with the analysis, the differences must be because of where I come from. In my mind, when I speak about women, I speak about humanity because there is equality in the Gitksan belief: the human is one species broken into two necessary parts, and they are equal. One is impotent without the other.

When I look upon the western world today, I see this human species broken into a siamese twin relationship where one wounded partner is being dragged behind the other. There is no cooperation, or pragmatic understanding, which is necessary for the species to be whole.

A North American Indian philosopher has likened the relationship between women and men to the eagle, which soars to unbelievable heights and has tremendous power on two equal wings—one female, one male—carrying the body of life between them. The moment one is fractured or harmed in any way, then that powerful bird is doomed to remain on the earth and cannot reach those heights.

We tend to think: male, female, two species. We are not. We are one. Therefore I am feminine to the largest degree but I cannot bring myself to hurt or blame that male part of me that has come from my body: my sons. Similarly, my husband. It's a wonderful feeling to be loved, after forty years, to have support and oneness with someone. It hasn't always been easy. As you can see I'm not a submissive woman and he came from a rather chauvinistic family; we had a lot of growing up to do. Coming straight out of our Gitksan background, however, was a deep commitment to our union. Though Jeff has been a loving father, the children are my responsibility—by my example I will mark them.

Judith Plant: Perhaps in a culture that is connected to the land, and isn't separated from the life process, there is a greater appreciation and understanding of the earth as Mother?

Marie: I don't look upon the earth as my mother. I don't believe the Gitksan ever did. They talked instead of the Power Larger Than Ourselves. They looked upon the land, the sea, the air, the creatures, as created life. Other native peoples did have a vision of the earth as mother but I can only speak for Gitksan.

The ground is throbbing with life, the dirt is not really dirt in a sense, it is full of life. We are a product of the dust of the stars, as others have said. This hand that I hold up is actually a multitude of different organisms living off of the kernel that is my life. There are thousands of different, created things within my body that have nothing to do with the spark that causes our energy to flow. We are the compost of the future. This is exactly the vision that Gitksan have. What do we cherish most in the corner of our gardens? The compost. Where do we put it? Around the tender new life to give it a good start in the new created life it will become. If I had any way of describing myself that would be the way I would like to be described. I believe this is why the Gitksan believed in reincarnation. They believed that the energy that I create cannot be destroyed—you can change its appearance but the influence remains.

The Gitksan did not have a god in the sky. They had a power larger than themselves which they recognized; they understood the limit of a lifespan and they lived comfortably within that limit. It was this understanding that was fundamental to the covenant created between humans and the land. They knew that the well-being of future generations depended upon caring for all life which the land itself represents. The land is the skin of the earth—without it, we die. And yet, we're ripping the skin of the earth without any thought at all. Not appreciating that that first inch of soil represents life.

Judith: The Gitksan's sense of spirituality would never have allowed the destruction of that inch . . . ?

Marie: Oh no! We believe that each created life is so born as to survive, knowing its own way. If we leave it alone, it will survive. We understand that we must use what we must to survive—that in order for one life to survive, another must be given. The Gitksan had ways of cleansing themselves before entering the animal world to take life— actually to receive life, to accept the gift. The hunters cleansed themselves not for a good hunt but so they would be acceptable to the animal. This is a total difference in attitude.

The Gitksan have no word for sin. Instead, you make bad judgments. Bad judgments have to do with people and have nothing to do with a god. All actions come back, full circle, and we have a lot to account for.

So my relationship as a woman is often different to the vision that non-Indian women have in their heads about being a woman. My vision as a woman is not bitter, although I think women have suffered bitterly in the world. I believe that there's no way that any woman can cut herself off from that—we are sisters. My feeling for women involves almost a pity for humanity because we have missed the boat so badly. The Gitksan are not alone. There are so many cultures who believe the same thing we do.

Judith: Yes, people who were not brought up this way are looking toward cultures like the Gitksan for some direction. . . .

Marie: The pity is that I believe that all people started out connected to the land. . . . People, like the Gitksan, copied nature because they were surrounded by it, not protected from it as we are. They saw the cycle of life, from the very smallest to the largest, all connected, and that the system itself punished any breaking of the cycle—not a god. The people saw and understood the checks and balances that were exhibited by the cycle and chose to base their fundamental truths and authority and responsibilities on something that has worked for millions of years. They fit themselves to the cycle of life.

What we are doing is putting into the English language what we have in our heads. This is very difficult to do. It can take months to define a few words: creation, philosophy, self-government, spirit.

Judith: How is respect for other life made concrete in Gitksan society?

Marie: It's made concrete through the rules. People have asked what is our law. We called them rules because we have no outside control. . . . we used inner control. We didn't have judges or lawyers or supreme courts or anything like that. So the people had to know themselves in order to control themselves. Individuals were under strict self-control and collectively this controlled the whole society.

The principles, or rules, were about hunting, about relationships between humans. Self-cleansing before hunting included fasting and meditation, and the hunters removed themselves from the women so that they could go deeply into themselves. In the kill itself there were certain things that had to be done in order to honor that creature: ways of disposing of what was not used, for example, though almost everything was used. Most of what they did was based on common sense which included reason and flexibility because no two situations are quite the same.

The criteria for judgment were that decisions must be good for the people, not just the decision-maker. While people of today dismiss this process as belonging to a primitive time when people were limited, does this mean that today peoples' lives are any less significant? And who will make the choice as to who is expendable and who is not? People in the so-called western world may be materially wealthy, but they are bankrupt in morals. The conditions under which people in less wealthy nations live—including the native peoples in this country—have meant that they are the recipients for decisions made by people who have set themselves up as gods.

You must realize that in my language there is no word for "rights." We have really struggled to find an equivalent in Gitksan-Wet'suwet'en and there is none. The closest we could come to an equivalent was jurisdiction and responsibility. We have obligation and control, and the responsibility that goes with it. Rights to us is a very selfish word.

Judith: Today, we may need more emphasis on responsibility—the other side of the rights coin. Women have clamored for rights—equal slices of a rotten pie—when we've had all the responsibility.

Marie: I have the same attitude toward women who reach points of great authority and they feel they must equate that authority to male authority. That is totally wrong because the moment they start pretending that they are not female, they turn into almost skirted males! I resent that because the world needs the power of women in these positions of authority. I never forget for a moment that I am female even though I am a highly political person. Men must become capable of discussing a woman's position, not her body. We must never forget who we are as women.

Judith: In fact, some of us have to remember. The world needs our voice. Do you feel it is possible to have caring, loving relations extended beyond the couple? Perhaps not with the same intensity but so that we are ready to take care of each other beyond just our families?

Marie: We do have real affection for young people who are having similar struggles as we have had. We needn't even know them. Children in the Gitksan were loved and taught, not as a privilege or a right, but as an investment in the future comfort and continuation of the society.

Judith: I was at a feast not so long ago and all ages of people were there—from the very young to the very old. It seemed to me that the young and the old were the most important people. The people that were my age were making it happen. On the surface it looked as if the children were being indulged, but there was certainly no obnoxious behavior. In fact, it was a joy to watch. In my world we have to be very careful when we indulge our children because they are apt to take advantage of the situation in a way that becomes obnoxious.

Marie: I think that the difference lies in that relationship between authority and responsibility. We celebrated passages of life, which isn't done any more. The great token gesture is becoming old enough to go into a bar! In our society, as in all "primitive" societies, you celebrate your position within that society. Children are well aware of this progressive move through life. They look forward to it. But they know that when they move from one stage of life to another that a death has occurred for part of their life. They can look back, with whatever feeling, but now it's over and they're into something different. All of the changes were celebrated by all the people, marking the change—not only physical, but in terms of responsibility and rewards. An example of this is the Nootka custom of young girls having to swim alone, after they've come out of their first menstrual period, from a very distant point in the ocean. The canoes leave the girl way out in the distance and she has to swim to the shore. The people stand in all their regalia, marking that it is important—her mother's people and her father's people. They cheer her on, sending out vibrations to give her strength when she is failing. And it is the oldest, wisest woman who puts the special robe on her.

Judith: Do you see a revival of these rituals? They seem so important to human groups.

Marie: Most of our customs became illegal under the authority of the missionaries. To get around the outlawing of feasting we developed the idea of parties. The church had no objection to Christmas parties, for instance. Incidentally, I reject this word feast. The actual translation for what we do is a gathering of the people. This meant feeding and housing the witnesses, who are extremely important, and entertaining them for about two weeks. There was an abundance of food and activity. The function of the song and dance was to imprint their memories forever.

Judith: Many of us who are trying to reconnect with the land are realizing that what is needed is a regeneration of culture. Fundamental to this is dealing with the great spiritual emptiness that so many of us are experiencing. What we are seeking is a religion that connects us to the land. Many of us can't help but try to emulate the native people. Some people feel uncomfortable with this.

Marie: It's too easy to take that approach to redeeming oneself. Essentially this is what non-Indians are looking for. We can say it's for the world, or it's for people, but really it's for self. I can't see it happening. Each of us springs from some original beginning. It would be uncomfortable for me to attempt to go to Africa and take up their tribal practices, though I could understand the purpose. I believe our shadows follow us, that we do not arrive in this world meaningless, that the child who is born brings things with her. The Gitksan believe this wholeheartedly. You know how a little child holds her hand like this? Every older Indian will say, "What have you brought for lunch today?" We believe that the child carries in her hands preparations for life from somewhere else.

Here again we have to talk about energy. It has nothing to do with anything mystic. It has to do with energy. I believe firmly that, coming from a long line of very strong women, I was literally born with this same strength. The energy of my great-grandmother, my grandmother and mother has exhibited itself in me, and I know which daughter of mine will follow me.

At the risk of sounding scornful or derogatory I have to say that the Indian attitude toward the natural world is different from the environmentalists. I have had the awful feeling that when we are finished dealing with the courts and our land claims, we will then have to battle the environmentalists and they will not understand why. I feel quite sick at this prospect because the environmentalists want these beautiful places kept in a state of perfection: to not touch it, rather to keep it pure. So that we can leave our jobs and for two weeks we can venture into the wilderness and enjoy this ship in a bottle. In a way this is like denying that life is happening constantly in these wild places, that change is always occurring. Human life must be there too. Humans have requirements and they are going to have to use some of the life in these places. I do believe that life does not need humans but, rather, humans do need the rest of life. We are very small within the structure.

Judith: So you don't take a stewardship perspective to the land—in the sense that the land needs our protection?

Marie: Oh, never! No, the land can do what it will with me. We cannot whip the waves back. When the waves come, they can strip the California beach of million-dollar homes with one contemptuous wave.

I worry about some of the young people who have been apart from their tradition for a long time, particularly in the cities. They don't have this true connection and they are going to have to struggle back to it as hard as you are going to have to struggle.

Judith: That's really what we have to do. Do you have any advice for non-Indian people who are struggling for their vision . . . ?

Marie: In Gitksan society, before you became adult enough to take on responsibility and power, you went out alone. Alone, we search for our full potential. After fasting for days and going into the sweat lodge and the cold waters of the stream, whipping oneself with the Devil's

Club, I imagine we were in a fine state of hallucination. We had visions, usually in the form of a creature, or an encounter with a natural resource like the sun. The intention was not necessarily to find the creature but rather our own full potential.

When people fast, their bodies are reverting to the survival mode of existence where only that which is absolutely necessary is being taken from the body itself. This is going back to the natural Gitksan: taking only what is required. Our territories are taken for need, not greed. We take creatures for need, never more than we can use. When the body is in this state, fasting is not at all painful. You are then able to reach this perception where smell, touch, taste take on a fresh sensitivity. Not only these things but also an increased perception of my place, my home, my children. So, imagine what happened to our people when they fasted for days. They became so empty that they were like snow in the spring—melting water drips through the snow and it becomes porous. This must have been the condition they were in—ready to receive.

The Gitksan accepted their intelligence for what it was, as they accepted their wonderful bodies. This intelligence, the product of the balancing between female and male, was the bridge between the body and the spirit. They could step lightly between each because they had such use of both sides of their intelligence. They had wonderful spatial vision because they used it and because there was no guilt on either side.

Judith: We have to rediscover this intelligence. My concern has been that non-Indian people have the tendency to think that we can have it all now; there it is, over there in that native culture, I'll just go and take it. We can't do that.

Marie: That's right. There's no way non-Indian people can really understand the emotion, the sense of defeat and elation, the way we've had to change our attitudes as we learned. None of this shows up. This has taken thousands of years for us to come to this point.

Judith: What do we do then? As people who are desperate for this meaning?

Marie: You will have to go back in your own history, as many Gitksan have had to do. We are drowning in statistics and yet we are aching for this knowledge.

23

The Subjective Side of Power

Margo Adair and Sharon Howell

Do you often censor yourself; that is, think one thing and say another?

Do you ever notice that some people frequently interrupt others and tend to dominate conversations?

Have you ever been in a meeting where a man's suggestion is enthusiastically supported, even though a woman who had just made the same suggestion was ignored?

Do you ever have that gnawing feeling that you just don't quite fit in?

These questions reflect patterns that permeate our society. They are cultural patterns of domination and submission that find their way into our lives, perpetuating themselves despite our best intentions. These patterns of power are a reflection of the larger inequities in society as well as a stumbling block for those who want to change it. This article is about breaking out of these patterns, and creating an atmosphere in which everyone's contributions are appreciated.

Shattering the hold of cultural patterns of domination and submission is an essential part of rebuilding communities that are life-affirming. Old ways of thinking which are so comfortable and ordinary to us can only lead to further destruction of the earth and one another. To secure the future we need to create new principles and values to guide our lives.

Ecofeminism is essential to our creation of these values. Affirming the sanctity of the earth and all life, it transforms rigid ways of thinking and being, deepening our capacity to consciously create and recreate our culture. Feminism and ecology give us a very different view of nature and our place within her.

Power

From its inception, industrial society has depended on the domination of nature. The desire for amassing wealth necessitated the exploitation of nature and established a hierarchical social order, in which entire classes of people were devalued and subjugated while others lived in opulence. Thus, from the very beginning, industrial development required the labeling of some people as "different," "less developed," as "others" in the way of "progress." Over the centuries this has been the justification for the degradation of those who stood for respect for nature. The destruction of indigenous peoples perpetrated by industrial societies reflects an inability to tolerate those who stand for living in harmony—for intrinsic to nature is her balancing force—equilibrium is what maintains health.

Resisting this assault is a natural response. To maintain control, those in power must be vigilant in exercising a combination of physical force and psychological domination. Fundamental to the continuation of patriarchy and privilege is the creation of a mindset in which we are taught to mistrust our experience, to hand over our power to "experts," technicians, and authorities. The more we have internalized this patriarchal view of ourselves and nature, the less overt force is needed to keep us in "our place."

Contemporary culture is dependent on separating us from the natural world. Replacing trust in nature with trust in technology, we have traded connection with the land and each other for material comforts.

Those peoples who have managed to maintain a connection to their land and traditions have a spiritual and cultural basis distinct from that of industrial civilization—a strength which enables them to challenge the onslaught of development and industrial values. For those of us who find ourselves living *within* industrial societies, ecofeminism provides a similar spiritual and cultural foundation, guiding us to reclaim the sacredness of the earth and to build communities of resistance. Ecofeminism offers a very different sense of power—power that comes from living in harmony rather than in hierarchy.

Exploring and transcending the patterns of power in our lives is a necessary part of the rebuilding of culture. For patterns of domination and submission reside not just in our institutions and political processes, but within each of us. These patterns limit our vision, stunt our creativity, and keep us alienated from ourselves and one another. In order to challenge these patterns both in our daily interactions and in our society, we must first develop a framework for talking about power differences and for naming the dynamics we experience.

The Power Taboo

Nobody talks about power. Those who have it spend a great deal of effort keeping it hidden. Those who don't, rarely risk raising the issue.

Power is the ability to do what one chooses—the more power one has, the more options one has. Those without power are led to believe this is a personal failing; those with it come to consider it a sign of personal success.

Instead of talking about power, we have learned to talk in terms of "freedom": the right of an individual to do what s/he chooses. Defining freedom in individual rather than collective terms keeps us from looking at the way society's resources are distributed and controlled. This emphasis on individual freedom obscures the power arrangements. It hides the fact that the options available to some are made possible only at the expense of others and of the earth. It is no wonder that freedom is the only word we hear. Naming power is taboo. *To raise the question of power is to threaten the freedom of those who have it.*

We live in a culture in which the measuring stick for normalcy is defined as white, male, Protestant, middle-class, heterosexual, able-bodied, and serious. The narrowness of this measure leaves most of us feeling that we never quite belong. We must prove we are just as good as the white, male, Protestant, middle-class, heterosexual, able-bodied, serious person in order to be considered competent. We have to trivialize or hide the particular aspects of who we are that don't fit the mold. "Passing," usually thought of in terms of blacks pretending to be whites, is something we all do to have access to privilege. The price we pay is the fragmentation of ourselves.

Because mass culture devalues and marginalizes the lives and experiences of everyone except those who fit the "norm," claiming the power to define oneself is the beginning of liberation. This involves acknowledging all the different aspects of who we are, the ways in which each of us has experienced both privilege and oppression. For example, a gay, white, working-class man experiences privilege by virtue of being white and male, *as well as* oppression by virtue of being gay and working-class. Privilege on one power axis does not negate oppression on another.

The Dual Reality

The force necessary to maintain power is not acknowledged. But power means control of physical survival—income, jobs, homes, education, food . . . When acting alone, people dependent upon those in power cannot afford to alienate those in power. Therefore, the exploited, dehumanized, trivialized, and dispossessed are forced to live hypocritically—thinking one thing and saying another.

Everyone has experienced this dual reality in the workplace when they say or do what they need to for the boss, despite what they are thinking. If they were to say what they thought, it would only get them in trouble. This gives rise to a dual reality which creates the subjective climate that holds power in place: the visible one for which there is supposedly a social consensus, and the invisible one, which is the experience of those who, in any given situation, are locked out.

As a condition of oppression, their sense of self is perpetually inside of their own minds. *The power struggle gets relegated to the realm of the subjective.*

Because of the mystification of power it is a serious mistake for anyone with privilege to assume that the only reality operating is the visible one. Invisible currents underlie our interactions, regardless of our intention. Only by making all realities visible can we break the imposed consensus. The narrow, dehumanizing context is transformed. For instance, at the workplace, if people begin a conversation about their families—which are assumed to be heterosexual—and a lesbian is present, she will be identifying with her inner thoughts rather than the sanctioned view of reality. So to change the power dynamics, the invisible lesbian experience must be acknowledged.

Our willingness to grapple with different experiences enables us to create a common context for relationships and true community. The content of the invisible realities differs with the particularity of oppression. Each oppression, whether it be based on a particular cultural heritage, sexual orientation, physical ability, appearance, age, etc., has its own array of experiences which have been distorted or ignored.

People in the dominated group have always had to know more about the dominators than those at the top have had to know about the experiences of those at the bottom. Survival depends upon not making a mistake. This is why coming to know the content of these invisible realities is vital for those with privilege. By understanding the particularity of the many oppressions in our society, we begin to see how our everyday interactions are unconsciously fraught with divisiveness that keeps power in place. For example, it is not uncommon to hear progressive people talk about Native Americans in the past tense, as if their cultures no longer existed. Nor is it uncommon to watch a differently-abled person treated as if s/he were incapable of any independent activity. When we are in a dominant group we need to become aware of the assumptions we have that result from our socialization and privilege.

Naming invisible realities cracks the silent conspiracy that upholds the status quo, forcing us to shift our orientation. In a society riddled with inequities, what on the surface often appears as casual conversation usually has undercurrents of silent agony and alienation.

When experiences kept from view are addressed, people are no longer forced to deny themselves. We no longer have to choose between self and other. Experiences, no longer invisible, become part of what everyone grapples with and not just "their problem." The boundaries of the situation expand, our humanity is enriched, and the basic assumptions of the power structure have to be re-examined. Naming power begins our process of reclaiming it.

Patterns of Power

Patterns of surviving operate on both sides of each oppression. They dictate our spontaneous responses to everything. Growing up in a hierarchical society, each of us has learned the kind of behavior expected, given class, gender, race, sexual preference, physical condition, age. . . . Socialized behavior does not instantly die when our intentions are to equalize relations.

Frequently, the behavior we aspire to, the most accepted and normal in our society, is that of the dominators. They are our most visible role models. Even those of us who have lived with enforced submission find ourselves capable of dominating others. Oppression does not make us immune from hurting others. All too often, it serves as a lesson in how to behave once we get whatever power we can. The following are generic patterns which apply to any situation of domination and submission. The hierarchical and competitive nature of our society gives everyone plenty of opportunities to experience both sides.

Behavioral Patterns that Perpetuate
Relations of Domination

Individual of the Dominant Group	Individual of the Oppressed Group
Projects an aura of authority.	Projects an aura of subservience.
Defines parameters, judges what is appropriate, patronizes.	Feels inappropriate, awkward, doesn't trust own perception, looks to expert for definition.
When in disagreement with status quo is seen as, and feels, capable of making constructive changes.	When in disagreement with status quo, is seen as, and feels, disruptive.
Assumes responsibility for keeping system on course. Acts unilaterally.	Blames self for not having capacity to change situation.
Self-image of superiority, competence, in control, entitled, correct.	Self-image of inferiority, incompetent, being controlled, not entitled, low self-esteem.
Views self as logical, rational. Sees others as too emotional, out of control.	Often thinks of own feelings as inappropriate and a sign of inadequacy.
Disdains nature.	Disdains own nature.

Believes certain kinds of work below their dignity.	Believes certain kinds of work beyond their ability.
Presumptuous, does not listen, interrupts, raises voice, bullies, threatens violence, becomes violent.	Finds it difficult to speak up, timid, tries to please. Holds back anger, resentment, rage.
Seeks to stand out as special.	Feels more secure in background, doesn't want to betray peers, feels vulnerable when singled out.
	Feels confined by circumstance, limits aspirations.
Assumes anything is possible, can do whatever s/he wants as an individual, assumes everyone else can too.	
Does not acknowledge constraints in current situations.	Sees current situations in terms of past constraints.
Initiates, manages, plans, projects.	Lacks initiative, responds, deals, copes, survives.
Sees problems and situations in personal terms.	Sees problems in social context, results of system, "them."
Sees all experiences, feelings as unique, individual, feels disconnected, often needs to verbalize feelings.	Sees experiences and feelings as collectively understood and shared. No point in talking about feelings.
Sees solutions to problems as promoting better feelings.	Sees solutions to problems in actions that change conditions.
Thinks own view of reality is only one, obvious to all, assumes everyone agrees with their view. Disagreements are result of lack of information, misunderstandings, personalities.	Always aware of at least two views of reality, their own and that of the dominant group.
Demands others articulate feelings while remaining invulnerable. Sees others as sullen, uncommunicative.	Witholds feelings in face of dominant group, resorts to silence and evasions.
Does not believe or trust ability of others to provide leadership.	Does not believe has capacity for leading.
Unaware of hypocrisy, contradictions.	Sees contradictions, irony, hypocrisy.

Fears losing control, public embarrassment.	Laughs at self, others, sees humor as method of dealing with hypocrisy.
Regards own culture as civilized, regards others' as underdeveloped, disadvantaged.	Feels own culture devalued, under assault.
Turns to others' culture to enrich humanity while invalidating it by calling it exotic.	Uses cultural forms to influence situation, humor, music, poetry, etc., to celebrate collective experience. Sees these forms as being stolen.

In whatever ways we have access to privilege, we have been carefully socialized to accept, protect, and maintain it. In whatever ways we are likely to be oppressed, we are socialized to accept it, protect ourselves and one another. This patterning is why we duplicate the very relations we are trying to transform. As we become aware of the impact of domination on ourselves and others, we are appalled by how we have somehow participated in its perpetuation and how much it permeates our every interaction from the intimate to the occasional.

Precisely because these patterns are so deep within us, the process of identifying them creates tremendous anxiety. The question is not whether we behave based on these patterns—we all do. The issue is our willingness to change them. Altering either side forces change on the other. Power exists as a relationship. Changing our own tendencies toward domination or submission cultivates a context of trust and cooperation that includes everyone's contribution.

The process of breaking out of these patterns necessitates reflecting on how they apply in our own lives by asking such questions as:

—Is the humanity, intelligence, sensitivity, and contribution of each person respected?
—Am I taking up more or less time than others?
—Do I interrupt others?
—Do I censor myself?
—Is information available to everyone?
—Are people dismissed for making mistakes or supported in changing?
—Are differences minimized or is pride encouraged in each of our ethnicities and struggles?
—Are decisions about the use of resources shared?
—Is there an awareness of the differences in our access to resources?

—Is there a generosity of spirit or are guilt and blame operating?

—What are the assumptions motivating activity?

—Do I make judgments based on principle or do I respond to personalities?

—Are distinctions drawn between where someone comes from and what s/he stands for?

—Are the activities of care for one another and the land at the center of what is valued?

—Do we create ways of sharing and celebrating the sanctity of life?

Healing in a Troubled Time

Replacing the unconscious and silent assumptions that have governed our relationships for so long with new principles of respect, accountability, and harmony must become the core of our efforts to create change collectively. Evaluating whose interests are being served, and whether or not we are moving away from domination and control should be the basis of decisions.

Because behavior patterns that perpetuate the status quo are so deeply ingrained in us, it is inevitable that we'll feel awkward, inappropriate and disruptive when we raise questions of power. To do so necessarily means breaking the power taboo and making the struggles visible. Though it may make us uncomfortable, this process will profoundly alter the context of our interactions. Trust begins to emerge, blame and guilt dissolve, it becomes possible to create an atmosphere where everyone is important.

We've all been damaged by society. This is why social change cannot be about some people trying to "fix things" for others. Real change is based on the recognition of what we have all lost. As we regain our wholeness by learning to trust others, or to trust ourselves, we give up control and are empowered to successfully organize against the power brokers.

In our efforts to build new ways of living together, we'll make mistakes with one another. Our challenge is to create contexts where we can support each other to change. When we listen, share and respect diversity, we create an expansive atmosphere, one in which we can honestly express what we are experiencing and make principled decisions.

By breaking the power taboo and naming the power dynamics that are operating, bringing the invisible realities to the surface, by reclaiming our heritages and our integrity, and by placing principles in the center of our relationships, we can build new ties and ways of being together that heal us and reestablish communities that are once again sustained by the sanctity of life.

24
Community—Meeting
Our Deepest Needs
Helen Forsey

In the early 1960s, the Ottawa Section of the Alpine Club of Canada maintained a tiny cabin perched on a pine-clad outcropping of the Luskville Escarpment—the southern edge of the Precambrian Shield where it overlooks the broad expanse of the Ottawa Valley. Members of the Club, scouting Gatineau Park a few years earlier for cliffs to climb, had come upon the cabin, at the time nothing more than a run-down shack. They arranged to rent it from the Federal District Commission for $25 a year, and proceeded to convert it into a home base for their rock climbing, skiing and hiking in the area.

I was sixteen when I first visited the Cabin, and it quickly became the center of my life. Over the next several years, about a dozen of us spent every weekend together, sometimes organizing excursions to other climbing and skiing areas in the Laurentians or the Adirondaks or, in summer, when the bugs drove us from the cliffs, canoeing the lakes and rivers of the Shield farther north. But for the most part we were at the Cabin. We developed an intimate acquaintance with the surrounding rocks and valleys, trees and streams, and we formed strong bonds with each other, some of which have lasted through a quarter century. I did not know it then, for at the time I was able to give it no name, but I was experiencing community, and that experience has profoundly influenced and inspired my search since then.

Many a winter evening, we would ski a mile across the frozen fields from the road to the base of the Escarpment, then strap our skis to our packs for the steep climb up. Sometimes there would be someone there ahead of us, and a fire would be glowing in the squat old wood-stove and the lanterns lit to welcome us home. "Home" was the golden sunsets above the great river, seen through the pines on the point; it was sleeping outside under the stars with the branches whispering and embracing overhead; it was washing in the cold sparkles of the stream first thing in the morning, then hauling water back up to the Cabin to make tea. It was the first spring climb as the sun warmed the south-facing boulders, before the snow was off the ground; the Cabin Day each November when thirty or more people participated in a massive clean-up and laid in a supply of wood for the winter's fuel. It was sharing a meal after a day on the rocks, then sitting round the little table with the oilcloth and the candles on it, reading aloud to each other or telling climbing stories or singing songs until it was time to stumble outside to bed.

We fixed up the Cabin and made it cozy and snug. We reshingled the roof, built a stone "patio" outside for storing wood and packs, decorated the walls with mountain scenes from old calendars and with sketch maps of the routes on the nearby cliffs. We built a rope ladder to the attic, where we kept emergency supplies, spare skis, extra climbing equipment, and sleeping bags. We had mouse-proof tin boxes filled with food—a common supply from which everyone drew and to which each contributed as need arose. We baked bread in the oven of the old stove, and one New Year's Eve roasted a goose, complete with stuffing, for a feast for seventeen people!

All of us did everything. There were no set roles, defined by gender or by anything else. We each prepared our own food, or took turns cooking and washing up. We all chopped wood, cut trails, repaired skis, built things. We all belayed each other on climbs, taking responsibility for the safety of the person on the other end of the rope. We shared our skills with one another—cooking, gymnastics, languages, as well as climbing. Anyone could lead a climb as soon as they reached the necessary level of skill and confidence. We shared climbing and camping equipment, even clothing when it was needed. We organized carpools for our expeditions, and shared tents with whomever needed a place to sleep. Women and men slept matter-of-factly side by side with never a hassle.

We were a crazy bunch. Early one winter before much snow had fallen, we trooped up the stream about a mile to the beaver lake for a hockey game. We used stones for pucks and dead saplings for sticks, and played "Canadians" versus "Europeans"—some of whom had never been on skates in their lives before! We built a mock bobsled run down the upper part of the trail from the Cabin, painstakingly hauling buckets of water over the ridge from the stream to ice the sides, and then went sliding down our "bum-run" on pieces of cardboard boxes. Once, in the spring, we tried damming the stream with rocks and branches to make a swimming pool, but the beaver must have had the last laugh; along with an attempted igloo, the pool was one of our few failures.

I lived for the weekends. School and the city were irritating and depressing; I was shy, awkward, and a tomboy who never measured up to what society expected of a teenage girl. But at the Cabin, all that was irrelevant and forgotten. There, all of us were individuals; none of us fitted any stereotype anyway, and we accepted and enjoyed each other for ourselves, simply and unquestioningly.

Now, of course, I would question more. With the wisdom of hindsight I can see incredible contradictions in that group of people. Practically all of us lived pretty "straight" weekday lives in the city, and espoused, if anything, rather conservative social and political views. Employers included the nuclear energy and "defense" establishments, as well as multinational corporations. We probably all believed to a greater or lesser extent in the patriarchal family, and saw urban middle-class values, privilege, and affluence as legitimate and normal. Yet the fact remains that each weekend for years, we laid aside those mainstream assumptions and briefly lived a reality that was radically different—one that bore the seeds of changes more fundamental than we could have dreamed!

What I can see now is that this experience embodied basic elements of community, certain principles of feminism and ecological practice, but in a very incomplete way—without our being aware of, let alone analyzing, the significance of what we were doing. When changes happened, therefore, we had no way of assessing their effect on our group life, no guidelines or points of reference to help us determine future directions, no clear commitment to essentials. This meant that the entire experience, although tremendously powerful, was inherently unstable; and, not surprisingly, it failed to survive changing circumstances.

Although I have a clear understanding now of the meaning and importance of what we shared at the Cabin, my awareness was a very long time coming. For years I saw "that part of my life"—my love of the woods, the rocks and the water, my energy for wilderness pursuits— as a diversion, a cherished but isolated fragment of my identity, quite separate from, for example, my work in Third World "development" or my increasing politicization. Then I read George Manuel's account, in *The Fourth World,* of his people's struggle to maintain their native heritage in the face of alienating power, greed, and injustice. His insights, and the way the elements of his people's culture and their struggles were integrated in the life he described, helped bring the fragments together for me, and eventually I understood that my love for the Earth, my feminism, and my search for peace and justice were all strong threads in the whole cloth of my life. That understanding freed me at a personal level from fighting parts of myself, and freed up my mind to see connections where I had tended to see separate issues before. It was another step on the way.

Perhaps all this was necessary before I could finally seek community and find it satisfying. In fact, though, my search was not all that purposeful; I never set out to "look for community." It was more a casting around, in search of a way of living that would have simplicity and balance, comradeship and challenge; that would meet my need to feel grounded, to touch the earth and put down roots. I wanted a place where I could try to live the principles that had become so vital to me, to explore personal politics in a supportive environment without constantly having to swim upstream. I sought a home base for carrying on the continuing struggle—not a refuge from the "real world," but the nucleus of an alternative which could influence and inspire broader change.

Many of us who come to community from activist backgrounds seem to come in somewhat this way. At some basic level we feel the sickness in mainstream society killing us, draining our spirit and nullifying our work. We feel a need for hope, for possibilities in the midst of despair; for integrity and wholeness in the struggle against alienation; for nurturing and closeness based on equality and respect, not on obligation and exploitation. These needs dictate the journey, and many of us find what we seek in community.

When people have plumbed the depths of despair and degradation, when we finally know just how bad things are, when we have tried for improvements and reforms and realized what we are up against, that experience helps us begin to define the kinds of changes—and the depth of change—that will be necessary. Thus, women and men who have struggled against the worst of colonial and imperialist exploitation, feminists who have suffered the concrete effects of male domination and violence, and environmentalists appalled by the increasing horrors of industrial devastation, all develop insights into the radical changes that are going to be needed if we are to survive. When we put our insights together, our visions can evolve into holistic realities that may just be capable of resisting fragmentation, may just survive well enough to evolve further, into a continuing future for life on Earth.

The traditions of male dominance have been notoriously bad for the human imagination. The patriarchal penchant for polarization has locked people into "either/or" modes of thought which have stifled our creativity and regimented our despair. What the visionary writers, the Third World revolutionaries, and those of us from the industrialized world who are experimenting with radical community alternatives are all attempting is to break through the barriers of those rigid patriarchal assumptions to imagine and create ways of living that correspond to our deepest needs.

Perhaps, too, humanity may be on the verge of completing a primeval cycle, one that will link us back to our roots in an ancient past. Perhaps we are at last beginning to turn again to the wisdom of prehistoric societies and of aboriginal peoples whose cultures integrated and honored both female and male, and who understood the need for sustainable, harmonious relations with the earth and all its creatures.

Interestingly, in certain patriarchal philosophies the concept of connectedness, union, nirvana, exists; but it has been narrowly conceived by men in exclusively spiritual terms. Women's cultures, on the other hand, have always recognized connectedness, relatedness, oneness, as being physical as well as spiritual—as a basic principle of the natural universe. The supposed division between the spiritual and the natural is another of patriarchy's lies—lies that divide us from our true nature and from each other.

When we look at human needs across cultures and over time, another recurring theme is the need for roots in the earth, for a reliable, sustained relatedness to a particular area or locality. Again, the multiple visions of people seeking and creating balanced, egalitarian, harmonious communities all have in common that element of sturdy rootedness. Bioregionalists call it "living in place;" most people would call it home. But the concept of "home" has been viciously distorted—co-opted by capitalism to refer to an exchangeable piece of real estate; corrupted by patriarchy to mean a man's castle, where women and children are neither free nor safe. In this context, "homelessness" takes on for us a new and broader meaning, referring not only to the harsh realities faced by those who actually lack shelter, but also to a pervasive phenomenon of modern alienation even in the midst of creature comforts. It is time we reclaimed the concept of "home," and made it synonymous with the kind of community that ecofeminism strives to create.

Human beings have always created ways of living together; we are social animals, after all. But under patriarchy, those ways have been oppressive and harmful to people and to the earth. More and more of us are realizing now—with the hope that it is not too late—that we must turn that phenomenon around.

So, in our various spots on this planet, groups of us cluster together again, more or less intentionally, in homesteads, neighborhoods, and networks, to forge new ways of living and working together, new models of community that will comprise this essential turnaround. And we ask: How can we make the most of these efforts to create a new reality out of our best visions? What pitfalls do we need to watch out for and avoid, so as not to fall back into the old oppressive patterns? How can we build, from our small scattering of communities, a network of growing strength that can truly help to bring about the enormous cumulative changes that the world so desperately needs?

A fundamental part of the answer is that we need to be ready and able to draw on both our experience and our understanding, and allow the theory and the practice to nourish and deepen each other. Unless we can become aware of the meanings of our experience and reinterpret those meanings in our actions, we risk losing the valuable lessons we can learn from the experience. Many of the important teachings of my Cabin years were inaccessible to me for a long time, because I was unable to recognize and understand the elements and the connections that made it all so significant. The ultimate demise of the Cabin community itself reflected—and was perhaps in fact caused by—our collective lack of self-awareness and conscious direction in what we did.

As we build community, we need to learn to listen to each other and to ourselves, to be aware of our experience and to hear our own inner voices. Reflecting on those times in our lives where we have experienced wholeness, empowerment, joy, we can see those experiences as signposts for our deepest needs, indications of how those needs can be filled. This process is part of what the feminist poet and nonviolent activist, Barbara Deming, calls "remembering who we are." Whether the "relevance" of what is going on is immediately obvious or not, we need to allow our awareness and our understandings to surface. If something feels right, or wrong, there is probably a reason, whatever the experts or the bosses or the politicians may try to tell us. We need to begin to trust both our intuition and our common sense—as the feminist movement has long been encouraging women to do—and be willing to spend the time and energy, individually and collectively, to fit these together and build from what we learn.

Our experience and understandings as feminists and as ecologists are, of course, absolutely vital to this process. So much of our search is for an alternative to the alienation that permeates modern industrial society, where our interrelationships with other humans, animals, plants, and the earth itself are distorted through power hierarchies and prescribed roles, electronic technology, plastic packaging, and layers of concrete and asphalt. The basic causes of that alienation lie in patriarchal attitudes and structures, distance from nature and lack of knowledge and respect for its cycles and systems. If we fail to recognize this causality, we are apt to find ourselves recreating those same alienating structures in our attempts to build community, and any hope for the evolution of a true alternative will be doomed.

In fact, as we attempt to practice community, we find that this effort by itself does not automatically change our old behavior patterns and our accustomed ways of relating to each other and to the earth. And to go on relating in the old ways threatens to destroy the community and the integrity of the alternative we sought. This contradiction has spelled the end of countless experiments in collectivity, with people coming to the tragic—and mistaken—conclusion that such alternatives run counter to human nature. I believe that it is not human nature itself which is at fault, but rather the stifled and distorted attitudes and behavior that *un*-natural and oppressive societies have cultivated.

Thus, in order to make possible the necessary fundamental changes in all our relations, we need to continually develop our understanding and analysis of what must be changed and why, as well as our determination and ability to live and interact differently in our daily lives. Without such understanding, the old destructive patterns will tend to dominate our actions, preventing any real change; whereas theory alone, without practice, is sterile.

Alternative communities can, of course, take a multiplicity of forms, and this potential for endless variety is one of the most hopeful aspects of the communal movement. Communities can be neighborhoods or villages, small homesteads or more geographically dispersed webs of commonality and interaction. We are not talking here about the patriarchy's repeated attempts to define "community" in its own oppressive terms, but rather about the many kinds of social experiment which are consistent with ecofeminist principles. To explore the characteristics that such communities tend to have in common would form the subject matter for an entire book, but I want to touch on a few of the elements that my experience tells me are essential for building sustainable alternatives.

First, community living is life-affirming and nonviolent. Community people come together out of love for each other and for the earth, commitment to certain basic values, and a hope, however tenuous, for a better future. This commitment often involves anger, struggle, and pain, but that in no way cancels out the love or the continuing possibility of joy. Community does not represent a withdrawal from the struggle; instead, it is an affirmation that better ways do exist, and an expression of our determination to live those better ways in the here and now.

Communities value autonomy and self-reliance based on equality. Community people have a common urge to make their own decisions, control their own destinies, both as a group and as individuals. This implies responsibility, "knowing what it takes to live," as one community woman put it, an ability to cope, and a willingness to share those capabilities. It also requires both an internal and an external balance—equality and respect within the group regardless of sex, race, class, age, or other differences, and freedom from intervention from the outside. Once again, everything is connected. If inequalities and exploitation exist within the community, those attitudes and modes of behavior will threaten not only the cohesiveness of the group, but also its relations with its homeplace and the creatures who coinhabit that place. And if control of decisions or resources is imposed from outside, the balance and cycles of the community's life are likely to be disrupted or destroyed. Without implying isolation, there needs to be a degree of autonomy which will permit the community to grow and flourish in the context of its own ecofeminist values.

Community demands openness, clarity, emotional connectedness and the ability and willingness to communicate about the things that matter. The inevitable problems faced by people living together cannot be resolved without honest and sensitive communication which builds trust and understanding. This is nowhere more true than in a group of people committed to new and better ways of relating. People in community must be willing to be vigilant and self-critical, as well as patient and generous, in addressing the group's internal dynamics; ready both to challenge and to affirm, keeping constantly in mind the principles of respect, equality, cooperation, and caring they have committed themselves to.

The issue of tolerance is a thorny one. How much are we willing to tolerate actions and attitudes that go against our cherished values? How do we handle such contradictions when they arise? Is it elitist or unrealistic to demand that everyone in the community be committed to ecofeminist ideals and practice? How accessible are these ideas to a wider public, and might our insistence on them prevent the growth of the very movement we wish to see spread?

How we answer these questions, and how, in practice, our communities deal with these situations, is indicative in each case of our own relatedness and respect for ourselves, other beings, and the earth. Surely there are many answers, and none of them are simple. Community is not a simple solution to the world's problems. We know by now that simple solutions don't exist in any case; they are another of the patriarchy's lies. What community may be, however, is humanity's next evolutionary step, giving more and more people the opportunity to live in ways consistent with our deepest needs. If we can understand those needs, and practice what it takes to meet them, we can find the strength to grow, and perhaps also to bring about the kind of changes that must be made if the planet is to survive.

Community develops quite naturally, then, out of ecofeminist ideals. The many and varied forms that our communities take, from northern Mozambique to eastern Ontario, from Ata to Mattapoisett, evolve according to the myriad factors which influence any group choosing to live and work together in harmony with the earth. Both the commonality of principle and the diversity of practice are characteristics of the ecofeminist movement, as indeed they are of the natural universe itself. By honoring both, we in our communities can help to build the kind of future we dream of for ourselves and for the Earth.

25
Consensus and Community
An Interview with Caroline Estes

Caroline Estes, skilled facilitator, teacher, and life-long communitarian, was interviewed by **The New Catalyst,** *a quarterly bioregional journal from British Columbia, in the spring of 1988.* *

The New Catalyst: Consensus seems to be catching on in a range of groups, from small households up to large gatherings such as the North American Bioregional Congress. Is that your impression, too?

Caroline Estes: Yes. In at least the western culture, the idea of individual rights has been very strong over many years and we're now seeing the results of too much reliance on that, and the need for coming together and making a unified statement or mode of action. And consensus is clearly the most efficient and effective method of doing that, honoring many different sides of the question which might be obscured in other forms of decision-making. It gives everybody the power to be part of the process.

TNC: Can you give an example?

Caroline: Yes, I'll take my own home as an example: all of our decisions are made consensually. There is a lot of tension around a lot of subjects, and sometimes it's hard to get to them. For instance, let's take the vegetarian issue which is facing many people these days. In our particular case, we faced this both ethically and from a practical point of view of money. We drew out from every person that was participating in this decision their personal place on how they felt about their diet, the impact of their diet on the world—things that normally you don't get into in a regular decision-making process. We found that we could honor each other in our different places and come to a decision, in our case eating vegetarian with additions of milk and cheese and eggs,

*The New Catalyst, no. 12: "Building Sustainable Cultures." P.O. Box 99, Lillooet, B.C., Canada V0K 1V0 eliminating red meat and occasionally adding fish or chicken. Now this did not meet any one person's total expectations. But, in hearing every person's point of view, we were able to satisfy everyone well enough to feel good about the diet that we have at Alpha Farm—which runs from twenty to thirty people.

TNC: What would you say, then, is the objective of consensus?

Caroline: To find decisions together that everyone can agree with and feel comfortable with, and participate in. Not just have someone else do it. This is where I have always been uncomfortable with Robert's Rules of Order kinds of decision-making where, yes, you can come to a decision, and the majority has clearly carried, but it's their decision, it's not our decision.

TNC: Can you tell us briefly how consensus works in your experience?

Caroline: My understanding of consensus comes from an investigation of two streams. One is the Society of Friends who have practiced it for about three hundred years, and the other is from the native traditions where they've practiced it for maybe millenia.

Consensus is where a question is asked (and the question must be phrased positively, not negatively), and then everyone who is there speaks their mind, shares their truth, gives their opinion—and out of all of the sharing, there starts to emerge a common answer to the question that moves the group to a decision. An important point is that you must be present to take part in consensus, there is no absentee voting. Depending upon whether you have someone who is serving the group as a facilitator, it can go quicker or slower. If a facilitator is there, they can be paying more attention to this gathering agreement, and possibly move the group ahead a little quicker.

At some point a decision is self-evident. At that point, it needs to be stated, and a search made of the group to see whether the decision has indeed answered all of the various questions that people have, and has satisfied them to the point that they can agree. It does not mean unanimity, that everybody is in absolute, total alignment. That is something that I think we reach very seldom. But in consensus it is fairly easy to arrive at a unity place where people can get behind and move forward together.

Now it is possible that, for some people, what is being decided is wrong, or they have not yet felt comfortable enough with it to join it. At that point, people are called upon to say that they are stepping aside from this decision. They need to be minuted or registered as having stepped aside, so that they no longer have to participate in the action that falls out from the decision. It does not mean that they are holding the group up. In my particular experience, I find that if two or more people start stepping aside, we have not done enough work to arrive at the very best decision. And there are those very few and far between cases where someone in the group has the very clear understanding that they, at that particular moment, have more wisdom and light than everyone else, and they have the responsibility of holding the group from moving ahead. This is what we call blocking.

TNC: Is it right that this is not frequently used in true consensus?

Caroline: In my twenty-five to thirty years of being involved with consensual groups, I've seen it less than a dozen times. And that's stretching. . . . It's very rare that any of us has the audacity to think that we have more wisdom than the collected wisdom of the group. And when those occasions occur, it is very difficult for us to take that stand. You must be terribly sure. Not so much intellectually terribly sure, but at that feeling gut level that says: this is wrong. I am not able to let these friends make this mistake, and I have a responsibility to stop them. It's very difficult.

TNC: You spoke about the role of the facilitator. Could you expand on that a little more?

Caroline: In my experience so far, the facilitator—who is just that: a person who has the role of making easy the movement toward decision— is fairly crucial at this particular time in the emergence of consensus as a decision-making process. We are not yet all good at taking part in meetings on an equal basis. We have not been trained to do that, to have full ease at sharing our thinking and our feelings. So in a meeting, if there is one person who basically steps out of the content that's being discussed, and pays attention only to the process, it greatly facilitates the discussion and the ability of everyone to take part. Because that person is making sure that everyone's bit of the truth is being added to the collective. This is a nudge for people to start realizing that their truth is really important. And it is also a person or a place that helps some people who may have been used to talking more than their proportionate share to understand the need to have a little bit more control over that and to allow space for people who aren't used to talking. It's someone who simply watches the process and makes sure the people stay on track.

TNC: Do you see it as an interim institution, before we can perhaps do this without facilitators, or is it something that we really need to have on a permanent basis?

Caroline: I would say any group over thirty needs a facilitator. Simply because it's hard to facilitate yourself. Under thirty I would hope that, as we move forward with the use of consensus and the honoring of each person's position, we become so trained and sensitized to the understanding of truth that we could indeed facilitate ourselves and wouldn't need a facilitator.

TNC: This is a worthy ideal. However, many people's experience with using consensus has been little short of disastrous. Consensus has been blamed as the problem—I'm speaking here, say, about political parties' attempts to use consensus—and frequently the comment is made that consensus can't work in impersonal or large gatherings. What's your response to that?

Caroline: I don't see any particular reason why consensus can't work in any face-to-face situation. So long as there's a common purpose, even if people don't know each other, there is no reason why consensus can't be used. The largest group I ever saw was five thousand, and it was a very powerful group that was brought together with great unity. This was the free speech movement in Berkeley. There were some pretty stiff differences sometimes, but still the commonness of their goals made it fairly easy. It was an awesome experience. I think that when people get into trouble sometimes in large groups, it is because they really are there for different purposes.

I think it's true that consensus has often failed in groups and my experience around this is that true consensus has not been understood. It grew out of the late fifties/early sixties experience of large groups of people operating with something like consensus where the word caught on, and the power of the process was so large that they took it back to their own individual groups and they scattered around the country, without understanding where it came from, what its basis in *fact* is, and how much you have to work to unify the group to be sure it has a common purpose before you make any decisions. Part of what I have been doing over the last four or five years is going around and cleaning up disaster areas by bringing forth again the whole basis for consensus: where it comes from, and how you *must* practice it.

In one sense consensus is much more than a decision-making process, in that it requires us to be the very best that we can be. It does not let us keep all our shortcomings unchallenged.

TNC: Could you give us an idea of the history of consensus?

Caroline: Historically, there was a man named George Fox who started the Society of Friends in England, three hundred years ago. Growing out of his very deeply held and resonating feeling with many other people that there is that of God in every person, came the idea that, when you are making a decision, you should listen to all of it. And it should all be incorporated into the decision. And if there were people who didn't agree, and that which was of God in them was saying "No," then you needed to listen to that. They called this the sense of the meeting. The word "consensus" is not a Quaker term.

The sense of the meeting is just that: that out of the meeting to make decisions, came a sense of the correctness of how you proceed.

That was then minuted, and on that rested the actions that followed. That's one direction that has come forth pretty much unchanged through the years.

The other side has to do with the native people in the United States—and that's all I've done research on so far. The way they made decisions was by a number of forms of consensus. In one tribe all of the men would sit in a circle and all of the women would sit in a circle behind them. And the decision was made by the collective of everyone there. And they never made a decision without that completeness.

TNC: How does this compare historically with Robert's Rules of Order and that whole tradition?

Caroline: When Colonel Robert wrote his Rules of Order—it was during the gold rush chaos of San Fransisco in 1867—it actually was a gigantic step forward in group decision-making. Prior to that, each group sort of made up its own rules of procedure. It was a great step forward, because everyone's rights were spelled out very clearly: it accommodated the minority by giving them certain power; and it gave the groups an ability to move forward in an orderly fashion, with everyone knowing the rules.

But Robert's Rules of Order can be manipulated. The parliamentarian is the strongest person in a Robert's Rules of Order group. And today we recognize that we can no longer have majorities and minorities; we need collective unity.

TNC: How does consensus help the process of forming communities, do you think—both intentional communities intending to live together, as well as peoples' less coherent attempts at forming community?

Caroline: The whole process requires knowing each other, exposing our truth. And to the extent that we do that, we build community. It's an integral part of the consensual process, because you have to share that. If not, you are short-changing the group. Completely.

So let's say you're a neighborhood group, and not an intentional community. Just the act of being in a group that is using consensus means that the neighborhood gets to know each other as individuals much better than just acting on a set of rules. Many of us have backgrounds that allow us to have very different perceptions on different aspects of the question. And as we expose our backgrounds, we become more whole to other people. It's this slow recognition that we need to know each other that seems to me to be very helpful.

TNC: Many intentional communities have fallen apart over the last decade or two, after many different attempts at coming together. Alpha Farm is one intentional community that's managed to stick together.

Is that because of consensus? And if so, can you tell us how it works within your community?

Caroline: I think consensus was absolutely crucial to how we began, in that we didn't know each other, and this was the process of coming to know each other. The basis of consensus, the ground on which it rests, is trust. Without trust, consensus really hobbles along. But it also engenders trust. It's sort of a circle. The more you do it, the more trust you build, and the larger the base on which you're resting. And the more you use it, the more trust you have, the more consensus is easy. And then what you do is easier, because the power behind unity is tremendous.

I think Alpha Farm in the beginning would not have made it without consensus. Fortunately we had the process correctly in order. Some groups who came together did not, and did not understand how to use consensus, or the importance of parts of it, and therefore allowed what I would consider a manipulation of the process. But it's very difficult to manipulate a true consensual decision-making process. I've never really seen it happen.

TNC: What about passing the skills of consensus on to children. What's your experience of that?

Caroline: I think it's a lot easier to advance the idea of consensus in households, which is basically where children of Friends learn. You don't necessarily need a facilitator, although it does help. And in a few families I know, they did take minutes at their family councils. And sometimes the children would go back and point out the minutes to the adults! So it was a very empowering thing for children, and we don't have a lot of ways of empowering children specifically. Consensus obviously needs to be used with discretion among children—children don't always have all of the light completely grown in them—but to the degree that that starts evolving, the more it's brought into family council probably the better the family's interrelationships. It's a way of starting to train people up in our society to feel empowered, and to be OK with empowering other people; that it's not scary; it's their right, and it's their right to empower others.

TNC: So if you had a recipe for building sustainable cultures what would the primary ingredients be?

Caroline: Well, real love and respect. Consensus could be a very important part of bringing about those two rather vital ingredients. I do think the more feminine traits need to be integrated in a much more equal way in any society that we're going to evolve that is going to be sustainable. And it is true that consensus is a feminine form of decision-making: it is unifying, it is sharing, it is caring, it is nondominant, it is empowering. This integration is going to be essential for our survival.

The civil rights movement and the antiwar movement had a tremendous amount of male domination—very large male egos in them. And the whole thrust of consensus and the feminine aspect to making these two movements work never got a full chance in them. That's not true now. I'm thinking now of the antinuclear groups—both Abalone and Clamshell Alliances: two very large gatherings of six thousand and three thousand people—which used a consensual process to arrive at their decisions. And the power that was behind those! Those places are still closed. The police just could not understand how six thousand people could make decisions in five minutes that they couldn't make! In nuclear issues it's that survival factor that raises the consciousness of the need for unity.

My guess is that the bioregional movement is kind of the same thing. Bioregionalism is striking at the very base of our chaos: our lack of place. As lost souls, or individuals, we're searching desperately for ways to answer this survival need. Consensus has been a natural outgrowth. Part of the power of the bioregional movement has grown out of its success with consensus. There has not been the need for minorities to be putting forth their positions all the time. Which, if you look at parties or units of social movements, that's often been the technique that's done them in—all that back-biting. I'm watching the Green Party with interest to see whether or not they can get themselves together well enough to use consensus and recognize the power behind it. Once you have a unified decision, I'd suggest everyone get out of the way, because you can go far with very little!

26
The Circle Is Gathering . . .
Judith Plant

The circle is gathering. It isn't going to be easy. Peoples' feelings are high and tense. He'd lost his temper and behaved outrageously, as just about everyone agreed. That he was provoked could not be denied, but macho and insulting behavior simply couldn't be ignored. To go to such an extreme, in public, and when representing our community, meant that an element of doubt was cast over us all. We can't allow such an example to be set for the children—especially the boys.

He's here. I see him over there with his partner. I sense that others are also looking around, in some vague subconscious way, for someone to tell us what to do, how to handle this situation—perhaps even deal with it for us. The funny thing is that we were brought up by individualists to be individuals, so where's the guidance on how to go about creating a whole world? There is none. Only us.

The circle begins. Each friend and neighbor takes their turn. Interestingly enough, it's the men who are hardest on him. No one condones his actions, though most everyone appreciates the stress he was under at the time. He sits among us, listening, saying nothing.

It's my turn. Some of the women are expecting me to really blast him. I look at this person, this man who has, in my eyes, behaved very badly. He's here, I thought, and I respect that act of will; that he is willing to face criticism from his friends takes humility, and to accept the possibility of change takes courage. As I look at him I am remembering other things about him and I begin to fill with warmth. He looks at me, expecting to be torn to bits. "Others have spoken my mind," I said, passing my turn. And it was true.

I have not always missed opportunities to make people feel small and insignificant because of their blunderings. In fact, in some circumstances, it's been a very effective way to take control, or to gain a little more power and status on the hierarchical ladder. But here, in the heart of community, I am compelled to act differently. Others had said my words—to repeat them again was for whose benefit? Power-over is not the issue. Instead, we have consciously decided to seek power-

242

from-within to give us all the strength to face ourselves and become who we want to be.

Besides, who wants to destroy the whole person? *He* is not the enemy. . . . merely aspects of his behavior. *We* are our own worst enemy. We have been taught to jump on each other not only to gain power, but also to do so the moment our individual persons feel threatened. Yet within the boundaries of community and the context of the caring relations of daily life, it is impossible not to see the humane side of ourselves. And, knowing each other closeup, as we do through day-to-day relations, it is clear to us all that not one of us is any pinnacle of virtue; each of us knows that we may well take a turn in his shoes. Indeed, we are all capable of hurting others in defense of our fragile egos—exactly what had happened.

And the next day, he brought me two dozen of his wonderful eggs. It feels like what might be called love. Not the passionate kind, but a wider, kindred feeling. And perhaps the greatest achievement of our difficult circle was not the remaking of this individual. More the fact that as a group we are willing to support each other in our struggle to find and develop this personal power, enabling us to take on the challenge of change. Power from the heart bonds people, unlike power-over which separates. And in bringing our hearts and minds together, sharing this power in our circle, we transform ourselves and our community.

.   .   .

Taking responsibility for our own health and well- being is our natural right; yet we are all suffering from the illusion that someone, or something else, will look after us in a sustainable way. We have even created institutionalized caring for our babies and elders—paying trained humans to do the work which cultures used to wholly embrace. In separating ourselves from these most basic facts of human life we are denying ourselves the nurturing relations of people and place that once made us whole.

With the creation of massive institutions, we have lost the ability to think for, and care for, ourselves. These structures function for the benefit of the few at the expense of the many. Furthermore, the many—most of the people in the world—no longer look to themselves, their elders, their people or the land for security, instead looking toward government or industrial solutions. Yet, it is these same institutions that are raping and poisoning the earth which is the source of all life.

.   .   .

As we were brushing off our skis, the kids and I, after our three mile ski to the village school, we noticed that the flag was at half mast.

Who died, we wondered? Some dignitary, some important person in some other place, I thought.

In the high school staff room of this small, North American Indian village, people's faces are long; some of the Indian teachers aren't there; a woman's eyes keep filling with tears. There's been a drowning, I am told. My friend's next door neighbor lost her son in the river last night. He'd been drinking and they shouldn't have tried to come home. The boat tipped, the river is fast, he was gone in a flash.

The village acted quickly. Where white people never know quite how to act in such a situation, Indian people know exactly what to do. Almost immediately a feast was called. Of course, we went. As long-staying visitors we were not only welcomed, but it was expected that we would participate. Feasts are usually six or seven hours long, endless speeches in their own language, a real endurance test. This one was different.

The whole village showed up. Tables were laid out and the aroma of the ceremonial moose stew filled the hall. There was a tension in the air, yet people were talking, quietly, and gradually taking their places. We sat still, waiting. Soon the family came, all surrounding the mother especially, whose head was held up, though her eyes were swollen. She would have to burn all of his possessions, that is the tradition when someone dies accidentally. I thought of my son and it was all I could do to keep my tears inside. And she had to come here to publicly present her grief—something very foreign to non-native people who tend to hide it in their little individual selves and homes. This is one of those times when her Indian-ness comes to the surface and takes care of her. Support. So much of it for her in this most difficult time.

After we'd had our stew, bread, and tea, the ceremonies began. Much to our shock, from the back of the room, came many, very wildly dressed people, masked, and doing their very best to make people laugh. You couldn't help it. They teased and tormented each other and friends and relatives so much that, soon, the tension that had permeated the room fell away and people began to sit back in their chairs, ready for what was to follow.

Elder after elder spoke—reaching out to the mother, the family, . the clan of this lost boy. She never broke down, her husband beside her, holding on to her arms and hands the whole time. I kept sneaking a glance, knowing this was wrong, yet marveling at the strength of this person. Presently a line began to form. A long line that went right around half the hall . . . everyone eventually joined it. We were advised by friends that it wasn't just *any* lineup, that there was an order to who was at the front, the middle, the end. We were at the end. This line was for public giving of money to the family, for it is felt by these people that the expense of funerals is not borne by the parents but rather the community. Booming male voices announced, so much from so-and-so, and on and on for hours—every amount accounted for. Even small children proudly gave what they could, encouraged strongly by their families, learning at a young age what keeps their people together. That night several thousands of dollars were raised and handed over to cover all the costs.

I watched her from a distance for over a year, wondering if she would ever recover from such a loss. As the months passed, a smile returned to her face. She came out of her house and into the rhythm of her tribe. At the end of that year she took off her black clothes and I could see that she was going to be alright. Again, I am overwhelmed at the power of culture, the power of ritual grounded in the day-to-day caring of real, living security.

.   .   .

There's a strong attraction that "civilized" people often experience toward tribal people. Sometimes it even feels like a longing to belong— even though we were brought up to believe that these peoples are inferior to civilized society. Yet to be civilized means to control and regulate all that is natural, thus separating us from relations of caring which our species depends on for its survival. What are relations of interdependence within tribal society are services bought and paid for by civilized "man." Real caring—love—for one another cannot be bought, controlled or regulated. This essence of our humanness has been shattered and all but lost through a desperate attempt to have power-over all of life; indeed, to conquer the fear of our own mortality. Our task in this modern age is to recognize what remains, salvage what we can of what has been lost, and create new cultural forms— making very sure we do not repeat the old order.

It would be very typical of the "taking" attitude of western society to think that Indian ways, traditions and rituals could simply be transferred to non-native people. This would be stealing, once again. And, as is the case with stolen goods, they can never really belong to the thief. For we would be taking the products of thousands of years of cultural refining, having a depth of meaning that is specific to a particular people and place, something we can never hope to understand as they do. These are *their* ways and, while we can respect the philosophy from which these traditions arise, we cannot hold them as our own. Indian people can, if they are willing, act as guides, as teachers, as wise elders, for people who are trying to make a home for themselves that goes way beyond the suburban bungalow.

.   .   .

He came into our lives as quite a surprise. Working away in the garden, miles from any road, I looked up from my work and there he was—long black braids, sitting quietly under a tree on the hillside, looking down at me for who knows how long. It was a shock to see someone just appear like that, let alone an Indian man complete with medicine pouch and walking stick. He said he'd come to give us a sweat; and that his purpose in life, given to him by his elders, was to take the message of the Indian sweat to the world.

It wasn't long before he had most of the commune entirely involved in this project. Needless to say, the children were thrilled—totally captivated by this larger-than-life Indian, who knew how to do real things with wood, fire, and water. Some of us were a little uncomfortable. After all, our whole day's work stopped dead when he arrived, and we had to adjust ourselves to this man who commanded so much authority.

"I need two young people," he said, "to go into the forest and find twelve willow trees." Our two eleven year olds jumped at the opportunity. He, meanwhile, drew a large circle on a flat near the creek.

"I need twelve holes, right here." The willows arrived and he, and a couple of us, under his careful direction, and in his very particular way, put the willows into the holes, placed at equal points around the circle. Carefully bending the green wood, the tops were interwoven to form the dome shape of the sweat. He told us that once the willows are stuck into the ground, the sweat is alive and must be treated as one would treat one's mother.

"We have lots of black plastic," someone offered.

"Never use plastic," he scoffed. "Get me canvas or old rugs." Luckily, we had both. The sweat really began to take some shape.

"Find at least twenty medium-sized rocks, and lots of firewood. . . . We're going to build a *big* fire."

On it went until everything was ready. The new sweat, with fresh cedar boughs lining the inside, waited while the rocks, carefully placed in a certain way, were heated by the blazing fire. It was dark by then, well past supper time—our whole routine had been entirely thwarted, but we all felt this was surely worth the disruption.

"Have you got a hand drum?" We supplied a set of bongos! Soon his magical, high-pitched voice rose from the fire to the tops of the trees and beyond. We couldn't believe what was happening. . . . Some of us bravely tried to join in but the high falsetto needed for Indian singing doesn't come easily to our tight throats.

"Alright, it's time," he said, entering the sweat lodge. "Men to my right, women to my left." Wait a minute, we thought. This is going too far. We're liberated people here. Quickly we consulted with each other as to how to deal with this situation. Let it go, we decided. . . . We're having a cultural experience and we must respect his ways.

It was like being in the belly of the earth. Dark, wet, and very hot. There were fourteen of us, shoulder to shoulder, though we couldn't see a thing. Give yourself to the process, I told myself over and over again, warding off possible claustrophobia.

Silence for a long time. He splashed the rocks with a fir bow covered in water. "We give thanks to grandmother and grandfather rocks." As the heat intensified, he led us in a traditional prayer, ending with a chorus of "All Our Relations."

"The energy from the rocks, wood, and water, is to heal our bodies and our minds. If the rock cracks, it is to show us that anything can change."

"All Our Relations."

"I thank you, Indian brother, for reminding us not to take each day for granted," one of us said.

"All Our Relations."

We did the required four rounds, all of us, young and old, and by the end we had all expressed our thanksgiving to this man, this sweat, for opening our eyes to each other and the world around us.

.   .   .

Trying to sort out the complexities of a network of caring human relations in hierarchical terms—where some are right and others are wrong—is tempting, since this is the method we all grew up with. It's such a simple-minded way of explaining things, where some dominate others, some lead and the rest follow, some think and others are told what to think. The truth is, human beings need a method or structure that supports diversity, otherwise we cannot create the fluid, yet whole, human organization which is required to fulfill our part of the ecological reality we face. It simply won't work for some to tell the others what to do. The time has come for all of us to grow up and assume a thinking, responsible role in a context where the well-being of all human and nonhuman life is central.

On what basis can we come together? Historically, we have been organized around belief in some outside authority, some all powerful being that will take care of everything, provided we obey—do what we're supposed to do. Today the prevailing belief is in the wizardry of science and technology with its complex bureaucracy and all powerful military which is, indeed, compelling. But, should we reject the power-over approach to human organizing, what *could* bring us together and what will keep us going?

.   .   .

I was feeling great, full of vibrant energy, flushed from an exhilarating ride on the horse through the valley. I was ready to settle in for the afternoon among most of the adults in our community to try to deal with some of our most difficult problems. We had decided a while back to put an afternoon and evening aside, once a month, to place these thorny issues in the center of our circle, and gently uncover the old wounds. After over a decade together, in some form or another, there are bound to be "unintegrated differences" that can really get in the way. It is in this aspect of community building, where our emotions and intellect come together, that some feel the real work of creating culture lies.

As the meeting time drew closer, I began to feel a knot developing in my stomach, anxiety so intense that I feared my voice would shake if I spoke. There was nothing new about this feeling. I've had it for as long as I can remember in situations where there's a chance I might get hurt.

We started a temperature round and when it came to me I decided, for the first time, to tell people how I really felt instead of the usual stalwart, "Oh, I'm a little tired, but okay." Someone said that in sharing my feelings I was helping to take some of the load off myself.

The conversation was difficult and upsetting, as I had anticipated. It's so easy to alienate people because of this unknown area called appreciating differences. Anyway, I was right in the thick of it and, when a break was called, I headed straight for the outdoors to walk off some of my anxiety. What is it that's at the root of this anxiety? What's causing this tightness? I asked myself these questions and wasn't really getting anywhere. Putting a name to my feelings, I realized that I was experiencing a fear of exclusion. I don't want to be left out and I want to be accepted for who I am. In this day and age it seemed a reasonable enough feeling and I headed back to the meeting with a little more understanding of my own part.

We reopened the circle with a round. Since I'd just had this revelation about my feelings out by the pigpen, I volunteered to begin. Realizing as I was speaking that I was taking quite a risk—because speaking from one's feelings is being about as honest as you can get—I explained that, for me, community means inclusiveness, caring for each other, keeping each other in mind in spite of differences in our lives. I've heard these words thousands of times before, but never had they held so much meaning because they came from my real need. Lofty idealism and rhetoric can sound hollow next to words that flow from the heart (or gut, in my case).

•   •   •

It seems that one of the most difficult concepts to grasp is that humans need each other. We have hurt each other for so long that we cannot imagine throwing in the towel for the collective well-being. Centuries of fear and hatred are the source of this inertia. Yet each other is really all we have. No amount of money or accumulation of things will settle the longing to belong. The freedom myth of individual independence—actually possible because of the servitude and suffering of other peoples—reinforces a society of separation and domination. For human survival is not a question of "solitary man," or dollars and cents, but of culture.

The idea that some people are better than other people, more worthy and intelligent, inhibits interdependence among modern people. Not realizing that no *one* holds the truth, that in diversity there is wholeness, we tend to hold ourselves and chosen companions above others. This wall, which we inevitably build, prevents the richness that different experiences, different ages, different practices can provide. Not only this, but it keeps us from building true ecological community. For in nature, no one species dominates. We have tried to describe the natural world in hierarchical terms—like the image of the lion as king of the jungle. But in actuality this is not how it works. An ecosystem is a web of differences. If one species eats all its food—that is, "dominates"—it soon must leave that neck of the woods, or die. Organic organization is much more complex than human hierarchical imagination would like to believe.

·   ·   ·

We were sitting around late one afternoon at the end of a long, hot day, drinking beer, sharing stories—mostly their stories. Are their stories more interesting or are they just better storytellers? Both must be true.

Anyway, one of the things I had wanted to know how to do for years is tan hides. I had done a little bit, and read on the subject, so I was keen to hear how native people do it. It turned out this is women's work.

"She's just a small woman, no taller than this." He gestures about five feet from the floor. "You have to work the hide for about five or six hours, without stopping. It's real hard work." Our friends' families provide tanned hides for another family who make a lot of Indian crafts. One day, when the dust settles around here, for sure I'm going to go and learn some of these skills, I thought to myself. They're tanning just the way they've always done it. I've got to learn this before it's too late.

After exhausting this topic, the conversation turned. "Did you see our pictures in the village paper?" They laughed uproariously. "We *graduated*," they said, tongue-in-cheek. "They made us take Life Skills, to help us get a job. We don't want no job. What kind of a job is going to let you off fishing for six weeks?"

I couldn't believe it. Yet, of course, I could, as I used to teach Life Skills in an Indian village. But I didn't tell them.

"*Life Skills?*" someone else shrieked. "You should be teaching *them* life skills! You can do so many things that most people wouldn't have a clue about, things that really count when it comes to survival."

"You and us, we're different," he said, "but we're sort of the same, too. You want to learn to live off this place, we already can do this. You value the salmon, we value the salmon. You don't trust the government, neither do we. Not all Indian people are like us. Not all white people are like you. We're the natives and you're the naturals." He roared with laughter again, reaching for his beer.

.   .   .

The feast is served. Great platters of salmon. Salmon fried, barbequed, and dried. And lots for everyone. I am reminded of the Indian woman who spoke in the afternoon around the sacred fire. "My great-grandmother," she said, "wouldn't have turkey for Christmas. Salmon was her food." This fish is these people, these people are the salmon.

.   .   .

The !Kung bush people, living in one of the most inhospitable areas of the world, spend about twenty hours a week gathering and hunting for their food. The rest of their lives is spent in leisure, recreating their culture. Their bodies are finely tuned in complete harmony with the carrying capacity of their environment.

We, on the other hand, are starving on factory food, thinking that such variety of packaging is part of a privileged way of life. With our arrogance and superiority we are selling our souls to the marketplace, spending less and less time in what little remains of our culture. We have been civilized to the point of insanity.

If we are what we eat, if the integrity of physical existence comes from what nourishes the body, could it also be that what feeds the soul are our cultural relations with each other and the natural world which connect spirit and body? And that in re-creating culture in daily life these vital relations are nurtured and sustained? So it is, for example, that people who have lived in the northwest of Turtle Island see the salmon as themselves. To mediate the production and consumption of food with money, allowing others to literally starve, is an expression of our collective madness. To turn the effort of feeding ourselves into a commodity—creating a dependency based not on love, but on profit—cuts us off from an experience which makes us understand our place in the organic swim of life.

.   .   .

"I guess you know why we're not eating as much salmon this year?" I was talking to a Shuswap friend who, for the past few years, has always brought us fresh fish—spring, sockeye, steelhead. We've canned it, frozen it, and wished that we knew how to smoke and dry it, like they do. It's felt good to know that every season we can count on it, and that it comes from right here, from the rivers we drink from, and that water the gardens.

Last year the Tribal Council commissioned an environmental assessment of the river and found deformed salmon, some with cancerous tumors. The scientists said it was because of the effluent from the many mills up and down the Fraser River. Now some of us won't eat it at all. Not even the wind-dried salmon that's excellent for hikes in the mountains because it's light and solid protein.

My friend looked right at me, his gentle eyes trying to make me understand his words. Crossing his fingers to show me what he meant, he said, "The salmon and us, we're the same. We can't stop eating them! We've been together since the beginning of time. If the fish die, we die." The enormity of what he was saying hit me with the sharpness of truth. In his person rests his ancestors. Will his life bring an end to their immortality?

.   .   .

Hierarchy destroys. Based on power-over, it has no capacity for compassion. Given the hierarchical requisite to take, in order to gain, it cannot empathize with people's needs and feelings. Rather, there are rules, tenets, within which we must mold ourselves to fit—thus destroying so much of our human need to create. How, and on what basis can we move away from these death-dealing ways?

To consider human feelings as necessary information for intelligent decision-making is a much different starting point. Working toward a framework for collective life based on people's needs, that is, on who they really are, makes infinitely more "organic" sense. Since we know that the hierarchical way won't create ecological community, we have nothing to lose by trying to put feelings up front. A compassionate framework would be flexible, ever-changing, because people's needs change, especially if they're being met. So, unlike a process based on principles, or commandments, we would have a process which was flexible, respected people for who they are, was inclusive, and allowed for growth.

Getting in touch with our feelings isn't going to be easy for any of us since we've been heavily encouraged to undervalue them and hide them from ourselves and others. Women have had much more experience with sharing feelings with each other and we will have to show the way. Men will have a terrible time with it, many thinking that idealism expresses their feelings. It may do, but chances are it's rhetoric that is masking what's going on inside. For men to speak from their hearts—and I don't mean eloquence—in a mixed group of peers will not happen overnight.

.   .   .

One of the things about native peoples' way of life that stands out in sharp contrast to non-native society, is their uninhibited relationships with their children. Our ways of raising children are riddled with uncertainties and feelings of inadequacy, yet their ways seem free and easy-going. There's a sparkle in their children's eyes that one cannot always find in other cultures' children.

In talking with Indian friends about this difference they have told me that they don't indulge their children, as I had suggested. They don't see it this way. Rather, children, like elders, have significant roles within the community. Children pass through stages of development, marked by ceremony and ritual, receiving added responsibilities on their way to maturity. What I had interpreted as indulgence was, in fact, very deliberate, guided experimentation with cultural ways—teaching behaviors that would be of value in adult years.

Within tribal life, taking responsibility seems to be what makes people whole, unlike modern society where rights are what people seek. Rights are granted by governments to citizens. To pass on responsibility from generation to generation to individuals who are ready and able to assume it is a much more organic process. How empowering it must be for young people growing up to know that they have a real role to play in the continued well-being of their people and place.

How can we transform our own communities such that our children feel they belong; feel there is a role for them, that they are wanted and needed and don't have to leave home at the age of eighteen? Is the answer to this question not part of the answer to sustainable human organization? For without a life that belongs to the children, we leave them no other choice than to join the alienated life in the cities and suburbs of twentieth century monoculture. Without a web of connectedness of which they form a part, we will, undoubtedly with great sadness, perpetuate the very system that we have spent our lives trying to change.

It is too early yet to know if our own attempts at forming a community that will make room for our children will work or not. We know we've not done as good a job as we'd have liked. For we've been distracted, to say the least. Each of us has had to arrive here first. Then settle in, making a home over the years; growing our own organic food; dealing with our adult anxieties and crises of identity; and, always, always, there are the struggles of resistance—against logging, mining, toxic waste incinerators, or some other depredation. Among all this, inevitably, the children have sometimes been forgotten or neglected.

But whatever our children *don't* have, at least they begin their own struggles through adult life knowing they have a people, of sorts, to which they belong; they know, too, that this movement for social change is happening all over the world and that, in a sense, they also belong to an emerging planetary community; and they have the beginnings of a set of cultural ways—including, most importantly, the consensus process of which the circle forms a vital part—that will take them a long way along the path to healing the wounds of people and place.

All Our Relations.

Recommended Reading

Going back to the first awakenings of ecofeminism in my life, I find myself picking raspberries with a close sister-friend. As we pick and eat we are sharing our lives. I am living a communal life in the mountains and am trying to figure out how to fit my feminist experience into the world around me. It's a searching kind of conversation because I am trying to find the words to describe a new kind of feminism—new to me, that is. It's about valuing women's work as life-sustaining, not something to get done as quickly as possible so we can get on with catching up with the men.

"It seems to me that we are valuing the same old priorities in our efforts to create a new world," I say to her. "And the work that women have always done to keep body and soul alive and well is still taken for granted, often dismissed as trivial, sometimes not even noticed."

"Yes, it's so hard to find new ground." She went on, "We have to keep trying, though. Anything less isn't worth the trouble."

We agreed together that people and the earth are literally dying for lack of attention grounded in caring and nurturing, and that all of humanity must recognize and act upon this fact before it's too late. She encouraged me, the next time I made a trip to the city, to search the bookstores and alternative literature for others having similar thoughts.

In the meantime I continued to read everything I could on the women's peace movement because it is from within this movement that ecofeminism, in part, has sprung. *Greenham Women Everywhere: Dreams, Ideas and Actions from the Women's Peace Movement,* by Alice Cook and Gwyn Kirk (London: Pluto Press, 1983) and the Greenham Women's Peace Camp itself, shows how women's values, exemplified by nonviolence and a deep commitment to life, were in sharp contrast to the diabolical madness of the arms race—organized, controlled and run by men. *Greenham Women Everywhere,* because it is rooted in feminism, connects the mentality of the political war machine with the everyday, personal mentality that allows the rape of women. In *A Handbook for Women on the Nuclear Mentality* (Norwich, VT: Wand, 1980), among the first books that I read which used the term "ecofeminism," authors Susan Koen and Nina Swaim share their vision of future directions wherein "we begin to design a world that is safe for all to live in. . . . "

Further connections with women's actions against militarism as a struggle against the oppression of women were made for me by Ynestra

King, whose work appears in this collection. This particular piece, "The Ecology of Feminism and the Feminism of Ecology," first appeared in *Harbinger* magazine (Vol. I, No. 2, Fall 1983), and extends the analysis to include the domination of nature. She explains that, in caring for human life, we must also have concern for all life, and that a culture based on militarism has priorities that cannot reflect this kind of caring. Ynestra King's work, by widening and deepening my understand of feminism, reinforced my musings in the raspberry patch. Here was a strand of feminist thought that, indeed, was not interested in an equal share of the same old carcinogenic pie (Ynestra's words), instead placing a high priority on the work of caring and nurturing life—work traditionally associated with women.

Finally I made it to the city and the bookstores and found *The Death of Nature: Women, Ecology and the Scientific Revolution* (San Francisco: Harper & Row, 1980), by Carolyn Merchant, the only copy left on the shelf. I knew I held an important book and that it would help me, inevitably, to defend ecofeminism. On the basis of extensive research, Merchant explains how the scientific revolution and the rise of a market-oriented culture replaced an organismic view of the world—which held the female earth as central to its values and concepts—with a mechanistic view. So, by the mid-seventeenth century, society had rationalized the separation of itself from nature. With nature "dead" in this view, exploitation was purely a mechanical function and it proceeded apace.

Just as women struggle for peace, so too, must we join the life struggles in nature. Since women have been associated with nature, with all that is natural, in taking a stand on the war on nature and by confronting the oppression of the earth, we confront the oppression of ourselves. The association of woman and nature, made by Susan Griffin in *Woman and Nature, The Roaring Inside Her* (San Francisco: Harper & Row, 1978), is fundamental to an ecofeminist library. No other has yet been able to touch my anger, indeed my rage, as this work does. We read it out loud on a cross-USA drive, through the ravaged landscape of America, and when we came to Mount Rushmore and the terrible destruction of nature so obviously done to immortalize the patriarchy, as well as make a cheap buck on the tourist trade, we were sickened. What Griffin writes about in this text is so real and so deep that readers' perspectives cannot help but be profoundly affected. At the same time as laying bare the terror of this association, she recalls, in another voice, the deep memories of being part of nature, memories which are within us all.

One of the first books to be published on ecofeminism is an anthology edited in England by Leonie Caldecott and Stephanie Leland, *Reclaim the Earth: Women Speak Out for Life on Earth* (London: Women's Press,

1983). As well as introducing the theory of ecofeminism, this collection of writers from around the world demonstrates how women are fighting for life through practical issues that range from defending the forests of the Himalayas to demonstrating for peace.

And then I heard about witches, and Goddesses, the spiritual dimension of this new "ism." Brave territory to enter into when all around people are shaking their heads as if you have now gone completely mad! Confirmed in my opinions about religion—the opiate of the masses—I now found myself realizing that some of my most spiritual experiences were in moments of awareness of my oneness with the natural world. That there has never been a way to celebrate this feeling of connectedness with friends shows the spiritual void of the movement for social change. More than this, though, this feminist spirituality is a process of healing and growing into maturity. In *Dreaming the Dark: Magic, Sex and Politics,* by Starhawk (Boston: Beacon Press, 1982), the reader is taken on a witch's journey, entering the dark—the other half of light—to those places where our culture has forbidden entry; where, with courage and determination, we may find the place where power-from-within dwells.

While there are many other writers placing their "pieces of the truth" in the circle of literature that is ecofeminism, these particular works formed my initial experience. Other books on my shelf include Rosemary Radford Ruether's *Sexism and God-Talk: Toward a Feminist Theology* (Boston: Beacon Press, 1983), an excellent read on feminist liberation theology which connects the struggle against sexism in Christianity with the oppression of other peoples and the earth.

Most recently, Vandana Shiva's *Staying Alive: Women, Ecology and Survival in India,* (New Delhi: Kali for Women; London: Zed Books, 1988), confirms that this movement for life on earth is not limited to the western world, to the privileged. For women everywhere have been central to the ages-long work for the health of people and place. If the authority that comes from assuming this responsibility could have been valued, instead of maximizing profits, it is surely a fact that at least parts of the world would have been spared exploitation. Instead, cultures which once understood that this work was central to their survival have been colonized, "developed," infused with the European idea of surplus for market. With the movement toward sustainable lifestyles in this part of the world, and the necessary shaking-off of the myth of security-in-consumerism, we here in the western world, are beginning to discover the strength that our sisters in the "less-developed" world have never lost. What power-from-within one must experience with the knowledge that comes from knowing that the world around us, in which we live, is sacred; its well-being a reflection of our well-being.

The strength of the ecofeminist movement lies in the fact that it did not emerge solely in the halls of academia, or the mind of one person or even one culture. For while I was struggling for words in the raspberry patch, others elsewhere, quite unknown to me, were also piecing together this perspective. The roots of this view of the world are firmly grounded in various strains of thought, action, and experience throughout the world. From India, Africa, Native American cultures, midwestern universities in the United States, and mountain gardens in northern Canada, the theory and practice of ecofeminism continues to be pieced together.

Contributors' Biographies

Susan Griffin is one of the most influential feminist writers of this age. Author of *Woman and Nature: The Roaring Inside Her* and *Pornography and Silence: Culture's Revenge Against Nature,* and a new collection of poetry, *Unremembered Country,* she is currently at work on a book about war.

Ynestra King has been a pioneering ecofeminist theorist and activist for over a decade. She is the author and editor of the forthcoming book, *Feminism and the Reenchantment of Nature,* and co-editor with Adrienne Harris of *Wrecking the Ship of State: Toward a Feminist Peace Politics* (Westman Press). She lives in New York City.

Corinne Kumar D'Souza from India is in the Collective of the Centre for Informal Education and Development Studies at Bangalore. She is a human rights activist working with several civil liberties groups. Her interest is in studying the issues of justice and peace in the context of women, and providing alternatives to present justice/peace initiatives.

Sharon Doubiago, poet and writer from the Pacific Northwest, is known for her incisive questioning of the alternative movement. In the late seventies she wrote "Where is the Female On the Bearshit Trail?"—an investigation into the sexism of Gary Snyder and other west coast poets. She has recently written *The Book of Seeing with One's Own Eyes,* a portrait of her life, published by Graywolf Press.

Ursula K. LeGuin has written about sixty short stories, many poems, and fifteen novels. Much of her work has received literary honors and awards, including the Nebula Award and the Hugo Award. Her work has stimulated the imaginations of so many involved in the movement for social change, inspiring the struggle for a better world.

Ellen Bass has published several volumes of poetry, the most recent being *Our Stunning Harvest* (New Society Publishers). She is also co-author of *The Courage to Heal: A Guide for Women Survivors of Child Sexual Abuse.* She lives in Santa Cruz, CA with her partner, Janet, and children, Sara and Max.

Anne Cameron is a writer from the Pacific northwest coast. Among her many publications is *Daughters of Copper Woman.* She belongs to no political party and believes that if voting made any difference it would be illegal. She would love to see an actual breakdown of what it costs the United States in direct and indirect grants, subsidies, and tax exemptions to make it possible for the multinationals and major corporations to rape, pillage, and plunder the Earth.

Pamela Philipose is a journalist from India and is the senior assistant editor of *Eve's Weekly*. She represents the Forum Against Oppression of Women (FAOW), which deals with all forms of oppression against women. She is also a member of the subgroup concerned with the portrayal of women in the media. Her other involvements include a campaign against injectable contraceptives and raising awareness about the coercive family planning program of India and its repercussions on women's health.

Gwaganad is a Haida woman and member of the Ts'aalth clan. She is forty years old with two teenage children and has been the community health representative for Skidegate in Haada Gwaii (the Queen Charlotte Islands) for eighteen and one-half years.

Vandana Shiva, a well-known Indian physicist, is associated with the Research Foundation for Science, Technology, and Natural Resource Policy near Delhi. After receiving a doctorate in theoretical physics, she worked for the Indian Institute for Management in Bangalore for three years. She is currently a consultant to the United Nations University. In keeping with her family's tradition of activist women, she devotes time and energy to the Chipko movement, speaking, writing, and helping out as circumstances demand. She is married and has a young son.

Rachel Bagby is a writer, composer, performer, scholar. She sings and tells tales about creating sustainable relations. With Gwyn Kirk, Rachel has hubbed WomanEarth Institute since 1986.

Marti Kheel is a vegetarian, ecofeminist, animal liberation activist, and writer. She is cofounder of Feminists for Animal Rights and has been active in the animal liberation movement for the last ten years. Her articles have appeared in *Environmental Ethics, Between the Species, Creation, Woman Spirit,* and *Woman of Power.* She is currently a doctoral student at the Graduate Theological Union.

Deena Metzger is a poet, novelist, playwright, essayist, and therapist concerned with personal, political, spiritual healing. She is the author of *The Woman Who Slept with Men to Take the War Out Of Them* and *Tree,*—two books in one volume, Wingbow Press; and has just finished a novel, *What Dinah Thought.* She is writing a book, *Writing For Your Life: Imagination, Creativity and Healing.* J. P. Tarcher, and Parallax Press will bring out her next book of poetry, *Looking For The Faces of God.*

Charlene Spretnak is author of *Lost Goddesses of Early Greece, Green Politics: The Global Promise* (with Fritjof Capra), and is editor of *The Politics of Women's Spirituality,* an anthology. She is also author of

"Ecofeminism: Our Roots and Flowering" in *Reweaving the World: The Emergence of Ecofeminism,* edited by Irene Diamond and Gloria Orenstein.

Dale Colleen Hamilton is a freelance writer living near Rockwood, Ontario. She has had several plays produced and short stories published and has been involved in environmental and native issues for the past decade. "The Give and The Take" is based upon her experiences during the height of the Meares Island Protest in British Columbia, when she served as the Victoria coordinator of the Friends of Clayoquot Sound. She is presently working on a new play about the suburbanization of agricultural land.

Rosemary Radford Ruether is the Georgia Harkness Professor of Applied Theology at Garrett Evangelical Theological Seminary and Northwestern University. She is the author or editor of twenty-one books and numerous articles on feminism, theology, and social and political issues. She is also an activist in feminist, peace, and global justice issues. These include concerns for ecology and animal rights. She is interested in interreligious and intercultural dialogue around human and planetary survival concerns.

Margot Adler is currently a reporter at the New York Bureau of National Public Radio. She is the author of *Drawing Down the Moon* (Second Revised Edition, Beacon Press, 1986), a study of ancient nature religions and modern groups that are attempting to revive these traditions.

Dolores LaChapelle has been a life-long climber and skier. Having lived in the mountains of Utah and Colorado most of her adult life, she has combined her work and her life by specializing in various forms of experiential education within the context of the natural environment. She is currently a tutor for the New Natural Philosophy program of International College and teaches Tai Chi at Fort Lewis College in Durango, Colorado; as well, she directs the Way of the Mountain learning center in Silverton, Colorado. Her latest book, *Sacred Land, Sacred Sex: Rapture of the Deep,* is available through the Way of the Mountain, Box 542, Silverton, CO. 81433.

Radha Bhatt was born in a remote village of Almora district in the Himalayas. Since 1951 she has worked with the women and children in the rural areas of the far-flung Kumaon Himalaya. During the past twenty years she has been actively involved in various social and development issues in the hills, including the prohibition movement, the grassroots struggle to protect the forests known to the world as the "Chipko Movement," and in recent years has been struggling against mining activities. Her guiding principle has always been to arouse the latent strength within women and encourage grassroots initiatives to arise from below. She has been very committed to developing a network of such women throughout the Kumaon and neighboring Garhwal hills, so that women in their individual valleys can gain strength and inspiration from the struggles of their sisters elsewhere. In these efforts Lakshmi Ashram is not alone, for alongside are numerous other small non-governmental organizations—all united in their vision of a decentralized society where the people have control over their own lives and live in harmony with their natural environment.

Starhawk is the author of *The Spiral Dance: A Rebirth of the Ancient Religion of The Great Goddess* (Harper and Row, 1979) (*Der Hexenkult Als Ur-Religion Der Grossen Gottin,* Bauer, 1984); *Dreaming the Dark: Magic, Sex, and Politics* (Beacon, 1982); and *Truth or Dare: Encounters with Power, Authority and Mystery* Harper and Row, 1987). A feminist and peace activist, she teaches at several San Francisco Bay Area colleges and travels widely lecturing and giving workshops. She works with the *Reclaiming* collective in San Francisco, which offers classes, workshops, and public rituals in the Old Religion of the Goddess, called Witchcraft.

Dorothy Dinnerstein is a semi-retired psychologist at Rutgers University, a writer, and is primarily concerned with the ways in which normal human psychology are dangerous to the Earth. Author of *The Mermaid and the Minotaur,* she is currently writing another book, *Sentience and Survival,* which will look at why people cannot think about what they must think about if we and the Earth are to survive.

Joanna Macy is Adjunct Professor at the California Institute of Integral Studies in San Francisco, Starr King School for the Ministry in Berkeley, and John F. Kennedy University in Orinda. Her principle fields of scholarship are Buddhism, general systems theory and social change theory. Dr. Macy is the author of *Despair and Personal Power in the Nuclear Age* and *Dharma and Development,* as well as various articles relating to psychological, cognitive, and spiritual resources for social action. The shift to an ecological sense of self is the subject of her most recent book, *Thinking Like A Mountain: Towards a Council of All Beings,* written with John Seed, Pat Fleming, and Arne Naess. She travels widely as a speaker, trainer, and workshop leader in the United States and abroad.

Marie Wilson, born in 1919, came into this world "kicking and screaming" and has not stopped since. She has lived most of her life in Hazelton, in the territory of the Gitksan-West'suwet'en, except for a brief period in Europe during World War II. Since 1979 she has worked as a cultural researcher for the Tribal Council, establishing who the Gitksan-Wet'suwet'en people were prior to intervention, where they lived, and, importantly, the details of their philosophy and its effect on the social, political, and economic lives of her people.

Margo Adair, born in 1950 into an upper middle class academic family, moved throughout her childhood. She settled in the Bay Area in 1965. She has a practice in which she leads support groups, works with people individually, teaches workshops, does mediations and consulting. She is the author of *Working Inside Out: Tools for Change* (Wingbow, 1984). She is politically active and a member of the Green Letter editorial collective. She has no formal academic training—she never finished high school. She is currently coauthoring a book with Sharon Howell: *Patterns of Power.*

Sharon Howell was born at the end of World War II in the heart of the Allegheny Mountains. She was raised in a small community of miners and foundry workers who have lived there for generations. She now lives in Detroit and is involved in community organizing, speaking and writing. She is the author of *Reflections of Ourselves: the Mass Media and the Women's Movement* (Peter Lang, 1988). She has a Ph.D. and teaches at Oakland University. She is currently coauthoring a book with Margo Adair: *Patterns of Power.*

Helen Forsey from Ottowa, Ontario, worked for many years in international development. In 1984 she joined Dandelion, a sister community of Twin Oaks, with her two teenage boys. She is a writer on feminism, peace, and community. Her current interest is sustainable agriculture and resistance to patriarchal destruction of the planet.

Caroline Estes, long-time member of Alpha Farm, an intentional community in Oregon, is an accomplished practitioner and teacher of facilitation and consensus.

Judith Plant is actively involved in the bioregional movement—both at the community level and the wider, North American Bioregional Congress. Her writings on ecofeminism and bioregionalism have been published in "green" journals both on this continent and in the U.K. She is coeditor of *The New Catalyst,* a journal for social and political change, from the Pacific Northwest.